Better Homes and Gardens®

COMPLETE GUIDE TO
QUILTING™

Better Homes and Gardens® Creative Collection™
Des Moines, Iowa

Better Homes and Gardens®
COMPLETE GUIDE TO
QUILTING™

Director of Editorial Administration	MICHAEL L. MAINE
Editor-in-Chief	BEVERLY RIVERS
Executive Editor	HEIDI KAISAND
Art Director	MELISSA GANSEN BEAUCHAMP
Senior Editor	JENNIFER ERBE KELTNER
Editor	DIANE YANNEY
Graphic Designer	MARY-BETH MAJEWSKI
Editorial Assistant	MARY IRISH
Contributing Graphic Designer	JANN WILLIAMS
Contributing Writers	JILL ABELOE MEAD, TERRI PAUSER WOLF
Contributing Copy Editors	DIANE DORO, JENNIFER SPEER RAMUNDT, MARY HELEN SCHILTZ
Technical Editors	LILA SCOTT, CINDY MARUTH, LISA FLYR
Proofreaders	ANGIE INGLE, MARCIA TETER
Photographer	PERRY STRUSE
Contributing Photo Stylists	JANET PITTMAN, CHRISTA BAHR
Contributing Quilt Designer	MABETH OXENREIDER
Contributing Technical Illustrator	CHRIS NEUBAUER GRAPHICS
Vice President Publishing Director	WILLIAM R. REED
Publisher	MAUREEN RUTH
Consumer Products Marketing Director	BEN JONES
Consumer Products Marketing Manager	KARRIE NELSON
Associate Business Director	CRAIG FEAR
Production Director	DOUGLAS M. JOHNSTON
Book Production Managers	PAM KVITNE, MARJORIE J. SCHENKELBERG
Marketing Assistant	CHERYL ECKERT

CORPORATION

Chairman and CEO	WILLIAM T. KERR
Chairman of the Executive Committee	E.T. MEREDITH III

Meredith Publishing Group

President	STEPHEN M. LACY
Magazine Group President	JERRY KAPLAN
Creative Services	ELLEN DE LATHOUDER
Manufacturing	BRUCE HESTON
Consumer Marketing	KARLA JEFFRIES
Finance and Administration	MAX RUNCIMAN

For book editorial questions, write:
Better Homes and Gardens® Complete Guide to Quilting™ • 1716 Locust St., GA 205, Des Moines, IA 50309-3023

Like having a trusted quilting friend by your side. . .

Whether you're a seasoned quilter or a novice who's always wanted to learn to quilt, this one-stop, quilter-tested reference guide will show you, step-by-step, all you need to know. We've included a variety of methods and techniques that will spark your creativity and dozens of tips that will make quilting easier and more fun. This book will guide you every step of the way—from buying supplies to sewing on binding and everything in between.

The easy-to-use tabbed sections will make finding the answers to your questions a breeze. The comprehensive index at the end of the book can be used to look up specific references. Fill the pages at the end of each chapter with notes on things such as sewing machine settings that work well for a particular technique, needle sizes you prefer, notes from quilting classes you attend, or plans for your next quilt. In short, we hope that this book develops well-worn edges from being used often over the years—helping to make quilting even more satisfying.

A well-made quilt brings enjoyment to both the quiltmaker and the recipient. It's our pleasure to provide you with proven methods that will help you spread the joy.

Happy quilting,

Executive Editor
American Patchwork & Quilting

Senior Editor
American Patchwork & Quilting

QUILTER
TESTED
FOR ACCURACY

OUR PROMISE TO YOU

Prior to publication we test every

technique shown to verify the accuracy

of our instructions. Then an experienced

team of editors reviews the text,

how-to directions, photographs,

illustrations, and charts to make sure

the information we provide you is

clear, concise, and complete.

The American
Patchwork & Quilting® Staff

Tools, Notions, & Supplies

1

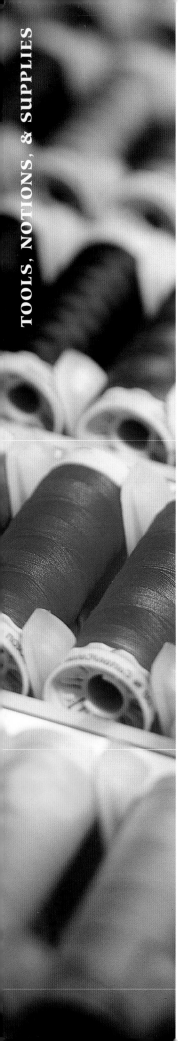

TOOLS, NOTIONS, & SUPPLIES

TABLE OF CONTENTS
Chapter 1—Tools, Notions, & Supplies

ONE OF THE JOYS OF QUILTING is that the supplies needed can be as simple as scissors, needle, and thread, or more complex with specialty tools designed for a specific purpose. There are literally hundreds of items to choose from to make quilting tasks easier, more accurate, or more fun. Whether you're a gadget-lover who wants every tool, or a minimalist looking to acquire the basics, knowing what the tools are, what to use them for, and why they're useful is essential to quilting success.

SCISSORS

Quilting requires a good pair of scissors. Most quilters use several pairs, each designed for a different purpose. Choose your cutting tools with care, making certain they are of the highest quality you can afford. It's better to have two or three sharp pairs of scissors than a drawer full of seldom-used, dull pairs.

Choose your scissors and shears from the following.

Thread clippers (A): Use for cutting threads. Single style used by both left- and right-handed persons.

Craft scissors and knife-edge straight trimmers (B): Use for cutting threads and trimming fabric edges. Left- and right-handed styles available.

Embroidery scissors (C): Use for thread cutting. Left- and right-handed styles available.

Appliqué scissors (D): Use for close trimming; special duckbill protects underneath layers of fabric. Left- and right-handed styles available.

Knife-edge bent trimmers or shears (E): Use for general cutting and sewing. Bent handle and flat edge provide accuracy when cutting on a flat surface. Left- and right-handed styles available.

Spring-action scissors (F): Small and large sizes available. Ideal for use by persons with weakened hands or for lengthy cutting sessions. Single style used by both left- and right-handed quilters.

> **TIP:** In a pinch with no scissors in sight? Use nail clippers to cut your thread.

ROTARY-CUTTING TOOLS

Although scissors are still often used for cutting fabric, the rotary cutter and mat board have revolutionized the industry and streamlined the process. To rotary-cut fabrics you need a ruler, mat, and rotary cutter (see Chapter 5—Cutting for information on how to rotary-cut).

ROTARY CUTTERS

Rotary cutters come with different types and sizes of blades and a variety of handle sizes. Try out the cutters before buying to find the grip and size that work for you.

A rotary cutter will cut through several layers of fabric at one time. Because the blade is sharp, be sure to purchase a cutter with a safety guard and keep the guard over the blade when you're not cutting.

Rotary cutters are commonly available in three sizes—28 mm, 45 mm, and 60 mm. A good first blade is 45 mm. The 28-mm size is good for small-scale projects, miniatures,

and corners. The 60-mm cutter can easily and accurately cut up to six layers of cotton fabrics.

Specialty blades, such as the 18-mm size, are used for cutting curves, miniatures, and appliqués; trimming seams; and cutting templates. Pinking and wave blades are used for novelty effects.

ACRYLIC RULERS

Accurate measurement is important for accurate piecing. To make straight cuts with a rotary cutter, choose a ruler of thick, clear plastic. Look for clear markings and accurate increments by measuring the ruler. Check to see if the 1" marks are the same crosswise and lengthwise.

Rulers come marked in a variety of colors. Try different rulers on cutting surfaces to see which is most easily visible for you.

There are rulers for every type of project and cutting need. Some rulers are almost like templates in that they create squares or right triangles in varying sizes. Some triangle rulers enable you to trim the points before joining the pieces together. If possible, try out rulers before you buy them or ask for a demonstration at a quilt shop and understand how to use them to get

SAFETY TIP: Rotary-cutter blades are extremely sharp. Develop a habit of retracting the blade after each cut. Just brushing your hand against an open blade can cause serious injury, as can dropping a rotary cutter with an open blade and striking your foot.

the maximum benefit from your purchase.

Rectangular rulers, such as a 6×24" ruler marked in ¼" increments with 30°, 45°, and 60° angles, are a good beginner's purchase. As you become more proficient you may wish to purchase additional acrylic rulers and templates in a variety of sizes and shapes.

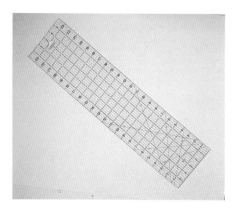

A good second ruler is the 6×12" size. It is easier to handle than the 24" ruler and can be used for smaller cuts and to make crosscut strips. It can also be used with the 6×24" ruler to cut 12" blocks or to make straightening cuts.

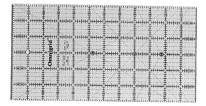

Square rulers, good for secondary cuts and cutting and squaring blocks, are available in a variety of sizes.

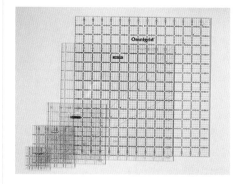

For squaring up large blocks and quilt corners a 12½" or 15½" square ruler works well. This ruler can also be used for making setting triangles.

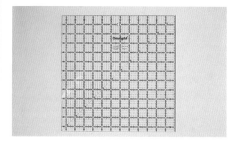

There are many rulers available that make cutting triangles, diamonds, and hexagons easy.

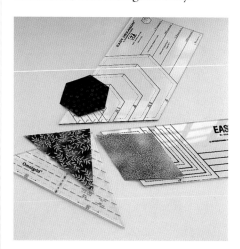

45° triangle rulers are useful for cutting half- and quarter-square triangles, mitering corners, and for cutting some diamonds and parallelograms.

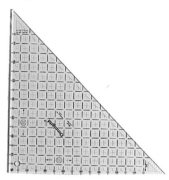

60° triangle rulers are helpful for cutting equilateral triangles, diamonds, and hexagons.

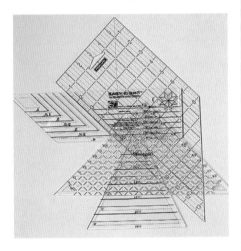

Specialty rulers and templates have been developed for cutting fans, arcs, Dresden Plates, Kaleidoscopes, some star patterns, and more.

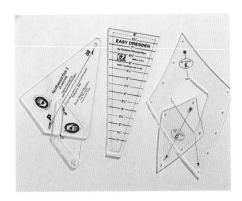

> **TIP:** Have a project that calls for a specific size of square or rectangle? If the size is right, consider using a specialty triangle or square ruler instead of making a separate template.

Curved rulers and templates help cut Double Wedding Ring and Drunkard's Path pattern pieces.

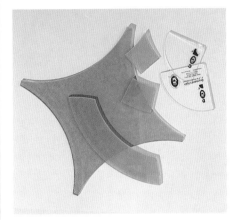

ROTARY-CUTTING MATS

A rotary cutter should always be used with a mat designed specifically for it. The mat protects your work surface and keeps the fabric from shifting while you cut. Often mats are labeled as "self-healing," meaning the blade does not leave slash marks or grooves in the surface even after repeated usage. Many sizes, shapes, and styles are available, but a 16×23" mat marked with a 1" grid, hash marks at ⅛" increments, and 45° and 60° angles is a good first choice. For convenience, purchase a second smaller mat to take to workshops and classes.

Cutting mats usually have one side with a printed grid and one plain side. To avoid confusion when lining up fabric with preprinted lines on a ruler, some quilters prefer to use the plain side of the mat. Others prefer to use the mat's grid.

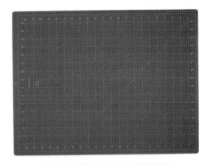

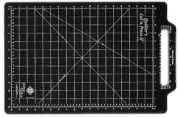

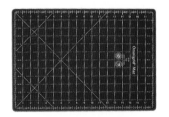

> **TIP:** Due to possible variances between manufacturers, it's preferable to use one brand of ruler throughout a project.

Mats are also available with a mat board on one side and an ironing surface on the other side. This combination ironing board/cutting mat is great to have at workshops. Some mats have a lazy-Susan-type turnstile affixed underneath so you can swivel the mat easily. The smallest mat boards (less than 12") work well for trimming blocks while you are seated at the sewing machine.

Store cutting mats flat or hanging on a wall. To avoid permanent bends do not store a mat on an edge or rolled up. Heat will cause a mat to warp and become unstable, so keep all mats out of direct sunlight, don't iron on them unless they have an ironing surface, and never leave them in a hot car.

Periodically treat a mat to a good cleaning with warm (not hot) soapy water or window cleaner. Dry gently with a towel.

MARKING SUPPLIES

Many products are available for marking sewing lines and quilting designs on a quilt top. Useful supplies include fabric markers, templates, and pattern guides.

Variances in fabric contrast (light to dark) and fabric quality make marking different for each project, and a variety of markers may be needed for a single project. Try markers on fabric scraps and wash the test scraps as you will the quilt to be sure marks will wash out. Templates and pattern guides will vary according to the needs of each project.

FABRIC MARKERS

Artist's pencil: This silver pencil often works on both light and dark fabrics.

Chalk pencil: The chalk tends to brush away, so it is best to mark as you go with these pencils.

Mechanical pencil: Use hard lead (0.5) and mark lightly so that stitching or quilting will cover it.

Pounce: This is chalk in a bag. Pounce or pat the bag on a stencil, leaving a chalk design on the fabric. The chalk disappears easily, so mark as you go with a pounce.

Soap sliver: Sharpen the edges of leftover soap for a marker that washes out easily.

> **TIP:** With any marking tool work with a sharp point to get a fine, yet visible line.

Soapstone marker: If kept sharp, these markers will show up on light and dark fabrics.

Wash-out graphite marker: Keep the sharpener handy for these markers that work well on light and dark fabrics.

Wash-out pen or pencil: These markers maintain a point and are easy to see. Refer to the manufacturer's instructions to remove the markings and test them on scraps of your fabric to make sure the marks will wash out. *Note:* Humidity may make the marks disappear, and applying heat to them may make them permanent.

TEMPLATES AND PATTERN GUIDES

A template is a pattern made from extra-sturdy material so you can trace around it many times without wearing away the edges.

Quilting stencils and templates: Precut stencils and templates in a variety of shapes and sizes are available from quilt shops. These may be made from template plastic or a heavier-weight acrylic plastic. They can be traced around multiple times without wearing away any edges.

Some quilting stencils also are made from paper. They are designed to be stitched through and torn away after the design is completed.

Template plastic: Template plastic is an easy-to-cut, translucent material available at quilt shops and crafts supply stores. Its translucency allows you to trace a pattern directly onto its surface with pencil or permanent marker to make a stencil or template.

Test a variety of materials as some are heat-resistant (helpful when ironing over template edges) and some are not. Other varieties are gridded for accuracy in tracing or shaded for better visibility.

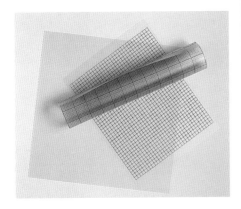

Freezer paper: Available at quilt shops and supermarkets, freezer paper allows you to create an iron-on template. You trace a shape onto the dull side of the freezer paper, cut it out, and press it directly onto fabric with an iron.

Graph paper templates: You can use the printed lines on graph paper to draw a pattern piece. Glue the graph-paper pattern to template plastic, tag board, or cardboard. Allow the adhesive to dry before cutting through all layers at once to make an accurate template.

Clear vinyl: Also known as upholstery vinyl, this material is used by hand quilters to make overlays for accurately positioning appliqué pieces on foundation fabric (see Chapter 8—Appliqué for more information on the overlay method).

Tape: Several types of tape are used to mark quilting and stitching lines—quilter's tape, painter's tape, paper tape, and masking tape are common choices. Quilter's tape is exactly ¼" wide; place it at the edge of your fabric and stitch alongside it for a ¼" seam allowance.

Specialty tapes in widths from ¹⁄₁₆ to 1" and wider are preprinted with lines to aid quilters in evenly spacing hand quilting or decorative stitches, such as a blanket stitch.

Some quilters use masking tape as a guide for straight-line machine or hand quilting. *Note:* Do not leave masking tape on fabric for an extended period of time as the adhesive from the tape may leave a residue. Painter's tape is less sticky than masking tape and also can be used as a guide for straight-line quilting.

> **TROUBLESHOOTING TIP:** Can't see the lines of your ruler on the fabric? When working with dark fabrics, choose a ruler with yellow or white markings. For light fabrics, choose one with black markings.

> **TIP:** Before working on your project, do a test to see how the thread and needle combination works. Sew together long strips of fabric to test piecing, or appliqué a patch. Create a little quilt sandwich (top, batting, and backing) and evaluate your quilting stitches.

THREAD AND NEEDLES

Thread and needles are at the heart of quilting as the two elements that literally hold everything together. Choosing the right type and size needle and thread can make a big difference in the success of your quilting project. Follow three general guidelines: match the thread type to the fabric fiber content, select the needle type based on the fabric being used, and select the needle size to match the thread.

> **TIP:** The fabric strength should be greater than that of the thread used for piecing. If seams are under stress, the thread will then give way before the fabric tears. For this reason, strong polyester threads should not be used for piecing cotton fabrics.

THREAD

Thread has multiple roles, from holding together patchwork to anchoring the fabric to the batting. Thread also plays a role in decoration, adding color, design, and texture to the quilt surface.

For piecing and most quilting, it's best to match the thread fiber to the fabric. Since most quilters use cotton fabric, 100% cotton thread is the best thread choice. Cotton thread is equal in strength to cotton fabric and should wear evenly. Synthetic threads, such as polyester, rayon, and nylon, are quite strong and can wear cotton fibers at the seams. For decorative quilting or embellishing, threads other than cotton may be appropriate (see Chapter 13—Specialty Techniques). Be sure your thread choice is suitable for the task; thread made for hand quilting, such as glazed cotton thread, should not be used in your sewing machine.

TIP: Typical thread weights are 30, 40, 50, 60, and 80. If the number of plies is equal, the higher number indicates finer thread. For example, a 50-weight three-ply thread is finer than a 40-weight three-ply thread.

THREAD TYPES

100% Cotton

Cotton thread is a staple in quilting. This thread works well with cotton fabric and is strong enough to create pieces that are durable. Hundreds of color choices are available in a variety of weights, although not all weights are created equal. Most cotton threads are two- or three-ply (see *page 1–8* for information on ply).

Cotton-Wrapped Polyester

Wrapping cotton around a polyester core creates a stronger thread with the finish characteristics of cotton thread. This thread is best used with fabric blends because it provides a little stretch. It's important to use a needle with a large eye to prevent stripping the cotton wrap from the polyester core.

Bobbin-Fill or Lingerie

Made from polyester or nylon and available in black or white, bobbin-fill works for machine embroidery, machine appliqué, or other decorative thread projects where multiple colors might be used in the needle. Prepare several bobbins filled with this thread and you can sew continuously without stopping to refill a bobbin. This thread is lighter weight than 100% cotton thread, which will cause the top thread to pull slightly through to the back side of the piece. Bobbin-fill is a more economical alternative to filling bobbins with specialty threads.

Metallic

The sheen and variety of colors available make metallic threads appealing for decorative stitching. However, metallic threads have a tendency to fray and break more often than cotton thread.

Using the right equipment will make the sewing process smoother. Work with a metallic or large-eye needle and a lightweight polyester, rayon, or nylon thread in the bobbin. Depending on your sewing machine manufacturer's specifications, you may also add liquid silicone drops to the spool to make the thread run through the machine more easily.

Monofilament

Available in clear or smoke color, this synthetic, lightweight thread comes in nylon and polyester. It generally is used for machine quilting when you don't want the quilting thread to show or where thread color may be an issue (i.e. quilting on multicolor prints). In the bobbin, use a lightweight cotton thread or bobbin-fill in a color that matches the backing.

TIP: Thread marked 50/3 (50 weight and 3 ply) works for both hand and machine quilting on cotton fabric. It's considered a medium-weight thread.

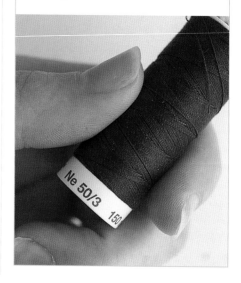

Perle Cotton

Soft and yarnlike, perle cotton is used for needlework projects or quilt embellishment. Typical weights used in quilting include Nos. 3, 5, 8, and 12. The higher the number, the finer the thread.

Polyester

This thread is designed for sewing with knits because the filament has the same stretch as knit fabric. Polyester thread should not be used with cotton fabrics for piecing or quilting, because it can be abrasive to soft cotton fibers and cause the fabric to tear at the seams.

Rayon

The soft, lustrous characteristics of rayon thread and the hundreds of colors available make it ideal for embellishment. It's often used for decorative quilting or embroidery. This thread is not strong enough and doesn't wear well enough to be used in piecing a quilt and should be alternated with a cotton thread when quilting a project that will get lots of wear.

Silk

Silk thread is stronger than cotton because it is a continuous filament, unlike cotton's short, spun fibers. Silk also has more stretch than cotton thread. Some quilters prefer to use silk thread for hand appliqué because it glides through the fabric more easily than cotton and is usually finer, thus making it easier to hide the stitches. It also is less prone to fraying, allowing a longer length of thread to be used.

Variegated

This term applies to thread in which the color changes back and forth from light to dark throughout the strand or revolves through a range of colors to create a rainbow effect.

TIP: Choosing a Thread Color

Match thread and fabric colors when you want the quilting design to blend in with the quilt top or backing, such as when stippling or quilting in the ditch (see Chapter 11—Hand & Machine Quilting).

When you want to accentuate the quilting, choose a thread color in contrast to the fabric color. This may be especially important when using decorative threads as a strong design element.

TROUBLESHOOTING CHECKLIST FOR THREAD BREAKAGE

If you're having trouble with thread breaking, check these possible causes.

- **Damaged or incorrect needle:** Change the needle, as it may have dulled from overuse or could have a burr or nick. If the needle is new, check that it is the correct size and the eye is large enough for the thread type and weight being used (see the Thread and Coordinating Machine-Needle Sizes chart on *page 1–9*).

- **Defective or old thread:** Lower-quality threads may have thick and thin spots that lead to breakage. Thread that is too old becomes dry and brittle as it ages, causing it to break easily.

- **Improperly threaded machine:** Check to see that your spool is properly positioned on the sewing machine. The thread may be getting caught on the spool cap end as it comes off the top of the spool. The solution may be as simple as turning over the spool on the spool pin.

  Or, if the presser foot wasn't raised when you threaded the machine, the thread may not be caught between the tension discs inside the machine. The quickest fix is to remove the spool and rethread your machine with the presser foot raised.

- **Operator error:** Pushing or pulling on the fabric or allowing drag to be created by hanging a heavy quilt over your work surface can increase stress on the thread and cause breakage.

- **Tension too tight:** Refer to your machine's manual and *page 1-19* to determine if this is the cause of your thread breakage.

- **Wrong thread:** You may have the wrong thread type for the fabric you've chosen. Change thread and sew on a scrap of fabric to see how a different thread performs.

It is available in both cotton and rayon.

Water-Soluble

This thread dissolves in water. Use it to baste a quilt or anchor trapunto or reverse appliqué. Once the project is completed, immerse it in water to dissolve the thread. Be sure to store the thread in a dry, humidity-controlled location.

THREAD FINISHES

After thread is made, finishes are often added to enhance its ability to perform under certain sewing conditions.

Mercerized Cotton

Mercerization enhances the dyeability, increases the luster, and adds strength to cotton thread. Mercerized cotton thread is often used for machine piecing and quilting.

Glazed Cotton

Glazed cotton threads are treated with starches and special chemicals

> **Choosing a bobbin thread? For general piecing and quilting, use the same type of thread on the bobbin as is in the top of the machine (except with metallic or decorative threads). Trying to save money by using a less expensive or different type of thread on the bobbin can lead to tension difficulties.**

under controlled heat, then polished to a high luster. The glazing process results in a hard finish that protects the thread from abrasion. Glazed cotton thread is used for hand quilting; it should not be used in a sewing machine.

Bonded Threads

These are continuous-filament nylon or polyester threads that have been treated with a special resin to encapsulate the filaments. The resultant tough, smooth coating holds the plies together and adds significantly to the thread's ability to resist abrasion.

THREAD QUALITY

Buy the highest quality thread you can afford for your projects. Skimping in the thread department can create frustration with breakage, bleeding, and other problems. Consider the total cost of your quilting materials and your time, and know that saving a dollar on a spool of thread may not be worth it in the long run.

Cotton thread is made from cotton fibers, which are only as long as what the plant produces. The fibers are spun into a yarn and yarns are twisted into a thread. Poor quality threads are made from the shortest fibers and appear fuzzy along the length of the thread. They tend to fray and break easily. Higher quality threads are made from

> **TROUBLESHOOTING TIP:**
> If you experience problems with breaking or twisting thread, the cause may be a needle mismatched to the thread type.

longer fibers of cotton and have a smoother finish.

Ply

Thread is made from yarns that are twisted together into a single ply yarn. Plies are then twisted together to produce two-ply or three-ply threads, which are the kinds most commonly used for piecing.

Filament

This term is generally applied to man-made threads, such as polyester, nylon, or rayon, created from a chemical spinning process where a single strand or "filament" is produced. Silk is the only naturally occurring filament. Polyester and nylon threads are quite strong and are not normally used for piecing cotton since the fabric will tear before the thread breaks.

NEEDLES

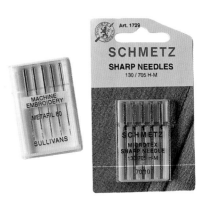

Whether you sew by hand or machine, using the correct needle size and type will make the task easier and the results more polished.

Machine- and hand-sewing needles have some similarities, but be aware that once you've mastered the numbers for machine-needle sizes, you'll need to learn a whole new set for hand-sewing needles.

It is important to change needles frequently as both kinds become dull with use. If a machine needle strikes a pin or the machine bed, it can develop a nick or burr that can tear your fabric.

Change needles at the start of a project and/or after 8 hours of sewing.

SEWING-MACHINE NEEDLES

The notions wall in your local quilt shop or sewing center can be intimidating if you're not sure what you need. There are dozens of sizes and shapes of sewing-machine needles, each designed for a different task. Understanding the terminology associated with machine needles can take the mystery out of making your selection and make your piecing and quilting go smoother.

MACHINE NEEDLE SIZES

When looking at a package of machine needles, you will often see two numbers separated by a slash mark. The number on the left of the slash is the European size (range of 60 to 120); the right-hand number is the American size (range of 8 to 21). Sizes 70/10, 80/12, and 90/14 are most commonly used for quilting. A lower number indicates a finer machine needle.

MACHINE NEEDLE POINTS

The needle point differentiates the type and purpose of a needle and is a key characteristic to consider

ANATOMY OF A MACHINE NEEDLE

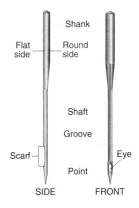

Shank: the part of the needle that goes into the machine.

Shaft: the body of the needle that extends below the shank.

Front Groove: the indentation on the front of the needle that allows the thread to lie close to the needle as it runs toward the bobbin. A deeper front groove can protect heavier thread from excess friction.

Scarf: the indentation on the back of the needle where the stitch is formed. When the bobbin shuttle swings into the scarf, it hooks into the looped thread on the needle to form the stitch.

Point: the tip of the needle. Select the point size based on the fabric being sewn.

Eye: the hole the thread passes through. Select the eye size based on thread type and weight.

THREAD AND COORDINATING MACHINE-NEEDLE SIZES

	60/8	70/10	75/11	80/12	90/14
Piecing and binding cotton fabric with cotton thread			●	●	
Piecing flannel					●
Quilting with monofilament thread	●	●	●	●	
Machine appliqué	●	●	●	●	
Sewing batiks, silks, or high thread-count fabrics with cotton thread		●			
Embellishing with decorative threads				●	●
Adding binding and borders			●	●	

when selecting a needle for a project. The needle point should match the fabric type. For sewing on quilting cotton, for example, use a needle labeled as a "sharps."

Needles last longer when the fabric and batting used are 100% cotton. Polyester or polyester/cotton blend batting tends to dull needles quicker.

> **For machine needles, the larger the number, the larger the needle.**

MACHINE NEEDLE EYES

A needle's eye must be large enough for the thread to pass through with minimal friction. If the eye is too large for the thread, it may produce a seam that is loose and weak. Large needles make large holes, so use the smallest needle appropriate for the thread. Some needles have eyes specially shaped for certain thread types, such as metallic threads, to minimize breakage (see the Thread and Coordinating Machine-Needle Sizes chart on *page 1–9*).

MACHINE NEEDLE TYPES

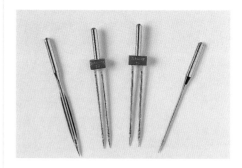

Sharps are the preferred needle type for piecing and quilting woven fabrics such as cotton. Sharps needles come in a variety of sizes and brands.

Universal needles can be used on both woven and knit fabrics but are not ideal for piecing because the needle points are slightly rounded. Choose this needle type if you want versatility when working with different fabrics.

Metallic needles are designed for use with metallic threads. A larger needle eye accommodates the thread, which tends to be fragile yet rough enough to create burrs in the eye of the needle. Burrs can cause the thread to fray and break.

Topstitch needles can handle heavier decorative threads but also leave larger holes in the fabric.

Specialty needles include double or triple needles, leather needles, and heirloom-sewing needles.

TROUBLESHOOTING CHECKLIST FOR NEEDLES

Your needle may be the culprit if these problems crop up while you're quilting.

- **Bearding** refers to the little white dots you see where your stitches come through the fabric. It occurs when batting comes through your fabric. Often the problem is caused by using too large a needle, a dull needle, or a needle that has a burr or nick.
- **Noisy machine stitching** (a sort of popping sound each time the needle pierces the fabric) is almost always a sign of a dull needle or damaged needle tip.
- **Skipped stitches** can be caused by a damaged or dull needle. If the needle is new, check to be sure it was inserted properly in the machine. Another problem may be a needle that is too small for the thread type. If the needle is too small, its front groove may be too shallow to protect the thread, causing stitches to be skipped.
- **Thread shredding** occurs for several reasons. The needle eye may be too small for the thread weight. If you have difficulty pulling the thread through the needle with ease, choose a needle with a larger eye. If you're hand quilting, you may have begun with a length of thread that's too long. If so, the thread may have become worn from being pulled through the fabric and batting too many times. If you're working with a metallic thread, be sure to use a metallic needle specifically designed to diminish thread shredding. Metallic needles have a larger eye to reduce the friction and heat caused by the speed of the machine needle piercing the fabric.

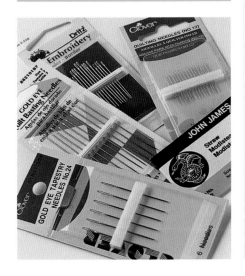

Make hand sewing easier by selecting the right needle. Myriad hand-sewing needles are available through quilt shops and fabric stores. Understanding the type, size, and uses of each needle will help you select the one most suitable for your project.

HAND NEEDLE SIZES

A hand needle's size is determined by its diameter. There are two ranges in diameter size: 1 to 15 and 13 to 28. The diameter of a specific size remains consistent across the various needle types. In each case,

the larger the number, the finer the needle; all size 12 needles are finer than size 8, for example.

HAND NEEDLE POINTS

Hand-quilting needles have a sharp point that pierces fabric readily. Working with a dull needle can be frustrating and produce less

> **TIP:** For hand-sewing needles, the larger the number, the smaller or finer the needle.

HAND-SEWING NEEDLES

SMALL ROUND EYES	TYPE	LENGTH / DIAMETER	SIZES	USES
#8 Sharps	SHARPS	Medium / 41–76 mm	4–12	Hand piecing; general sewing; fine thread embroidery; sewing binding
#8 Betweens	BETWEENS/ QUILTING	Short / 41–76 mm	4–12	Hand piecing and quilting; appliqué; sewing binding
#9 Straw	STRAW/ MILLINERS	Long / 53–76 mm	4–10	Basting; gathering; appliqué
#8 Glovers	GLOVERS	Medium with a triangular point / 86–102 mm	1–3	Leather
		53–76 mm	4–10	Leather
LONG NARROW EYES				
#8 Embroidery	EMBROIDERY	Medium / 53–102 mm	1–10	Wool thread embroidery
#9 Darners	DARNERS	Long / 46–102 mm	1–11	Basting; weaving; tying comforters
		127–234 mm	14–18	
#9 Long Darners	LONG DARNERS	Double long / 61–183 mm	1–15	Weaving; tying comforters
#10 Beading	BEADING	Double long / 25–46 mm	10–15	Bead and sequin work
LONG OVAL EYES				
#26 Chenille	CHENILLE	Medium / 61–234 mm	12–26	Heavy thread embroidery; tying comforters
#26 Tapestry	TAPESTRY/ CROSS-STITCH	Medium with blunt point / 46–234 mm	13–28	Needlepoint; cross-stitch

Tools, Notions, & Supplies

desirable results. Just as with machine sewing, switching to a new needle after several hours of sewing is optimal.

HAND NEEDLE EYES

Needles with small, round eyes carry fine thread (approximately equal in diameter to the needle itself) that slides easily through the fabric. Longer needle eyes accommodate thicker threads and yarns. The oval eye found in tapestry and chenille needles helps create an opening in the fabric for thick, sometimes coarse fibers to pass through. Use the smallest needle appropriate to the thread to minimize holes in your fabric.

HAND NEEDLE TYPES

Quilters have many different uses for hand-sewing needles—hand piecing, hand quilting, appliqué, embroidery, tying, and securing binding. The point of the needle, the shape of the eye, and the needle's length in proportion to the eye determine its type. Short needles are easier to maneuver in small spaces. For tasks that require long stitches or lots of stitches on the needle, like basting, weaving, and gathering, there are longer needles.

Betweens have a small, round eye and come in sizes 4 to 12. Betweens are short and made of fine wire, resulting in a strong, flexible needle that's ideal for hand quilting, appliqué, and sewing binding. This is the most commonly used needle for hand quilting.

Sharps have a small, round eye and come in sizes 4 to 12. They are used for hand piecing, appliqué, general sewing, embroidery work that uses fine threads, and sewing binding.

Straw, or milliners, needles come in sizes 4 to 10. They have a small, round eye and are very long. These needles are often used for basting, gathering, and appliqué.

Beading needles are extra long with long, narrow eyes. Available in sizes 10 to 15, these needles are used for embellishment, beading, and sequin work.

Chenille needles have a long, oval eye and come in sizes 12 to 26. A chenille needle is often used for heavyweight thread, embroidery, and tying quilts.

Darners have a long, narrow eye. This needle type comes in sizes 1 to 11 and is used for basting, weaving, and tying quilts. Darners are also available in finer sizes ranging from 14 to 18. Long darners (double long needles) come in sizes 1 to 15 and can be used for weaving or tying quilts.

Embroidery needles come in sizes 1 to 10 and have a long, narrow eye. They are most often used for embroidery work with thicker decorative thread and wool thread.

Experiment with different pins to determine which ones work best for your needs.

Extra-fine, or silk, pins have thin shafts and sharp points. These pins make a small hole and are easy to insert.

Glass-head pins allow you to press fabric pieces with pins in place and not melt the pins' heads.

Flat flower pins have heads shaped like flowers. The long shaft makes them easy to grab and helps the pins stay put in the fabric.

Appliqué pins range from ¾ to 1¼" in length. They are designed to securely hold work in place yet prevent the sewing thread from getting snagged with each stitch.

Safety pins are clasps with a guard covering the point when closed. Use safety pins that are at least 1" long to pin-baste a quilt. Choose stainless-steel pins that are rust-proof and will not tarnish. There are several devices, including a spoon, that can be used to help close the pins, preventing hand fatigue. In addition, there are curved basting safety pins that slide in place without moving the quilt sandwich.

GENERAL SEWING SUPPLIES

Whether you like to hand- or machine-quilt, there are a variety of general sewing supplies that are handy to have around.

NEEDLE THREADERS

Whether handheld or a machine attachment, this device makes getting the thread through the needle eye easier. Try several models to see which works best for your vision and coordination skills. Keep one close at hand to prevent eye strain.

SEAM RIPPERS

Although quilters don't enjoy "reverse sewing," sometimes it is necessary to remove a line of stitching. A sharp, good quality seam ripper can make the task of removing stitches easy and cause the least damage possible to your fabric. Choose one that is sharp and fits comfortably in your hand.

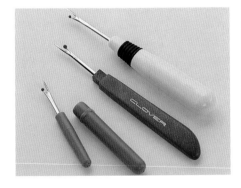

GRAPH PAPER

For pattern making or quilt designs use ⅛" (8 squares per inch) graph paper. If you're drawing a design on ¼" paper, enlarge the design on a copier by 400% to have a full-size copy. *Note:* Be sure to measure photocopies for distortion before using them as templates.

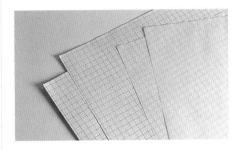

MEASURING TAPES

A measuring tape is essential for large measurements, such as border lengths or squaring up quilts. Make sure to purchase one that is long enough to cover your largest quilt measurement so you don't have to move the tape midway. Be aware that over time, a well-used cloth measuring tape may stretch and thus become inaccurate.

PINCUSHIONS

Pincushions are available in numerous styles, from the standard tomato shape so many of us are familiar with, to wrist, magnetic tabletop, and even decorative pincushions. Select a style that's easy for you to use. Some computerized machines may have problems with magnetic pincushions placed on or near the computer display screen. Check your machine manual for specific warnings.

The strawberry-shape needle cushion filled with emery that is often attached to a tomato-shape pincushion is an important aid in keeping your needles sharp and tarnish-free. Run all hand-sewing needles through the emery cushion before using them to remove any slight burrs, nicks, or residue.

STABILIZERS

Stabilizers are used beneath machine appliqué or machine embroidery work to add support to the foundation fabric, helping to eliminate puckers and pulling.

Stabilizers may be temporary or permanent. Temporary stabilizers are removed after stitching is complete. Permanent stabilizers remain in the quilt or are only partially cut away

CLASS OR WORKSHOP SUPPLY CHECKLIST

Use this list to be sure you have everything you need for a successful class.

- Supply list items specific to class (usually provided by instructor)
- Sewing machine with power cord, foot pedal, presser feet, and bobbin case
- Cutting tools
- Thread
- Bobbins
- Needles
- Scissors
- Needle threader
- Seam ripper
- Iron and pressing surface (unless provided)
- Extension cord
- Power strip
- Portable light

after stitching. Many brands are commercially available. Two of the most common types are tear-away and water-soluble. Freezer paper may also be used as a stabilizer.

Check the manufacturer's instructions on the package to select a stabilizer that is appropriate for your fabric and type of project. You may wish to experiment with a variety of stabilizers to determine which works best for you.

BIAS BARS

These heat-resistant metal or plastic bars may be purchased in a size to match the desired finished width of the bias tube you wish to make. They are a handy tool for making appliqué stems (see Chapter 8—Appliqué for more information on making bias stems).

REDUCING LENS OR DOOR PEEPHOLE

This device allows quilters to view fabrics and projects as if they are several feet away. Distance is valuable in determining design qualities (see Chapter 2—Fabric & Color for more information).

PRESSING EQUIPMENT

Proper pressing is essential to successful quilting. Even with the right equipment, understanding how to press can make a significant difference in the quality of your finished quilt. See Chapter 6—Hand Piecing and Chapter 7—Machine Piecing for information on how to press.

IRONS

Choose an iron that can be adjusted to a cotton setting and can be used with and without steam. There are a variety of irons available, including some small portable models that work well for classes or for special purposes, such as pressing bias strips or appliqués. If you plan to use your iron with fusible web, be sure to place a protective, nonstick sheet between your fabric and the iron to prevent the fusing adhesive from sticking to the sole of the iron. Or, consider purchasing a soleplate cover or second iron for use only with fusible web.

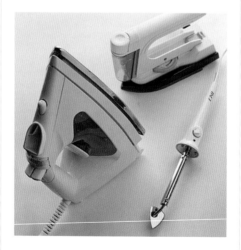

IRONING BOARD

Quilters have many choices in pressing surfaces, from the traditional ironing board with a tapered end to portable pressing surfaces/cutting boards in one. There are products available that allow you to create a pressing surface on a table, and there are large rectangular boards that fit over the traditional ironing board. The pressing surface can be covered with a purchased cover, or you can make one with batting and flannel or extra cotton fabric.

Do not choose a silver-color, teflon-coated cover for your pressing surface, as it reflects the heat, rather than allowing steam to pass completely through your fabric pieces.

STARCH AND SIZING

Some quilters like to work with fabric that has been starched, because they believe the fabric pieces are easier to handle and hold their shape better while pinning and stitching. Use a spray starch to add stiffening to prewashed fabrics or appliqué projects. Use spray sizing when more body but not as much stiffening is desired, such as when working with flannels. Wash the quilt after assembling.

ADHESIVES

BASTING SPRAY

Many brands of basting spray are available. The main point of difference is the ability to reposition the fabric. The sprays are often a good option for temporarily holding appliqués in place or for basting a small quilt or wall hanging together. Follow label directions and work in a ventilated area.

FABRIC GLUE

Fabric glue comes in several different forms. Whether you choose a type that comes in a bottle with a needle-tip applicator or a glue-stick version, important factors are making certain it is designed for use with fabric and is water-soluble and acid-free. When dry, fabric glue is more pliable than standard glue, and often its temporary bond allows you to reposition pieces without leaving permanent residue on your quilt.

FUSIBLE WEB

Available in prepackaged sheets or rolls, by the yard off the bolt, and as a narrow-width tape, fusible web is an iron-on adhesive that in nearly every case creates a permanent bond between layers of fabric.

Fusible web has adhesive on both sides with a paper backing on one side. It is most often used for machine appliqué.

The standard version for quilting is a lightweight, paper-backed fusible web specifically designed to be stitched through. When purchasing this product, check the label to make sure you've selected a sew-through type. If you are certain that you will not be sewing through the fused fabric (e.g. unfinished appliqué edges), you may wish to use a heavyweight, no-sew fusible web.

> **TIP: What is a BSK?**
> Basic Sewing Kit—You may see this abbreviation on class supply lists. Always bring along scissors, needles, and thread as part of your BSK.

The manufacturer's instructions for adhering fusible web vary by brand. Follow the instructions that come with your fusible web to ensure that you're using the correct iron temperature setting and know whether to use a dry or steam iron. These factors, along with the length of time you press, are critical to attaining a secure bond between the fusible web and the fabric.

BATTING

The material that goes between the quilt top and backing—batting—can vary from quilt to quilt. Learn the characteristics and properties of batting for the ideal match (see Chapter 10—Batting & Backing for complete information).

MACHINE QUILTING ACCESSORIES

Besides choosing needles and threads appropriate to your project, a couple other tools will make your machine quilting more successful. Personal preference dictates the use of many of the optional accessories.

QUILT CLIPS

Use quilt clips, or bicycle clips, to secure the rolled-up edges of a large quilt you are machine-quilting. These will help you better control the bulk of the quilt as you move it around while stitching.

WALKING OR EVEN-FEED FOOT

This foot evenly feeds multiple layers of fabric and batting for machine quilting, effectively providing feed dogs for the upper

fabrics to work in conjunction with the feed dogs on the machine bed. Some sewing machines come with a built-in dual-feed system, eliminating the need for a special foot. Other machines have brand-specific walking feet, while still others will accept a generic walking foot. (See Additional Accessory Feet on *page 1–19* for information on other specialty machine presser feet.)

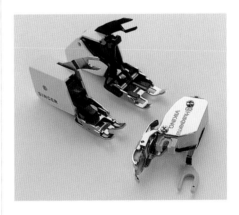

HAND QUILTING ACCESSORIES

Beyond the all-important needle and thread choices that hand quilters make, there are few other tools required. Personal preference dictates the use of many of the optional accessories.

THIMBLES

Protect your fingers while quilting with a variety of thimbles. Choose

from metal or leather, or consider special pads that stick to your finger. Try them all to determine the style that works best for you. For difficult-to-fit fingers or simply increased comfort, custom-made thimbles are widely available.

QUILTING FRAMES AND HOOPS

Wooden hoops or frames are often used to hold quilt layers together, keeping them smooth and evenly taut, for hand quilting. The layers of a quilt should be basted together before inserting them into a hoop or frame.

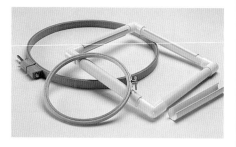

Some quilters prefer hoops because they are smaller and lighter in weight than frames, take up less storage space, are portable, and can be retightened as needed.

Quilting hoops, which generally are sturdier than embroidery hoops, may be round, oval, square, or rectangular. Semicircular hoops, which are good for stitching borders or other areas close to a quilt's edges, are also available.

Hoops come in all sizes, but one with a diameter of 10 to 20" should be able to accommodate most quilting needs. Some hoops have a detachable floor stand that frees your hands for stitching and permits the hoop to be tilted and/or raised.

Most quilting frames consist of wooden top rails in a rectangular shape supported by sturdy legs.

They come in a wide range of sizes (30 to 120") so they can handle quilts up to king size. When using a frame, a quilt's edges are pinned or stitched flat to the rails so the layers are smooth, straight, and secure. One or both pairs of frame rails can be rotated to roll up the quilt and facilitate working on a small area at a time. A quilt frame must remain set up and in place until the quilting is complete.

WORK SPACE DESIGN FOR EFFICIENCY AND COMFORT

Although quilting may seem like a sedentary activity, it takes energy and the repetitive actions can stress joints and muscles. To keep sewing comfortably, follow a few simple tips for posture and position.

POSTURE

Be aware of your body posture. A straight back with your head and neck aligned and feet flat on the floor gives you the most support. Sitting or working at awkward angles and performing repetitive motions create situations that can cause injuries.

90 DEGREES

Keep this angle in mind whenever you sit down to perform a task.

Your back and legs should be at a 90° angle. Your upper and lower legs should form a 90° angle at your knees. When your feet are flat on the floor your ankles will also be at a 90° angle. Next look at your arms. Your elbows should be at a 90° angle with your forearms parallel to the work surface. Keep your elbows close to your sides and your shoulders straight.

TABLE OR LARGE WORK SURFACE

A large work surface allows you to lay out long yardages of fabric when cutting or to handle a medium- to large-size quilt for basting. In addition, a large surface can give you room to spread out a project for machine quilting, preventing the project from dragging or pulling, which can result in uneven stitches.

ADJUST THE WORK SURFACE

Once you have determined your 90° positions, raise or lower your work surface and/or chair in order to hold these positions and work comfortably.

If you raise your chair so your arms are at the work surface, you may not be able to keep your feet flat on the floor. Put a sturdy box or platform step under your feet so your knees and ankles stay at their 90° angles.

There are several products available at quilt shops and fabric stores that can adjust the tilt of your sewing machine or foot pedal to make it more comfortable to use and easier for you to see the machine bed. Many quilters find these products ease the stress and strain on their bodies when they sew for extended periods. If possible, sit down and try the products at the shop to see if they would aid in making your work space more comfortable.

Give yourself time. If you have been working at awkward angles, your body may have adapted and it may feel strange when you adjust your posture. Stay with the correct posture and you will benefit in the long run.

Align your cutting surface to hip height to eliminate the need to bend over and unnecessarily put strain on your back and shoulder muscles. If you're rotary cutting, use sharp rotary blades and rulers with nonskid material to decrease the amount of pressure needed to cut fabric, thus reducing the strain on your body.

When hand-quilting with a frame, it is best to first position your chair with your body at 90° angles. Next measure the distance between your elbows (bent at 90°) and the floor. Set the front roller bar of the quilting frame at this height, then adjust the back of the quilting frame.

DESIGN WALL

Having a vertical surface on which to lay out fabric choices can help you visualize how they might look in a quilt. For a permanent or portable design wall, cover foam core or board insulation with a napped material, such as felt or flannel, that will hold small fabric pieces in place. Some designers use the flannel backing of a vinyl tablecloth which can be rolled up between projects or hung on a hanger.

LIGHTING

Quilting requires overall lighting and nonglare directional lighting to avoid eyestrain and produce high-quality results. Review your quilting areas for lighting and invest in the appropriate fixtures to eliminate the headaches and vision problems that can result from eyestrain.

Several specialty lamps and bulbs specifically designed for quilters are available at quilt shops. Some are designed to more accurately reflect the colors of fabrics, filtering out excess yellow and blue tones that common household bulbs can cast. These can be especially helpful when you are selecting fabric combinations for your quilts and if your quilting area does not have abundant natural daylight.

WORKSHOP AND RETREAT SETUP

Plan for your posture and comfort needs when going to workshops and retreats. Bring your own portable table and chair, or anticipate the type of chair (often folding) and table (often portable and 30" high). Borrow a folding chair ahead of time and note your posture and the 90° positions. Use pillows or boxes to adjust your height, and take them to your class. Being properly positioned will allow you to be more productive and reduce the chances of developing pain in your joints and muscles.

KEEP MOVING FOR PERSONAL COMFORT

Though it's easy to get lost in your quilting, it is important to your overall health to pause for a few minutes every hour to step away from your sewing machine or quilting frame and stretch. If you take time to reposition yourself periodically, you can reduce muscle fatigue and eyestrain, and enjoy several hours of quilting. Speak with your health care provider about specific exercises that can help strengthen your neck, back, shoulders, arms, wrists, and hands.

> **CHECKLIST FOR HEALTHY QUILTING**
> - No reaching up to the work surface
> - No hunching over
> - No reaching over or out to the work surface (elbows at your side)
> - Take 10-minute breaks every hour
> - Drink extra water

SEWING MACHINES

Essential to machine piecing and quilting is the sewing machine. A serviceable, basic machine in good working order is sufficient for most purposes. Newer machines offer some features and optional accessories that make piecing and quilting easier and more enjoyable. Select a brand that can have its annual maintenance and repairs handled conveniently.

Understanding your machine's features can help you avoid problems or fix them when they arise. Your machine's manual is the best resource for specific information and problem solving. Some basic information applicable to most sewing machines follows.

HOW MACHINES STITCH

Two threads coming together to hold pieces of fabric in place may appear to be magic. In reality, it takes sophisticated engineering for the two threads to create straight and decorative stitches. Understanding how thread travels through the sewing machine can be useful in preventing and solving problems.

The seams created by machine are a series of lockstitches or knots. To create lockstitches on most machines, the thread runs from the spool through tension discs and into the take-up lever. As the needle goes down into the bobbin case, the take-up lever also moves down. In the bobbin case, the bobbin hook creates a loop that interlaces with the thread coming through the needle eye. As the take-up lever and needle come back up through the fabric, the loop formed with the bobbin and needle threads is pulled up to create a stitch.

SEWING MACHINE FEATURES

Only one basic function is needed to piece and quilt by machine—sewing straight, uniform stitches to create a seam that doesn't pucker or pull the fabric. Optional features may include some or all of the following.

Adjustable Stitch Length

This feature enables you to change your stitch length from long stitches for basting to tiny stitches you might use to secure your thread at the beginning or end of a seam or quilted area. In many newer machines, this feature is expressed in millimeters (10 to 12 stitches per inch equals a 2.0- to 2.5-mm setting). If knowing the stitches per

inch is important to your project, create a sample swatch and measure the number of stitches in an inch.

Adjustable Stitch Width

This feature enables you to widen zigzag and other decorative machine stitches. It can be an important feature if you enjoy crazy quilting with decorative stitches (see Chapter 13—Specialty Techniques).

Zigzag and Satin Stitch

For a zigzag stitch, often used in machine appliqué, the needle swings from left to right. Adjusting the stitch length will produce stitches that are closer together. When the stitches form one against the other, filling any gaps, this creates satin stitching (see Chapter 8—Appliqué). Often the width of the stitch also can be varied.

Needle-Down Option

Once engaged, this feature allows the needle to stop sewing in the down position every time, allowing you to pivot or adjust the fabric without losing your stitching position. If disengaged, the needle will always stop in the up position.

> **READY-TO-SEW MACHINE CHECKLIST**
> - Machine in good working order
> - Foot pedal and machine plugged in
> - New needle in correct size for project
> - Correct presser foot
> - Bobbin wound
> - Threading done properly
> - Tension adjusted

Adjustable Feed Dogs

The ability to drop or cover the feed dogs is important if you want to do free-motion quilting (see Chapter 13—Specialty Techniques). When the feed dogs are in the up position, they grab onto the fabric as it moves under the presser foot.

With the feed dogs in the down position and a darning presser foot on, you can move the fabric freely on the machine bed, controlling where and at what rate the fabric feeds beneath the presser foot.

Easily Accessible Bobbin Case

When your bobbin runs out of thread, especially if you're in the middle of a project, being able to easily change or refill it is important. Look for a machine that offers easy access to the bobbin so that you don't have to take apart the machine bed or remove the machine from the cabinet.

Extended Machine Bed Surface

An extended surface is important if you do not have your machine in a cabinet with the arm in line with the cabinet surface and you're piecing or quilting large projects. Some portable machines come with a snap-on or slide-on tray that extends the bed of the machine. You may also purchase a surround that is customized to fit around the arm of your sewing machine to extend the work area. The larger, level work surface prevents the fabric from pulling and stretching under its own weight as you work with it.

Knee-Lift Presser Foot

This feature enables you to lift and lower the presser foot by pressing your knee on a bar that extends down from the machine front. It can be especially helpful when you need both hands free to hold your fabric.

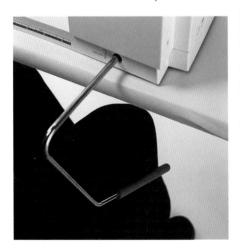

SEWING-MACHINE ACCESSORIES

Many machines come with a kit of standard accessories. Some have optional accessories you can purchase.

There are also a number of generic sewing accessories designed to work with a variety of machine models. Knowing your model brand and number when purchasing generic accessories is helpful, as the packaging often states the machines and brands with which the accessories will work.

Straight-Stitch Throat Plate

A straight-stitch throat plate has a small, round hole for the needle to pass through, rather than the larger opening of a standard throat plate. This smaller opening allows less area for the sewing machine to take in or "swallow" the fabric as it is being stitched and results in more uniform stitches.

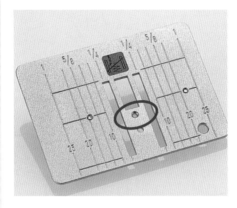

¼" Foot

Some machines allow you to reposition the needle so that it's ¼" from the edge of the standard presser foot. In addition, many machine models offer a special ¼" presser foot. With this foot and the needle in the standard position, the edge of the foot serves as the seam guide. For piecing, it is a useful accessory as you can watch only the edge of the fabric along the presser foot edge; you don't need to watch or mark a line along the throat plate or machine bed.

Additional Accessory Feet

An array of specialty feet, including open-toe appliqué and darning (used for free-motion quilting), cording, and binding feet, are available for a variety of machines. (See Machine Quilting Accessories on *page 1–15* for information on a walking, or even-feed, foot.) Check with your sewing machine's manufacturer for a complete list, or check the packaging of generic accessory feet to determine which models might be compatible with your machine.

(See Machine Quilting Accessories on *page 1–15* for information on a walking, or even-feed, foot.)

TENSION

When tension is balanced, stitches appear on both sides of the fabric without loops, surface knots, or broken thread.

For most piecing, your machine's tension will not need to be adjusted. Tension problems tend to be more prevalent when you're sewing with fabrics of different weights, heavy or decorative threads, or specialty needles. As with all sewing machine

Knowing what affects the tension on your particular machine is critical for professional results.

adjustments, check your machine's manual first when attempting to solve a tension problem.

ADJUSTING UPPER THREAD TENSION

When a "bird's nest" of thread appears either on top of or underneath your fabric, the likely culprit is your upper thread tension. To determine what to correct, follow these guidelines:

If loops appear on the underside of the fabric, the upper thread tension may be too loose.

If knots appear on top of the fabric, the upper tension may be too tight.

Before adjusting the machine's tension dial, check to be sure your machine is properly threaded. If the presser foot was lowered as you were threading your machine, it is likely the upper thread is not between the tension discs inside the machine. Or, you may have missed one of the tension guides or the take-up lever. Simply raise the presser foot and rethread your machine.

If the problem still occurs, you may need to adjust the upper tension dial. If your tension is too tight, adjust the dial to a lower number to loosen it. If the upper thread tension is too loose, adjust the dial to a higher number to tighten it. Refer to your machine's manual for specific instructions about making tension dial adjustments.

ADJUSTING BOBBIN THREAD TENSION

Although many machines allow you to adjust the upper thread tension, the bobbin thread tension is generally set by the machine's manufacturer. It doesn't usually need to be adjusted unless you're working with decorative or specialty threads (see Extra Bobbin Case, *opposite*).

If your bobbin thread is knotting up on the underside of your fabric, try removing the bobbin and reloading it, making sure to properly insert the thread through the bobbin tension slots as directed in your sewing machine's manual.

In some cases, you may need to try threading your bobbin thread through the hole in the bobbin case "finger" to increase the tension. Your machine manual will have instructions for this procedure if it is an option on your machine.

BOBBINS

For general piecing and quilting, use the same type of thread in the bobbin as in the top of the machine. Metallic and decorative threads are the exceptions (see *page 1–6*). Trying to save money by using a less expensive or different type of thread in the bobbin can lead to tension difficulties.

Use bobbins that are specifically designed for your machine.

There are two basic types of bobbin mechanisms. The first is a front-loading bobbin, in which a filled bobbin fits into a bobbin case that then snaps into the opening on the front of the machine.

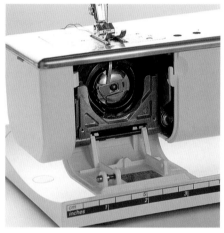

The second type of bobbin mechanism is the top-loading, or drop-in, bobbin. This type usually does not have a separate bobbin case. Instead, the filled bobbin simply drops into the bobbin casing in the bed of the machine, usually in front of the presser foot.

Winding Bobbins

For large projects, keep multiple bobbins filled by winding several at one sitting.

Follow your machine manufacturer's directions for bobbin winding. Be sure to start the thread in the correct direction and wind at a speed that allows for even filling. Winding your bobbin at too fast a speed can stretch the thread, resulting in a puckered seam.

Disposable, prewound bobbins are another option, depending on what your machine will accept and what your project requires.

Extra Bobbin Case

The bobbin case that came with your machine has been factory set for sewing with basic threads. If you plan to sew with specialty threads, consider purchasing an additional bobbin case (if your machine accepts one) for use with decorative or thicker threads.

You will need to adjust the tension for these threads by turning the screw on the bobbin case's tension spring. Turn it to the left to loosen the tension and to the right to tighten the tension.

For heavy, thick threads the tension generally needs to be loosened, and this should be accomplished in less than two complete rotations of the screw. Work over a bowl, box, or plastic bag in case the screw comes out.

Always sew a test sample after adjusting the screw.

Place a dot of nail polish or permanent marker on the second case to designate it as the case that has had its tension adjusted.

If you only have one bobbin case, make notes in this book or in your machine's manual to indicate changes in screw or tension settings when using different threads. For example, you might write "left 1½ turns for No. 5 perle cotton."

My Notes for Tools, Notions, & Supplies

My Notes for Tools, Notions, & Supplies

Fabric & Color

2

FABRIC & COLOR

TABLE OF CONTENTS
Chapter 2—Fabric & Color

SELECTING JUST THE RIGHT FABRICS IN JUST THE RIGHT COLORS is part of the fun of quilting. For some quilters, however, this step in the quiltmaking process can be the most daunting. Understanding how your fabric and color choices affect the overall appearance of a finished quilt can help make the selection process easier.

FABRIC

Understanding how fabric is made and what kind of finishes are applied can help you select fabric for your project.

FABRIC MANUFACTURING BASICS

Most quilting fabrics begin as greige (gray-zh) goods, which means unbleached and undyed. Fabrics in this state must be cleaned and prepared before any color can be added or design printed. Greige goods can range in weave from loose to tight and their surfaces may have imperfections. The number of threads per square inch varies according to each manufacturer's specifications. Each of these characteristics affects the finished product's quality, durability, hand (or feel), and price.

Because manufacturers try to meet different market demands for products and prices, it's common for a manufacturer to print the same design on different quality greige goods. The fabrics may appear the same and have the same manufacturer and designer names

printed on the selvages, but may vary in terms of durability or quality.

Homespuns are one of the few fabric types that don't begin as greige goods. Instead, they are woven with colored threads.

PRODUCING A FINISHED PRODUCT

Color and design are dyed, screen printed, or roller printed onto greige goods. Occasionally dyed fabrics may be overprinted, meaning they are first dyed, then printed.

Finishes are added to greige goods through mechanical or chemical means and range from temporary to permanent. Permanent finishes, as the label implies, endure for the life of the fabric. Durable finishes lose some of their properties with each cleaning, but, with proper care, should last nearly as long as the fabric. Semidurable finishes will last through several launderings, while temporary finishes are lost after the first washing.

Many quilting cottons have a finish applied to reduce wrinkling. This is beneficial when you're working with a fabric, and is important to know as it may affect your ability to press seams flat by preventing the fabric from holding a sharp crease.

Fabrics with a polished appearance on one side have been glazed. The finish tends to wear off over time, but some quilters find it helpful during quiltmaking as it adds a stiffness to the fabric.

More loosely woven fabrics are sometimes finished with a process called napping, which creates flannel. The fabric runs over a series of napping rolls that raise the surface nap of the fabric. Fabrics can be napped on one or both sides.

Because of the looser yarns and weave required to create the nap, flannel fabrics tend to shrink more than other woven fabrics do.

Cotton fabrics with an especially soft feel may have had a mechanical sueding finish applied.

FIBER CONTENT

The preferred fabric fiber content for quilting is 100% cotton. However, even within this category, there are choices to make. Other fiber content options also are available.

100% Cotton

Cotton is woven in many ways to create a variety of products. Some of these products work well in quilts, and others are better suited for home decorating and garment making. Poplin, chino, chenille, and velveteen can be 100% cotton, for example, but may not work well for intricately pieced quilts.

Always consider the intended use when choosing quilting fabrics, as different fabrics behave in different ways when sewn, pressed, hung, or laundered. If you plan to combine different types of 100% cotton fabrics in a quilt, know that the

pieced units will only be as strong as the weakest fabric, and you may have to deal with such complications as puckering, sagging, and pulling.

Several types of 100% cotton fabrics are often used in quiltmaking. They include broadcloth or plain-weave cotton, homespun, flannel, and chintz.

Broadcloth or Plain-Weave Cotton:
This fabric, often called quilters' cotton, has several benefits, including a weight, or body, that allows it to be sewn with little slippage. It creases well, so seams open flat. It is durable and doesn't readily fray. It also will tear along the grain line. When used in bedding, cotton's natural fibers wick moisture away from the body, increasing comfort.

Homespun:
Already-dyed threads are woven into a solid, plaid, striped, or checked design for these fabrics. They are often used when a primitive look is desired.

Flannel:
This fabric is woven of a bulkier cotton thread with a looser fiber, then brushed to give it a nap.

Chintz:
A high thread count and glazed finish make this fabric more difficult to needle than other 100% cottons. It frequently puckers when stitched, and needles and pins may cause permanent holes.

Other Fiber Choices
Fabrics with a fiber content other than 100% cotton, including wool and silk, can be used in quilting, though it's best to stick with the same content within a single quilt.

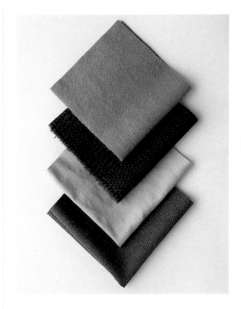

Wool: Working with wool offers quilters nearly as many options as working with cotton. Felted wool is especially easy to use in appliqué, as the edges don't need to be turned under since they will not ravel.

To felt wool, machine-wash it in a hot-water wash/cool-water rinse cycle with a small amount of detergent, machine-dry, and steam press. If you wish to use wool from a piece of clothing, cut it apart and remove the seams before washing so it can shrink freely.

Silk: This natural fiber has luster and can be smooth or have slubs (small threads) on the surface. Silk generally requires more care in cleaning than cotton does.

DETERMINING FIBER CONTENT AND THREAD COUNT
Check the Fabric Bolt End
The percentage of fibers is usually listed on the end of the fabric's cardboard bolt, along with information about special finishes, such as if the fabric is chintz or is permanent press. Care instructions,

style number, the fabric and manufacturer's name, and any processing, such as preshrinking, will also be noted.

Note: Some fabric stores rewrap fabric flat folds around unused cardboard bolts. Be sure to confirm that the information on the bolt end matches the manufacturer and fabric name on the fabric selvage.

Thread Count
The number of threads per square inch determines the quality and weight of a fabric. If the thread count is the same for both length and width, the fabric is said to have an even weave.

Quilting cotton has a higher thread count (68×68 threads per square inch) than lighter-weight cotton. Fabrics with low thread counts (less than 60×60 threads per square inch) are too lightweight to use successfully in a quilt, as they will ravel excessively when they are handled. Low thread counts also mean more shrinkage, less durability, and bearding (batting coming through the quilt top or backing). Pieces can fray and fall apart if seams need to be removed.

Higher thread counts and extremely tight weaves can be difficult to needle. It may be tempting to use a sheet for a quilt back, for example, but the finish and thread count make it difficult to work with and create puckering.

GRAIN LINE

Cutting pieces according to a fabric's grain line makes for more accurate piecing and a stronger finished quilt top. Following the grain line reduces stretching and distortion, enhancing the overall appearance of your finished quilt.

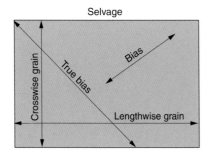

In weaving fabric, manufacturers place the lengthwise threads (warp) tightly in the loom to eliminate stretch. The crosswise (weft) threads are then woven into the lengthwise threads, but are not stretched as tightly, leaving a little "give" in the finished fabric.

Fabric pieces cut diagonally across the grain line, or on the bias, are susceptible to stretching because there are no stabilizing threads along the edges. If the design motif can only be cut on the bias, backing it with a lightweight fusible web can help to stabilize it.

RIGHT SIDE/WRONG SIDE

Most manufacturers print on one side of the greige goods. This means the fabric has two sides (right and wrong, or front and back). The back of the fabric, or wrong side, may have some color from the dye bleeding through. If you need a lighter shade of a fabric in your quilt, you may wish to use the "back" or wrong side of the fabric as the right side.

Batiks have very little difference between the right and wrong sides. Homespuns, which are woven from already-dyed threads, look the same on both sides.

SPECIALTY FABRIC CUTS

Two common specialty cuts of fabrics—fat quarters and fat eighths—are found in a majority of quilt shops. Many quilters find these sizes offer more versatility for cutting templates or strips than the actual ¼-yard and ⅛-yard cuts.

Fat Quarter

Although a traditional ¼-yard cut and a fat-quarter cut are the same amount of fabric, the difference is the shape. A traditional ¼-yard cut measures 9×44". A fat quarter is ¼ yard of fabric cut crosswise from a ½-yard piece of fabric—an 18×44" rectangle of fabric cut in half to yield an 18×22" "fat" ¼-yard piece.

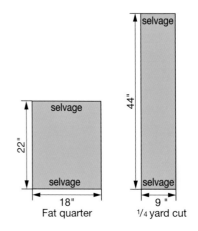

Fat Eighth

Although a traditional ⅛-yard cut and a fat-eighth cut are the same amount of fabric, the difference is the shape. A traditional ⅛-yard cut is 4½×44". A fat eighth is cut crosswise from a ¼-yard piece of fabric—a 9×44" rectangle of fabric cut in half to make a 9×22" "fat" ⅛-yard piece.

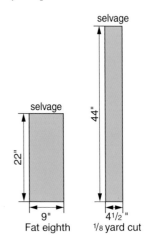

BEFORE YOU BUY FABRIC

Determine how much fabric you'll need for a project before you go shopping. Graph paper helps take out the guesswork.

Use graph paper to create a cutting diagram. Let each square equal 1" and map out the needed pieces. You may wish to purchase ⅛ to ¼ yard more fabric than your layout requires to allow for inches that may be lost in squaring up fabric edges, shrinkage during prewashing, and/or cutting errors.

Make template windows out of sturdy paper or cardboard to take to the fabric store for previewing fabric options. Do not include seam allowances in the window cut, but do leave a healthy margin of paper

around each window to help differentiate what's showing through from the rest of the bolt. Viewing a fabric through a template window can help you see what individual pieces look like more easily than looking at the whole bolt will.

Once you're in the quilt store or fabric shop, the array of colors and designs that fill the shelves can be both exciting and intimidating. When you're selecting fabrics for a project, consider the following suggestions:

Separate the bolts you're interested in from the other fabrics. Examine them away from other fabrics to avoid confusion or interference from other colors.

Stack the bolts horizontally to view how the fabrics may appear when cut into smaller shapes (if you don't have template windows) and how they work together.

Stand back about 10 feet and look at the bolts stacked horizontally. A view from this distance will give you an idea of how a fabric combination will work in a quilt.

Find optimum light. Fluorescent lighting can sometimes cast a yellow glow, altering the appearance of a fabric's true colors. Take the bolts to the area of the store that has the most natural light. Stand with the light at your back and let it wash across the bolts.

FABRIC PREPARATION

All fabrics are subject to loss of color from washing, exposure to light, and abrasion. Whether to prewash fabrics or not is a topic of much debate among quilters.

Many of those who don't prewash find it easier to work with fabrics that have the sizing and finish from the manufacturing process still on them. Others don't prewash because the shrinkage of the fabric after a quilt is complete can create the rumpled, old look of an antique that they desire.

Some quilters favor prewashing fabrics to reduce uneven shrinkage or colors bleeding once a quilt is complete.

Your decision about prewashing may change from one project to the next. Consider these color-retention factors when making your choice.

COLOR-RETENTION FACTORS

Whether you're prewashing fabric or laundering a finished quilt, several factors affect a fabric's ability to retain its color.

Hot water can be damaging to any fabric's color and finish. Cold water is safest for washing cotton. Check first to see if any color is released at this temperature by filling a clear

glass with cold water and dropping in a swatch of the fabric. If the water changes color as a result of dyes being released, prewashing the fabric will be necessary to rid the fabric of excess dye before using it in a quilt. After prewashing, retest a swatch in a clear glass to see if the dye-bleeding problem has been resolved.

Detergents can break down the binding agents that hold pigment on cloth. Detergents with chlorine bleach can damage fiber-reactive dyes. Gentle soaps and cleansers made specifically for cleaning quilts are widely available at quilt shops and some fabric stores.

As with any product, it is important to follow the manufacturer's instructions and use the correct amount. Soils remain if too little is used, and fabric is affected if too much is used and it's not rinsed out properly.

Abrasion, or the friction of fabrics rubbing against each other, may cause crocking, which is a transfer of color from one fabric to another. The friction may be caused by handling or from contact in the washer and dryer. Colors may leach out of a piece of fabric, causing a color loss in that piece, but the real concern is whether or not the dye will then permanently reattach itself to other fabrics.

If you are working with high-contrast fabrics, such as red and white, one method of testing for crocking is to pretreat the fabrics as desired, then vigorously rub them against one another. If any of the darker color rubs off on the lighter fabric, you must pretreat it again until the fabric passes the rub test.

Another test to determine if color will migrate from one fabric to another is to put the suspect fabric (usually a dark, intensely colored fabric) in a jar of water with 1 teaspoon of the detergent you might launder it in. Check for color loss after 10 minutes. If color is present in the water, add a piece of the light fabric to the water and shake the jar several times. Leave both fabrics in the water for 10 minutes, then remove the lighter sample and compare it to the original light fabric. If there is no transfer of color, the dark fabric should be safe to use even with color loss in the water.

FABRIC AND QUILT CARE

Caring for fabrics properly, both before and after they're sewn into a quilt, can increase their longevity. Whether your quilts are stored for a long period of time or are periodically rotated on display, follow these guidelines to protect them from fiber damage and keep them at their best.

SOURCES OF FIBER DAMAGE
Light
Fluorescent lights and ultraviolet radiation from sunlight cause fabric dyes to fade and fibers to become brittle. Rotate quilts frequently to prevent damage from exposure to light. Watch quilts displayed on beds, as the side exposed to sunlight from a nearby window may fade. Cover windows with shades when sunlight is direct. Make sure that quilts are not stored in an area exposed to direct sunlight to prevent the exposed portions from fading.

Folds and Creases
When folded fabrics or quilts are stored for long periods of time, the fibers along the folds begin to weaken, and permanent creases can develop. Some quilters refold their fabrics periodically to keep this from occurring. It's best to roll, rather than fold, quilts for storage, adding acid-free tissue paper between the layers of the quilt to help prevent creasing.

Acid
Paper, cardboard, plastics, and unfinished wood in shelves, drawers, and trunks release acid, which is damaging to plant-derived fabrics, such as cotton and linen. Prevent your fabrics and quilts from coming in contact with these surfaces by rolling them in acid-free tissue paper and storing them in acid-free boxes or white, cotton pillowcases.

TIP: Clean Hands Preserve Quilts
From the first cut of fabric to the last stitch of the binding, having clean hands and a clean work area will help preserve your quilt. Wash your hands often when working on a project and avoid contact with food and drink. Residues from the acids and salts on your hands and in food products may attract insects, which will cause damage. White gloves aren't only for quilt shows; use them when handling quilts that you want to preserve for generations.

Mold/Mildew

Mold and mildew flourish in warm, moist environments, so quilts shut in closed containers or wrapped in plastic and stored in areas of temperature extremes and excess moisture (attics, basements, garages) are susceptible to the growth of these fungi.

To avoid the irreversible damage caused by mold and mildew, and to protect your quilts from dust and other elements, store them in a cool, dry location (less than 50% humidity) wrapped in white, cotton pillowcases to allow air to pass through and let the quilts breathe.

Time

Antique fibers need to be handled with care. Vintage fabrics can be prone to damage by laundering. Unstable dyes and pigments, weave, and age make these fabrics especially sensitive to today's cleaning methods.

For example, some older fabrics were made with unstable dyes, and any contact with moisture may cause them to bleed. This is especially noticeable with brown

and black dyes in antique quilts. Other fabrics become brittle with time and may turn to powder.

Contact an expert, such as a quilt preservationist or appraiser at a museum or university, for recommendations on handling, cleaning, and preserving older quilts.

CARING FOR QUILTS ON DISPLAY

Rotate the quilts on display often to give them a rest. This will diminish their exposure to dust, light, and other potential sources of fiber damage (see Sources of Fiber Damage, which begins on *page 2–5*, for more information).

A quilt that doesn't have an obvious top or bottom can be turned periodically to prevent distortion or damage to the fibers along one end. You may wish to add a hanging sleeve to more than one edge to make rotating the quilt easier. (See Chapter 12—Binding & Finishing for information on adding hanging sleeves.)

CLEANING METHODS

Avoid washing a quilt unless it's absolutely necessary. Washing, even when done on a gentle cycle, causes

fabrics to fade and is abrasive to fibers. Clean and freshen a quilt using one of these methods.

Airing Outdoors

Annually take quilts outdoors on an overcast, dry, and windy day to be refreshed. Place towels or a mattress pad on the dry ground and lay your quilts on them. Cover the quilts with a sheet to prevent debris from falling on them. Avoid placing quilts on a clothesline to prevent stress on the seams.

Using a Dryer

Quilts can be freshened in a dryer on a gentle-cycle/air-dry setting without heat.

Vacuuming

Vacuuming both the front and back of a quilt can help preserve it by removing dust and dirt. Place a nylon hose or net over the end of a vacuum hose and gently draw the hose over the quilt's surface without rubbing it. You can also lay a piece of clean screening on the quilt, then vacuum it. Always clean a quilt with at least a quick vacuuming to remove airborne dust and dirt before storing it.

TROUBLESHOOTING TIP:
It's often too much time in an overly hot dryer that shrinks cotton fabrics unnecessarily, as most shrinkage happens near the end of the drying cycle, when the fabric is about 75% dry. If line-drying your fabrics isn't an option, remove them from the dryer when they're still damp and press them with a dry iron.

TIP: Evaluate antique quilts individually before attempting to clean them. Improper cleaning can damage a quilt. If a quilt has sentimental or monetary value, consult an expert before attempting to clean it. Contact a quilt museum, university textile department, or antique expert for references.

Washing

As a last resort, cotton quilts can be washed in cold water with a gentle soap by hand or in the machine on a gentle cycle. Do not wring or twist a quilt; instead gently squeeze out the water. Wet quilts are heavy and need to be supported when you are moving them to a flat area to dry.

Washing by Hand

1. Use a clean tub that is free from other soaps or cleaning materials.

2. Place a large towel or cotton blanket in the tub to support the quilt.

3. Thoroughly dissolve soap in water prior to adding the quilt to the tub. Be sure you have enough water in the tub to cover the quilt.

4. Place the quilt in the tub. Gently agitate (do not wring or twist) the quilt to release the dirt and soil.

5. Rinse the quilt by draining and refilling the tub. Repeat as needed to remove soap, as residue can build up on a quilt's surface.

6. Press excess water out of the quilt, starting at the end farthest from the drain and working your way across the quilt. Use towels to blot up excess water.

7. Remove the quilt from the tub, using the large towel or cotton blanket beneath it.

8. Spread the quilt flat on a clean sheet that has been placed out of direct sunlight. Let it air-dry, using a fan to speed the process.

Washing by Machine

1. Fill the washing machine with water and dissolve the soap.

2. Place the quilt in the machine. Let it soak for up to 15 minutes, checking it frequently to make sure the fabric dyes are stable and not running onto neighboring fabrics. If desired, agitate the quilt on a gentle cycle for up to five minutes. *Note:* A front-loading washing machine will not allow you to soak the quilt in the washer drum. Agitating on a gentle cycle is necessary in this type of washing machine.

3. Repeat steps 1 and 2 with fresh soap and water if a quilt is especially soiled.

4. Use a gentle spin cycle to rinse the quilt and remove the excess water. Continue to rinse and spin until the rinse water is free of soap.

5. Remove the quilt from the machine and spread it flat on a clean sheet that has been placed out of direct sunlight. Let it air-dry, using a fan to speed the process.

Dry Cleaning

It is wise to check references before selecting a dry cleaner to handle your quilts, as dry cleaning can cause cotton dyes to bleed or change color.

Take special precautions if you wish to dry-clean a wool or silk quilt. Dry cleaning should be a last resort, used only if vacuuming or spot cleaning doesn't remove the soil.

TIP: An unused bed makes an ideal storage spot for quilts. Spread your quilts on the bed, separating them with layers of cotton fabric, cotton sheets, or batting to prevent any dye transfer.

DESIGN CONCEPTS

Use the three Cs when selecting fabrics for your quilt—contrast, color, and character.

Although color is fun and exciting, it is contrast, or differences in values, that often makes a design successful. Without contrast in value between pieces in a block or the blocks in a quilt top, the colors will blend together and the design itself may get lost.

It's important to choose colors that appeal to you and suit the design. A block design may work with odd colors that have good contrast, but it may not be as visually pleasing.

The character of the fabric, or its motif, also influences a quilt. Motifs can range from polka dots or stripes to florals, calicoes, novelty prints, plaids, and large-scale patterns.

SEEING DESIGN AT WORK

Different quilts and styles of quilting attract different quilters for different reasons. Before you select fabrics, it may be helpful to thumb through quilting books, magazines, and patterns. Note the common qualities among the quilts that attract your eye.

Do you like quilts with stark contrast between colors, such as a quilt composed solely of red and white? Are you attracted to scrappy

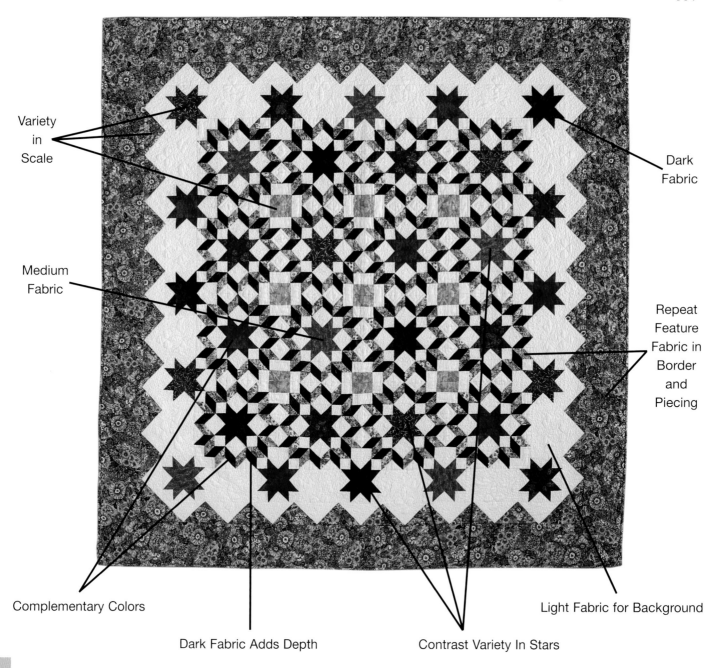

Variety in Scale

Dark Fabric

Medium Fabric

Repeat Feature Fabric in Border and Piecing

Complementary Colors

Dark Fabric Adds Depth

Contrast Variety In Stars

Light Fabric for Background

quilts with dozens of different fabrics included? Do you like quilts with muted tones where the colors seem to meld together?

Knowing what you like is the first step in selecting fabrics. For an idea of where to start, look at the quilt *opposite*. Study its design in terms of color, contrast, and character to learn how the fabric choices affect a quilt's overall appearance.

This quilt provides a good example of how to use a range of light-, medium-, and dark-value fabrics in a composition. The light background brings out the lighter colors in the other fabrics, while the light-color shapes and images in the quilt center appear to come forward.

The dark fabrics appear smaller in the overall quilt design. The dark shapes and images seem to recede, adding depth to the design.

The medium fabrics are a mix of light and dark colors, eliminating the possibility of a blended or flat design. The floral print used in the rings that surround the stars is repeated in the border, giving the quilt continuity. Its large-scale print also adds nice balance to the small-scale light and dark prints.

CONTRAST (VALUE)

One of the first design concepts to consider when composing a quilt is contrast. Many quilt patterns list the fabrics needed for a project in terms of their contrast or values—light, medium, or dark. Learning to see fabrics in these categories of contrast can enhance your fabric selection success.

WHY CONTRAST?

Contrast clarifies the design and makes depth apparent. Without contrast between the medium gold and the medium green in the block *below*, the pieces in the block blend together, and the design appears flat.

The shapes take on new dimensions when the fabrics—a dark purple, medium green, and light yellow—have more contrast.

TIP: Fabric manufacturers tend to produce more fabrics in the medium range. When you see light or dark fabrics that you like, add them to your stash.

Contrast, however, is a relative concept. The block *below* uses a medium-value purple for the center star and a darker purple for the background. Because there isn't too much difference between the medium and dark values, the contrast in the resulting block is subtle.

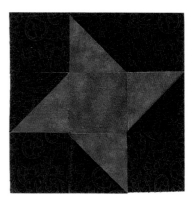

When the same medium-value purple is paired with a light purple background fabric, the resulting block *below* has a higher contrast than the first one because of the difference in values between the purples.

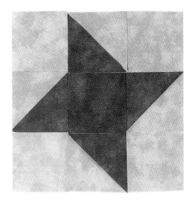

Understanding the relative contrast of color choices is helpful when selecting fabric for your quilt, so you'll achieve the desired contrast between elements.

VISUALIZING CONTRAST

Trying to ignore color and just study contrast is not an easy task. When looking at fabrics in a store or from your fabric stash, try these techniques to see the contrast or value.

Select your fabrics for a project, then perform one or more of these tests to see if you've included enough contrast in the group.

If you need more contrast, substitute lighter or darker fabrics until you have a variety of values.

Try squinting. Closing your eyes slightly limits the amount of light they receive and reduces your perception of color, so contrast becomes more evident.

Use a reducing tool. Purchase a reducing glass or a door peephole.

These tools reduce an image, making color less obvious and contrast more apparent when the fabrics are viewed. Taking instant photographs or looking through a camera also works in this regard.

Look through red cellophane. This technique obliterates the color and allows you to see the continuum of values from light to dark.

Make black and white photocopies. Photocopying completely masks color and can give an indication of contrast between and within pieces of fabric.

QUICK REFERENCE CHART
DETERMINING CONTRAST LEVELS FOR A QUILT BLOCK

Use the chart *below* and the photo at *right* to assess how changing the contrast between the background and block pieces will affect the block's overall appearance.

For example, if you've chosen a light background and light block pieces (*upper left*), you'll achieve a block with low or no contrast. In comparison, a dark background with light block pieces results in a block with high contrast (*lower left*).

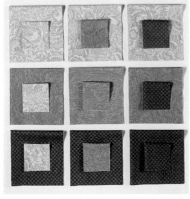

	BLOCK PIECES		
		LIGHT	MEDIUM	DARK
BACKGROUND	**LIGHT**	Low or no contrast	Some contrast	High contrast
	MEDIUM	Some contrast	Low or no contrast	Some contrast
	DARK	High contrast	Some contrast	Low or no contrast

COLOR

After contrast, color or hue becomes the next design element to consider when selecting fabrics for your quilts. Where contrast is an objective quality, color is more subjective and often evokes emotion.

Successfully combining colors takes observation, practice, and a little help from the color wheel. Study the color palettes of quilts, artwork, or fashions that appeal to you. Note the main color and how it is combined with other hues.

USING THE COLOR WHEEL IN QUILTING

Artists in many mediums use the color wheel. With paint the result of blending colors is a little more predictable than with fabric because paint is solid; it doesn't have pattern or texture. Even so, the color wheel is a useful guide in choosing fabric colors.

PRIMARY COLORS

All colors are derived from the three primary colors: red, blue, and yellow. Though you may think of them in terms of color, black, gray, and white are not on the color wheel.

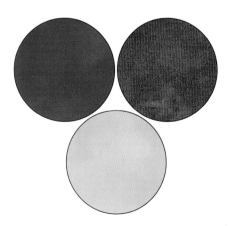

QUICK REFERENCE CHART
PRIMARY AND SECONDARY COLOR COMBINATIONS

PRIMARY COLOR	ANALOGOUS COLORS	COMPLEMENTARY COLOR
	Neighboring colors that coordinate with the primary color. These colors share the primary color, so they'll always work together.	The color opposite a primary color on the color wheel that contains the other two primary colors. A small amount of a color's complement can serve as an accent.
Red	Orange Violet	Green
Blue	Violet Green	Orange
Yellow	Green Orange	Violet

The six-piece color wheel shows the relationship of the primary and secondary colors. Use the information above to understand how analogous and complementary colors work together.

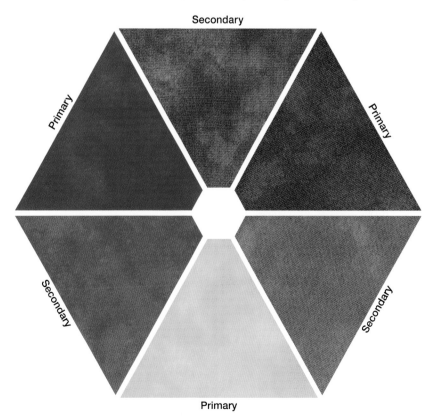

QUICK REFERENCE CHART
12-PIECE COLOR WHEEL (PRIMARY, SECONDARY, AND TERTIARY COLORS)

The middle ring of this color wheel shows the color or hue. The outer ring is the shaded color; black has been added for a darker value of the original color. The inner ring shows the tinted color; white has been added for a lighter value of the original color.

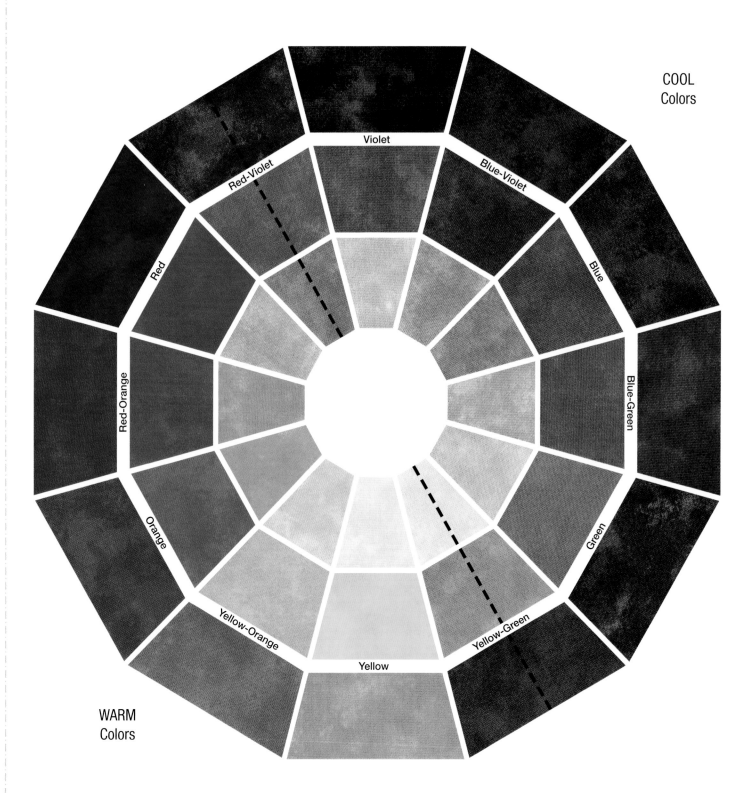

COOL
Colors

WARM
Colors

SECONDARY COLORS

When primary colors are mixed in different combinations, the secondary colors of orange, violet, and green are created.

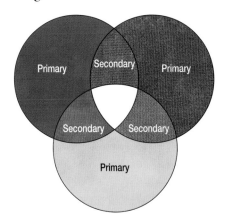

COMPLEMENTARY COLORS

The color that sits opposite a color on the wheel is its complementary color. When combined in equal amounts, complementary colors can vibrate. A popular pair of complementary colors is red and green. True red and true green are a vibrant combination. When they are shaded with a bit of black, they become the calmer colors that are often used for traditional Christmas designs.

A little complementary color can go a long way in adding excitement to a design. For example, include a sprinkle of orange in an otherwise all-blue quilt for a little punch.

TIP: What about neutral colors, such as beige or cream? These colors can be added to one-color and multicolor quilts. In the midst of color, neutral pieces give the eye a place to rest. They spread out competing colors and also add contrast.

QUICK REFERENCE CHART

TINTS AND SHADES OF PRIMARY, SECONDARY, AND TERTIARY COLORS

COLOR	TINT White is added for a lighter color.	SHADE Black is added for a darker color.
Red	Pink	Cranberry
Red-Violet	Magenta	Grape
Violet	Lavender	Eggplant
Blue-Violet	Lilac	Ultramarine
Blue	Periwinkle	Navy
Blue-Green	Aqua	Teal
Green	Seafoam	Forest Green
Yellow-Green	Mint	Olive
Yellow	Daffodil	Gold
Yellow-Orange	Peach	Mustard
Orange	Melon	Cinnamon
Red-Orange	Salmon	Burnt Orange

TERTIARY COLORS

Further divisions of colors are created in a 12-piece color wheel, on *page 2–12*. This wheel shows the primary colors (red, yellow, blue), secondary colors (orange, purple, green), and the tertiary colors, which are a combination of the primary and secondary colors— red-orange, yellow-orange, yellow-green, blue-green, blue-violet, and red-violet.

TINTS AND SHADES

Also shown in the 12-piece color wheel on *page 2–12* are some variations in the colors when they are tinted (white is added) or shaded (black is added), which alters the colors' values. When you consider the infinite amounts of black and white that can be added to make different tints or shades, it's easy to see that the number of colors is limitless.

If the fabric world only had primary, secondary, and tertiary colors, all quilts would be bright and vibrant. Fortunately for those who enjoy a more subtle palette to choose from, fabric designers create additional color options by adding white or black to colors.

TEMPERATURE

Fabrics, like paints, have a warmth, or lack thereof. In a quilt of predominantly cool fabrics (blues), a dash of warmth from orange or yellow can add zip to the quilt.

> **Good design works in color and in black and white.**

QUICK REFERENCE CHART
SPLIT COMPLEMENT COLOR COMBINATIONS

The split complement combination includes a primary, secondary, or tertiary color and the colors on either side of its complement.

FEATURE FABRIC	SPLIT COMPLEMENTS	
Red	Yellow-Green	Blue-Green
Red-Violet	Yellow	Green
Violet	Yellow-Orange	Yellow-Green
Blue-Violet	Orange	Yellow
Blue	Red-Orange	Yellow-Orange
Blue-Green	Red	Orange
Green	Red-Violet	Red-Orange
Yellow-Green	Red	Violet
Yellow	Red-Violet	Blue-Violet
Yellow-Orange	Violet	Blue
Orange	Blue-Violet	Blue-Green
Red-Orange	Green	Blue

Temperature, like contrast, is relative. The temperature of a color depends on what colors are around it. Look at the color wheel for guidance. Yellow-green and red-violet can be warm or cool depending on who their neighbors are. For example, yellow-green feels cool when used with pure yellow, which is warmer in comparison. The same yellow-green feels warm when paired with greens or blues, which are cooler in comparison. (See the dashed line on the 12-piece color wheel on *page 2–12*. It delineates the warm and cool sections of the color wheel.)

INTENSITY

When looking at a fabric, ask yourself if the color is pure (saturated, brilliant) or muted (grayed, subdued). The answer indicates the fabric's intensity.

Contrast differs from intensity. A dark navy fabric can be brilliant, and a pale yellow can have a low intensity.

In general, use intense colors sparingly, and choose less intense colors for larger areas. Intense colors will appear to come forward, while less intense colors will recede.

Intensity is also a relative characteristic; it changes according to the fabrics that surround it. Observe in the photo *above right* how intense the small red square looks when placed on the larger

TIP: The color wheel can help you classify a particular fabric, allowing you to select additional fabrics and colors to combine with it for a quilt.

black square; it pops out from the background.

When the same red square is placed on the larger white square, it appears to recede.

When combined with the muted gray square, the intensity of the red seems to lessen.

COMBINING COLORS

Remember that the color wheels and charts presented in this book are created from pictures of solid or marbled fabrics. The colors are bright and pure. Fabrics you choose may have similar colors, but could be influenced by pattern and additional colors in the fabric. Use these charts only as a guide.

Study individual fabrics and note their color combinations. Often the fabric manufacturer has printer's dots on the selvage that show the colors used to create the fabric design. Replicating these colors exactly can create a flat quilt, but

QUICK REFERENCE CHART
TRIAD COLOR COMBINATIONS

The triad combination uses three primary, secondary, or tertiary colors that are equidistant on the color wheel. There are four possible triad combinations, but your choice of tints, shades, and intensities within each is unlimited. Each triad shown below includes an example of colors that would work well together in a three-color quilt.

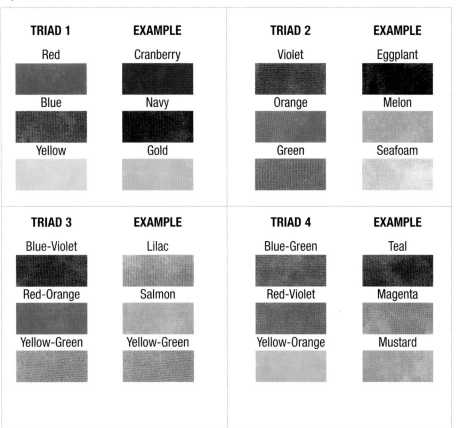

using tints and shades of the colors, as well as a variety of intensities (pure colors versus muted, grayed colors) and temperatures (warm versus cool colors) can enhance a design (see *pages 2–14* and *2–15* for more information on temperature and intensity).

Consider the following guidelines and types of color combinations when choosing fabrics for your quilt.

MONOCHROMATIC

While a monochromatic quilt uses a single color, every color has tinted and shaded variations. If you're interested in composing a single-color quilt, refer to the Quick Reference Chart for Tints and Shades of Primary, Secondary, and Tertiary Colors on *page 2–13* for possible color combinations in planning a monochromatic quilt. Choose one of the primary, secondary, or tertiary colors, then consider including all of the tints through shades of that color. A one-color quilt is most successful when the fabrics' designs, textures, and contrasts vary.

> **TIP: Where does brown fit in?** Brown is not on the color wheel because it has all the colors in it. Use brown when you don't want to add another color but need some type of contrast or transition.

SPLIT COMPLEMENTS

A split complement color scheme includes a primary, secondary, or tertiary color and the colors on either side of its complement.

For example, if you have a violet fabric and want its split complement colors, looking at the 12-Piece Color Wheel on *page 2–12* shows they would be yellow-orange and yellow-green. These are the colors on either side of violet's complementary color, yellow—directly across on the color wheel. If these pure colors seem strong, consider that violet, yellow-orange, and yellow-green could be eggplant, olive, and mustard, three warm and mellow colors. The Quick Reference Chart for Split Complement Color Combinations on *page 2–14* can help you devise a split complement color scheme.

ANALOGOUS COLOR COMBINATIONS

Think of analogous colors as neighbors. If you desire a quilt of this type, select a favorite fabric as your feature fabric and find its closest companion on the color wheel. Pull the remaining fabrics for your quilt from the neighboring, or adjacent, colors.

For example, if the feature fabric is a green, then pick a variety of light and dark fabrics in yellow-green, yellow, blue-green, and blue. This is one of the safest palettes to work with, but it can look dull if the fabrics don't have some interest in their patterns and variety in contrast.

TRIAD COMBINATIONS

A triad combination—three colors that are equidistant on the color wheel—results in a harmonious quilt. There are four triad combinations from which to choose, and you can select from an unlimited number of tints, shades, and intensities within those colors. The Quick Reference Chart for Triad Color Combinations on *page 2–15* shows the four triad combinations and a color combination example for each.

TETRAD COMBINATIONS

A tetrad combination—four colors that are equidistant on the color wheel—is another way to select quilt fabrics. There are three combinations from which to choose. Again, you can select from an unlimited number of tints, shades, and intensities within those colors. The Quick Reference Chart for Tetrad Color Combinations, *opposite*, shows the three tetrad combinations and a color combination example for each.

POLYCHROMATIC COMBINATIONS

Polychromatic, or multicolor, combinations are often scrap quilts—those composed of myriad fabrics in a wide range of colors and textures. Varying contrast, intensity, and temperature helps tie these quilts together (see *pages 2–14* and *2–15* for more information on temperature and intensity). Adding neutral fabrics to the mix provides balance among colors that might otherwise compete for attention.

QUICK REFERENCE CHART
TETRAD COLOR COMBINATIONS

The tetrad combination uses four primary, secondary, or tertiary colors that are equidistant on the color wheel. There are three possible tetrad combinations, but your choice of tints, shades, and intensities within each is unlimited. Each tetrad shown below includes an example of colors that would work well together in a four-color quilt.

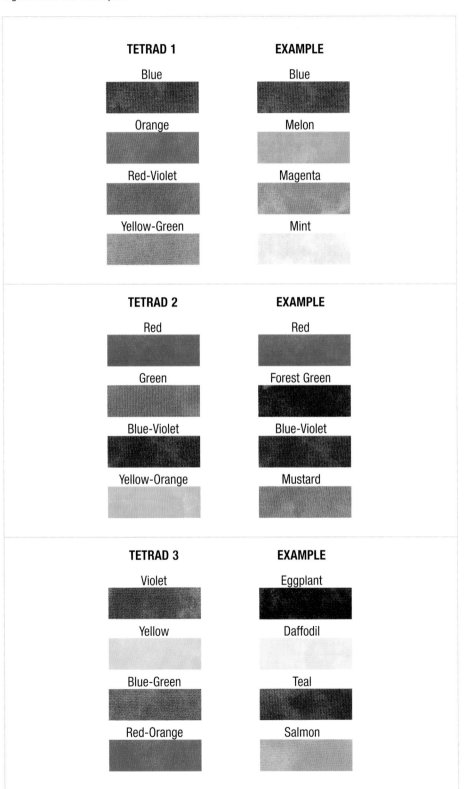

TETRAD 1 — **EXAMPLE**

Blue — Blue
Orange — Melon
Red-Violet — Magenta
Yellow-Green — Mint

TETRAD 2 — **EXAMPLE**

Red — Red
Green — Forest Green
Blue-Violet — Blue-Violet
Yellow-Orange — Mustard

TETRAD 3 — **EXAMPLE**

Violet — Eggplant
Yellow — Daffodil
Blue-Green — Teal
Red-Orange — Salmon

The third element that affects quilt design is the character of the fabrics, the features that change how each one works in a block or an overall quilt top. Prints may contain the same hues, for example, but may look different when placed in a block. One may be an elegant floral reproduction fabric, while the other is perhaps a stripe or a conversation print of animals. Consider each fabric's character when making selection decisions.

OVERALL CHARACTER

Color, contrast, and print style aside, fabrics have overall characteristics that should be taken into account.

Scale

Scale refers to the relative size of the print's elements. Quilts benefit from a range—small, medium and large—in scale.

Small-scale prints will look as though they're solid, but will contribute additional color and add visual texture.

Medium-scale prints tend to be quilters' favorites because they are easy to use and most readily

Fabric & Color

2–17

available. Even when cut or viewed from a distance, they tend to retain their design.

Large-scale prints are visually appealing on the bolt but require a little extra care when incorporating them into a design. Test large-scale prints with a window template to see what colors or parts will appear when cut into smaller pieces. (See *page 2–4* for information on making window templates.) Use care because a large-scale print can appear fragmented if used for small pieces within a block. They are best in borders and setting blocks.

Mood
Is the print busy or calm? Is the fabric elegant and formal or playful and lively? Coordinate fabric moods to convey the desired effect.

PRINT STYLE
Variations in Contrast
When selecting fabrics, be sure to look for variety in contrast, or values, within each color family. This adds more life to a quilt. Consider that an individual fabric can have contrast within itself—a red print, for example, that has areas of pink and burgundy—which brings interest to a monochromatic block or quilt.

Solid and Tone-On-Tone Prints
Solid-color fabrics or tone-on-tone prints (prints that look like solids when viewed from a distance) help set areas of the quilt apart from other prints or linear designs. Tone-on-tone prints add subtle visual texture without competing for the eye's attention.

Striped, Checked, or Plaid Fabric
Available in structured designs or wavy lines, stripes, checks, and plaids can add pizzazz to blocks or units. Try them as sashing or small inner borders.

Stripes also make fun binding. For example, cutting a striped fabric on the bias can produce the effect of a barber-pole stripe around the edge of your quilt.

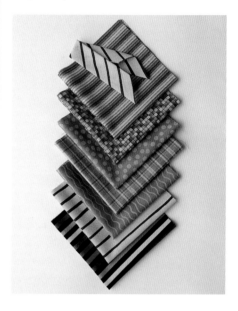

Black-and-White Fabric
Don't overlook black-and-white fabrics when shopping for color. Sometimes such a print can be the answer if you want to add some punch to your quilt design.

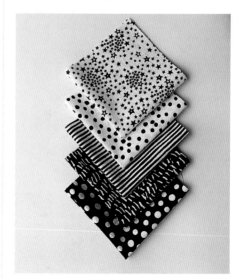

Large-Scale Prints

Large-scale prints, such as floral motifs, leaves, and paisleys, are often used as feature or focus fabrics. Use a window template to determine how a large-scale print might look when cut into smaller pieces. (See *page 2–4* for information on making window templates.) Purchase additional yardage if the fabric is going to be used as a border. Using a large print in both the quilt center and border helps bring unity to a quilt top.

Conversation or Novelty Prints

These prints depict themes, including sewing tools, holiday

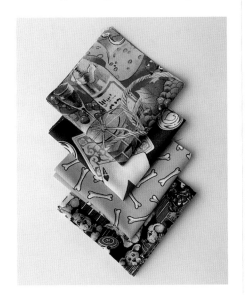

symbols, corporate logos, and even hobbies. If you're having difficulty working a favorite conversation print into a quilt top, use it for the backing instead. Or, if you're using it as the main motif in a block, try fussy-cutting it to center the desired area. (See Chapter 5—Cutting for information on fussy cutting.)

Reproduction Fabrics

Whether you're choosing fabrics for a Civil War-era quilt or a reproduction 1930s design, there are many fabric collections available

that re-create prints from bygone eras. The color and design elements of these reproductions may be such that it's easiest to combine them with other reproduction fabrics from the same collection or era.

Variety in fabrics results in an eye-catching quilt.

VARIETY CHECKLIST

Ask yourself these questions to determine if you've achieved variety in your selection of quilt fabrics.

Contrast
- Is there a variety of light-, medium-, and dark-value fabrics for the blocks, appliqués, and the overall quilt top?

Color
- Have I selected colors according to a certain color scheme or grouping of color families—primary, secondary, complementary, tertiary, etc.?
- Are there shades and tints within color families represented in the fabrics chosen?
- Do the fabric intensities work well together?

Character
- Have I chosen a variety of print styles?
- Have I included small-, medium-, and large-scale prints?
- Is the mood of the fabrics appropriate for the quilt I plan to make?

Abstract or Painterly Fabrics

Batiks and hand-dyed fabrics can be great choices when you're looking for subtle changes in color and texture, such as where you want a transition between colors.

TIP: Having extra fabrics on hand when working on a project opens up opportunities for substitutions and the additional variety quilts often need. Buy fabrics you like in the colors you enjoy. Working with fabrics you enjoy will help you maintain enthusiasm throughout the project, thus achieving the best overall results.

AUDITIONING FABRICS

Combining fabrics successfully may take experimentation, patience, and experience. Understanding the basics of contrast, color, and character will take some of the trial and error out of putting fabrics together.

Use the variety checklist on page 2–19 while making fabric choices for your quilt. The questions may help you determine what, if anything, is missing from a design.

Distance

One of the best ways to tell if your fabric combination will work is to step back from it. Fabrics that don't appear to work when viewed up close may be perfect from a distance, where you can see a fabric's contribution to the whole. Remember that each piece is just a fraction of the total finished product.

TIP: Why Scrap Quilts Work. Scrap quilts make the ultimate statement concerning the impact of contrast. It doesn't matter what colors are used in a scrap quilt, but rather how the pieces contrast with one another.

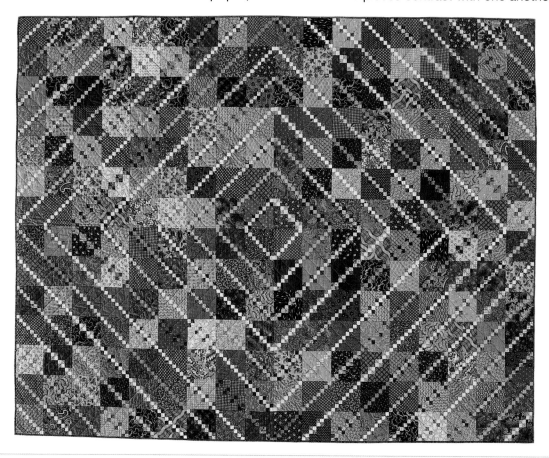

Color Photocopy

Photocopy your fabric choices on a color copier to test your options. (See Chapter 3—Planning Pieced Blocks for more information on testing fabric choices using photocopies.)

Design Wall

Having a surface to vertically lay out fabric choices can help you visualize how they will look in a quilt. For a permanent or portable design wall, cover the surface of foam-core board with a napped material, such as flannel, that will hold small pieces in place for viewing. Some quilters use the flannel back of oilcloth for a design wall, rolling it up between projects or hanging one in front of the other to view different quilts.

TROUBLESHOOTING TIPS

Having trouble choosing fabrics for your quilt?
Use these ideas to help find solutions to your color dilemmas.

IF YOU DON'T KNOW WHERE TO START

- Read quilt books, studying the designs and noting those you like best.
- Join a quilt guild. You'll gain inspiration and garner advice from fellow quilters.
- Identify a favorite feature fabric and use it as a starting point for choosing others.
- Study color combinations in favorite items.

IF YOU LIKE A PATTERN BUT NOT ITS COLORS

- Study color combinations in favorite articles of clothing.
- Look at home decorating magazines for possible color inspiration.

IF FABRICS CHOSEN HAVE NO COLOR CONTINUITY

- Replace some of the stronger colors with their muted versions.
- Try adding a complementary color.
- Choose a feature fabric to use in the blocks and borders to unify the overall design.
- Add neutrals or less intense colors to give the eye a place to rest.

IF CERTAIN PIECES ARE TOO DOMINANT

- Look at each piece and determine whether there is high contrast within the piece or with the pieces around it. Decrease the contrast accordingly.

IF BLOCK PIECES BLEND TOGETHER SO THAT THE DESIGN IS LOST

- Check the values of the fabrics involved and substitute fabrics in colors with higher contrast.

FABRIC SHOPPING CHECKLIST

Photocopy this checklist and take it with you when you're buying fabric for a quilt. Attach fabric swatches to the checklist as a reminder of what you've already purchased and to be certain you get enough variety in color, contrast, and character. (See Chapter 5—Cutting, Chapter 9—Assembling the Quilt Top, and Chapter 10—Batting & Backing for information on determining the yardages needed.)

PATTERN NAME _____   COLOR SCHEME _____

Batting Type _____ Size Needed _____   Sketch of quilt top (or attach pattern)

FEATURE FABRIC 1   Yardage Needed_____

Fabric 2
Yardage Needed_____

Fabric 3
Yardage Needed_____

Fabric 4
Yardage Needed _____

Fabric 5
Yardage Needed _____

Border Fabric 1
Yardage Needed_____

Border Fabric 2
Yardage Needed _____

Binding Fabric
Yardage Needed _____

Backing Fabric
Yardage Needed _____

My Notes for Fabric & Color

Planning Pieced Blocks

TABLE OF CONTENTS
Chapter 3—Planning Pieced Blocks

QUILTS AND QUILT DESIGNS OFTEN ARISE FROM A SINGLE BLOCK OR GROUPING OF UNITS. Understanding how blocks are created can help you dissect a quilt design, thus allowing you to duplicate its elements. Learning more about combining block elements also may enable you to design original quilt blocks.

COMBINING GEOMETRIC SHAPES INTO UNITS

Individual geometric shapes and their combinations are the foundation of every quilt block. On the following pages, several common shapes are shown. Study the different shapes in blocks. Knowing the shapes will make cutting and piecing easier to understand.

The term *unit* is used frequently in block design and pattern directions. Units are composed of at least two shapes sewn together. In this chapter, the shapes that combine to make a unit are

WHAT IS A BLOCK?
The majority of quilts are built on a basic unit called a block. Most commonly these block units are square, but they can also be rectangular, triangular, or another shape such as a hexagon. A single block style or several block styles may be used in a single quilt.

illustrated. For specific instructions on piecing methods for these units, see Chapter 6—Hand Piecing or Chapter 7—Machine Piecing.

Many blocks are built from common units such as the triangle-square and Flying Geese. Knowing how a block is divided into units can help you determine how a quilt is put together and allows efficiency in piecing.

SQUARES
Whether it is a simple setting block, the foundation for an appliqué block, or part of a unit, the square is one of the most common geometric shapes used in quilt designs.

Four-Patch Unit
Four equal-size squares sewn in two rows of two result in a Four-Patch unit. This unit acts as a block in some quilts.

Nine-Patch Unit
Nine equal-size squares sewn in three rows of three form a Nine-Patch block or a unit within a block. Often these units are composed of two alternating colors.

 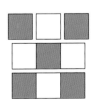

RECTANGLES
Rectangles can be combined into square units.

Two- and Three-Bar Units
Depending on the size of your rectangles and the desired size of your finished square, any number of bars can be used to create a square.

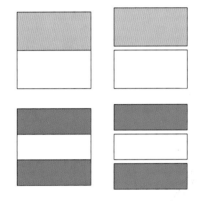

Alternating the direction of those squares produces a Rail Fence block.

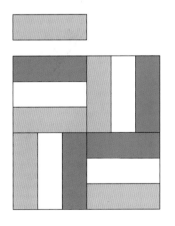

TIP: When you're ready to plan your own blocks, use colored pencils and the graph paper on *pages 3–17 to 3–23.*

Three-Piece Square Unit

Two small squares and a rectangle can be pieced into a square unit.

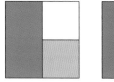

90° TRIANGLES

The square is also the starting point for many other shapes commonly used in quilting. Infinite design opportunities arise when squares are cut into 90° (right) triangles.

Two 90° triangles, or **half-square triangles**, are created when a square is cut in half diagonally. When you cut triangles from a square in this manner, the two short sides are cut on the straight grain and the longest side is cut on the bias.

Four 90° triangles, or **quarter-square triangles**, are created when a square is cut diagonally twice in an X. When you cut triangles from a square in this manner, the longest side of the triangle is cut on the straight grain and the two short sides are cut on the bias.

Knowing which edge is cut along the straight grain becomes

important when joining shapes into units and blocks. The straight grain should run along the outer edge of the block whenever possible to minimize stretching and distortion (see Chapter 5—Cutting for more information on fabric grain).

Triangle-Square Unit

Two 90° half-square triangles combine to make a triangle-square unit. Note that by using half-square triangles to create this unit, the bias edges are sewn together, leaving the straight grain along the outer edges (see Chapter 7—Machine Piecing for more information on making triangle-square units).

Hour Glass Unit

An Hour Glass unit is made with pairs of contrasting quarter-square triangles. Note that by using quarter-square triangles to create this unit, the bias edges are sewn together, leaving the straight grain along the outer edges.

Flying Geese Unit

Often used as a block, in sashing, and in borders, a Flying Geese unit is made of three 90° triangles in two different sizes. To keep the straight grain on the outer edges of this unit, the two smaller pieces are half-square triangles and the larger piece is a quarter-square triangle (see Chapter 7—Machine Piecing for

more information on making Flying Geese units).

Three-Triangle Unit

This versatile unit is made from a large 90° triangle and two smaller 90° triangles. To keep the straight grain on the outer edges of this unit, the two smaller triangles would be quarter-square triangles and the larger triangle would be a half-square triangle.

Square-in-a-Square Unit

Four 90° half-square triangles sewn to a square produce the square-in-a-square unit.

EQUILATERAL TRIANGLES

With equal-length sides and equal angles of 60°, this triangle can be sewn into hexagon-shape blocks or into larger equilateral triangles. This shape is used for tessellating designs (see box *opposite*).

TIP: The arrow symbol (←→) represents the direction the grain line should run when pieces are cut.

The Pyramid block is made of four equilateral triangles. A Hexagon block is made from six equilateral triangles.

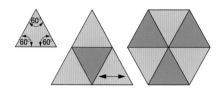

LONG TRIANGLES

When a rectangle is cut in half diagonally, the result is two long triangles.

ISOSCELES TRIANGLES

With two equal-length sides, this triangle is half of a diamond shape.

Triangle-in-a-Square Unit

Add two long triangles to an isosceles triangle to produce a triangle-in-a-square unit.

DIAMONDS

The diamond shape, also called a parallelogram, can be used for one-shape quilt designs or to make stars. With careful color placement of the

pieces, the diamond shape, when repeated multiple times, forms a mosaic and can create an optical illusion.

The Tumbling Blocks quilt is made with only the diamond shape, yet has many design possibilities. Consistent value placement causes a cubelike pattern to emerge.

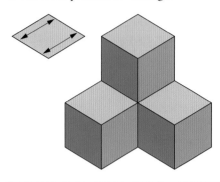

WHAT ARE TESSELLATING DESIGNS?

Tessellation occurs when a single shape is repeated and covers a surface without holes or overlap. Mosaic tile designs are examples of tessellating patterns. Quiltmakers take advantage of tessellation, creating dramatic quilt designs using a single shape.

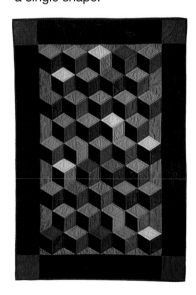

Diamond shapes combined with squares and 90° quarter-square triangles can be joined to make an Eight-Pointed Star block.

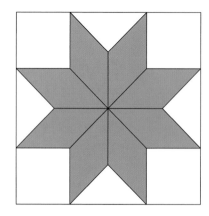

Four long triangles can be joined to a diamond to create a pieced rectangle unit.

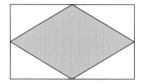

TIP: Pieces of a block will travel easily and stay in place if you lay them on a piece of batting and carefully roll them up inside.

HEXAGONS

With six sides, the hexagon can be pieced to other hexagons to form a tessellating design. English paper piecing is a popular technique used to join hexagon shapes (see Chapter 6—Hand Piecing). These shapes are often pieced into a design called Grandmother's Flower Garden.

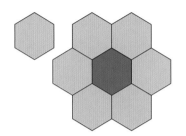

OCTAGONS

This eight-sided piece functions in quilt blocks just like a mosaic tile design. It appears most often in a block called Snowball.

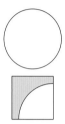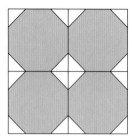

CIRCLES

Circles can be more difficult to piece than shapes with straight edges and are often appliquéd onto blocks. Sometimes one-fourth of a circle is pieced with a concave patch. When four such units are sewn together a complete circle is visible.

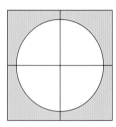

TESTING UNIT LAYOUTS

To determine your layout, make several of the same unit and experiment with various settings.

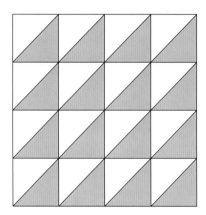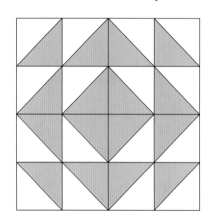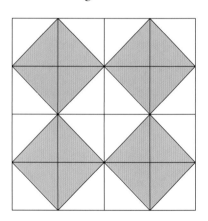

Changing the placement of a unit within a block will cause different designs to appear.

Change colors and a block's possibilities expand even further.

Planning Pieced Blocks

THE GRID METHOD

Many blocks are based on a grid or can be broken down into one. Working with a grid organizes a design and makes cutting and piecing sequences easier to determine. Some grids commonly used for quiltmaking follow.

2×2 Grid (Four-Patch)

A grid of four undivided or divided squares—a Four-Patch or 2×2 squares—offers multiple design options.

Grid of 2×2 squares (Four-Patch)

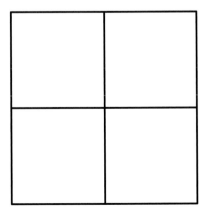

Four three-triangle units on a grid of 2×2 squares form a Windmill block.

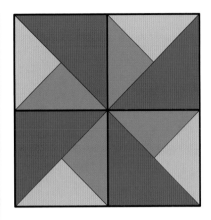

Grid of 4×4 squares

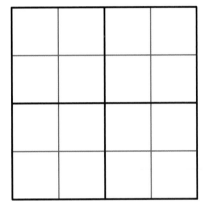

Triangle-square units placed on a grid of 4×4 squares form a Broken Dishes block.

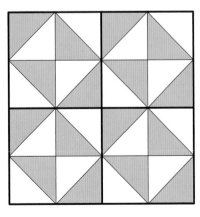

Grid of 8×8 squares

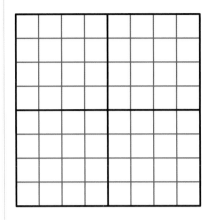

Squares and triangle-square units on a grid of 8×8 squares form a block called Northumberland Star.

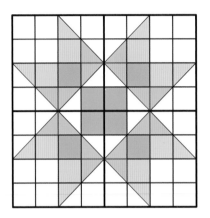

5×5 Grid

Five squares along each edge give this block design versatility and a center point.

Grid of 5×5 squares

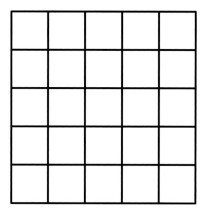

Triangle-squares and squares form a basket shape to make a Cake Stand block.

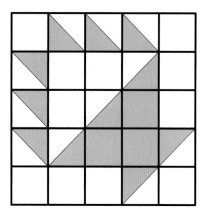

The same pieces in a different layout create a Checkered Star block.

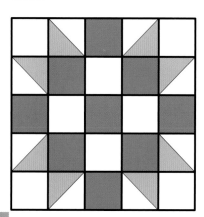

The New Mexico block, a variation on the Checkered Star, is formed with four Nine-Patch units and four three-bar units replacing the squares in the center.

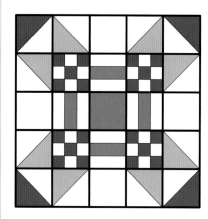

7×7 Grid

With 49 separate patches in this grid, intricate designs are possible.

Grid of 7×7 squares

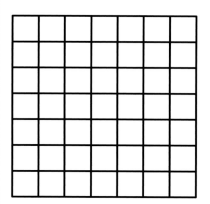

Sashing separates the four Bear's Paw units in this Bear's Paw block.

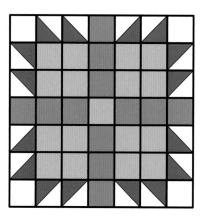

Triangle-squares and squares combine to form a Tree of Paradise block.

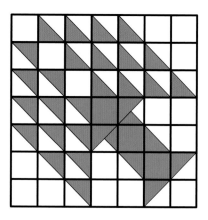

The design of a question block radiates from the center.

3×3 Grid (Nine-Patch)

A common block/unit in quiltmaking is the Nine-Patch. The Nine-Patch grid, like the Four-Patch, can vary in the number of squares it uses. In the case of a Nine-Patch, the number needs to be divisible by three.

> **TIP:** Should I use odd- or even-numbered grids?
> Even-numbered grids allow for symmetrical designs; odd-numbered grids can be oriented around a center point.

Grid of 3×3 squares (Nine-Patch)

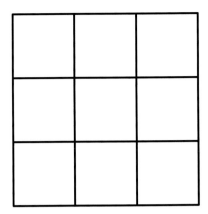

Grid of 6×6 squares

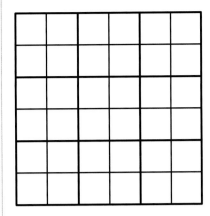

Four pieced units combine to make a sawtooth and star block.

Squares and triangle-square units compose a Friendship Star block on a grid of 3×3 squares.

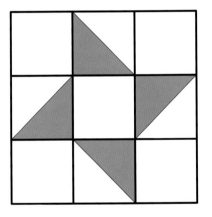

Jacob's Ladder blocks combine into many different patterns when placed together. Though based on the Nine-Patch grid, this block incorporates Four-Patch units.

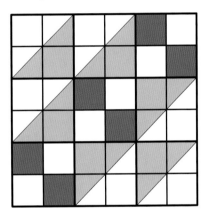

A Nine-Patch grid has a unit as its center point.

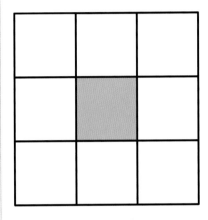

TIP: Can a Nine-Patch grid be 9×9 squares?
Yes, because any number divisible by three works in the Nine-Patch grid. It would have 81 pieces to assemble, however.

CENTER POINTS

A Four-Patch grid has a center point where the corners of the units meet.

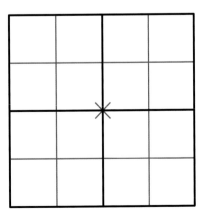

The Ohio Star block is based on a Nine-Patch grid with the center of the star as its focal point.

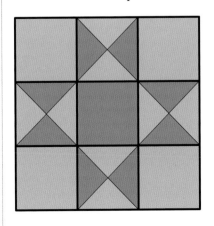

QUICK REFERENCE CHART
CHANGING BLOCK SIZES USING THE GRID METHOD

For blocks based on the grid system, changing size is a matter of redrafting the block on the new grid size. For example, if a Nine-Patch grid makes a 6" finished block but you want it to be a 9" finished block, use this chart to determine the patch size needed for the larger block. The chart shows that the new Nine-Patch grid would have 3" finished squares.

Note: Where no number is listed, there is not an exact whole or fractional number equivalent.

Grid Size/Finished Block Sizes (inches)

Block Size	← Grid Size →						
	2×2	4×4	8×8	5×5	7×7	3×3	6×6
	4-Patch	16-Patch	64-Patch	25-Patch	49-Patch	9-Patch	36-Patch
6"	3"	1½"	¾"			2"	1"
8"	4"	2"	1"				
9"	4½"	2¼"	1⅛"			3"	1½"
10"	5"	2½"	1¼"	2"			
12"	6"	3"	1½"			4"	2"
14"	7"				2"		
16"	8"	4"	2"				

TIP: How many grids should I have in my block design? Each division within a grid square means additional piecing. As the number of squares increases, consider the overall size of the block to avoid piecing tiny bits of fabric. For example, a 12" block with 64 squares would have 1½" squares. (Refer to the Grid Size/Finished Block Sizes chart *above* to calculate the size of grid squares relative to the finished block size.)

DRAFTING BLOCKS

Drafting allows a quilter to copy a block in a quilt, develop an original design, or change the size of an existing block. All you need is a pencil and paper (or a computer

SUPPLY CHECKLIST
- ⅛-inch-grid graph paper (8 squares to the inch allows the greatest flexibility)
- Plain paper
- Rulers
- Pencil (mechanical pencils help maintain line width)
- Colored pencils

---

design program, if you prefer) and a basic understanding of the grid method to draft your own blocks.

REPRODUCING A BLOCK DESIGN

If you're trying to re-create a block from an antique or heirloom quilt, identifying the block and grid can sometimes be difficult, especially with complex quilt tops. It is common for block designers to start with a base grid, such as the Nine-Patch, and further divide the patches into grids. For instance, the Double Nine-Patch block is based on the 3×3 Nine-Patch grid, but some of the squares have been divided into even smaller Nine-Patch units.

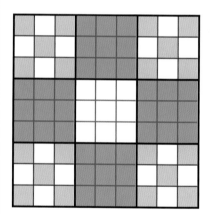

To determine the units necessary to reproduce a favorite quilt block, follow these steps:

1. Isolate the block on the quilt.

2. Visualize a grid superimposed over the block. Look for a repeating pattern across the block and count the number of times the pattern repeats.

3. Measure the block to determine the finished size.

4. Using graph paper, rulers, and a pencil, draw out the block. Remember that the pieces you are drawing are finished size. Once the drafted block is complete, you need to add ¼" seam allowances to all the edges before cutting.

Original block design: Use the grid system to organize an original block design and to make it easier to figure out cutting and piecing. To practice, draw several miniature grids and photocopy them. Draw lines throughout the grid to experiment with new block designs. Think about some of the basic units (see *pages 3–1 to 3–4*) and draw

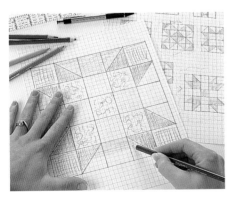

them in the grid squares. Keep doodle pads of grids available so you can design when inspiration strikes.

Computer programs: A number of computer programs are available for designing blocks and quilt tops. On a computer you can explore multiple block options quickly and without drafting—a timesaver if you're doing a great deal of original design work. The programs allow flexibility in creating thousands of designs, adding color, and seeing how blocks will work together.

Advanced block design: Blocks designed with tight curves and unusual shapes may not work on the grid system. These designs can be executed with different techniques, such as appliqué (see Chapter 8—Appliquéing Blocks) or foundation piecing (see Chapter 7—Machine Piecing). Some blocks require multiple methods.

Test fabric choices: Finalize block design and fabric selections by mocking up a block. Cut the fabric pieces to the finished size (leave off the seam allowances for this test only; these pieces will not be used in the finished project) and sketch the grid and block design on paper. Glue the fabric pieces in position on

the paper to create a mock block. Place the mock block several feet away to view the design and color combination. If desired, make additional blocks to test alternate fabric choices.

To further test the color and layout, make color photocopies of the mock block. Use the copies to begin planning the quilt top, watching for secondary patterns to emerge and checking color placement in adjacent blocks.

QUICK REFERENCE CHART
ADJUSTING BLOCK SIZE

You can see how a block you wish to enlarge or reduce will look by using a photocopier. The equations for determining the percentages shown in the chart are given *below*. You need to know the original block size and the new block size before using the copier.

Note: Only blocks with whole number percentages have been listed.

Enlarge: (New Block Size ÷ Original Block Size) × 100 = Percent Enlargement

Reduce: (New Block Size ÷ Original Block Size) × 100 = Percent Reduction

REDUCTION AND ENLARGEMENT PERCENTAGE CHART

New Size (Finished) →

Original Size (Finished)	2"	3"	4"	5"	6"	7"	8"	9"	10"
2"	100%	150%	200%	250%	300%	350%	400%	450%	500%
3"		100%			200%			300%	
4"	50%	75%	100%	125%	150%	175%	200%	225%	250%
5"	40%	60%	80%	100%	120%	140%	160%	180%	200%
6"		50%			100%			150%	
7"						100%			
8"	25%		50%		75%		100%		125%
9"								100%	
10"	20%	30%	40%	50%	60%	70%	80%	90%	100%

QUICK REFERENCE CHART
FIGURING PROPORTION

To figure dimensions on blocks that are not square, use these formulas.

HEIGHT FORMULA

If the desired width is known, use this formula to determine the block height:
- Desired Width ÷ Original Width = A (proportion factor)
- Original Height × A (proportion factor) = New Height

For example, if the original block is 5" high by 6" wide and you want it to be 12" wide, divide 12 by 6 to get 2 (proportion factor). Multiply the original height of 5" by 2 (proportion factor) to determine that the new finished height of the block is 10".

WIDTH FORMULA

If the desired height is known, use this formula to determine the block width:
- Desired Height ÷ Original Height = B (proportion factor)
- Original Width × B (proportion factor) = New Width

For example, if the original block is 3" high by 7" wide and you want it to be 4½" high, divide 4½ by 3 to get 1½ (proportion factor). Multiply the original width of 7" by 1½ (proportion factor) to determine that the new finished width of the block is 10½".

Looking for inspiration in choosing blocks for your next quilt? Trying to remember the name of a favorite quilt block? The following pages list some well-known quilt block designs. The possibilities for combining them into a one-of-a-kind quilt are limitless. Use the graph pages at the end of this chapter and colored pencils to create your own designs.

Attic Window

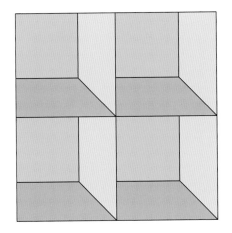

Bride's Bouquet

Card Trick

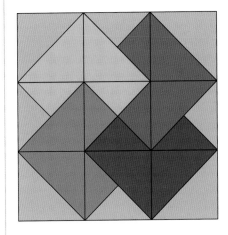

Bear's Paw

Broken Dishes

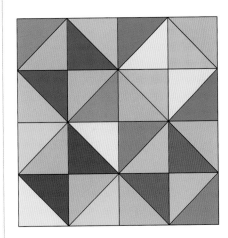

Checkered Star

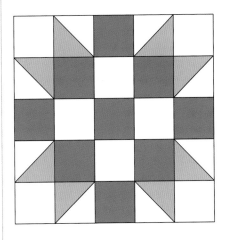

Bow Tie

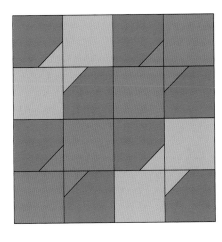

Cake Stand

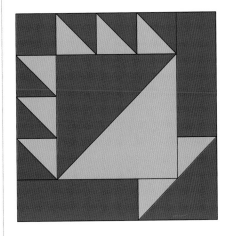

Churn Dash

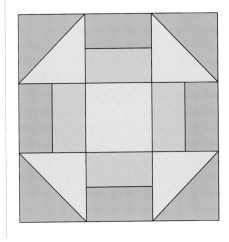

Planning Pieced Blocks

Delectable Mountains

Dresden Plate

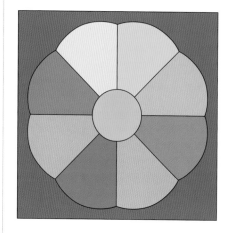

Feathered Star

Double Nine-Patch

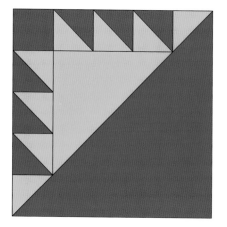

Drunkard's Path

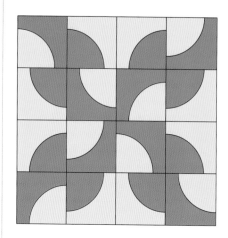

Flower Pot Basket

Double Wedding Ring

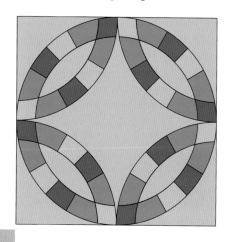

Eight-Pointed Star

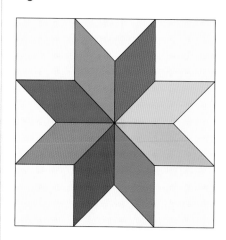

Friendship Star

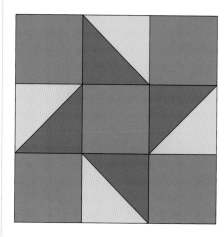

Grandmother's Fan

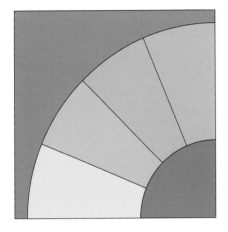

Grandmother's Flower Garden

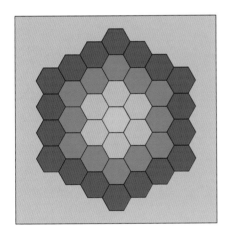

Hearts and Gizzards

Irish Chain

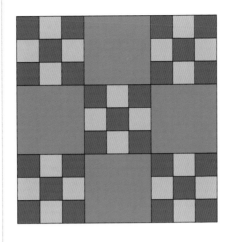

Jacob's Ladder

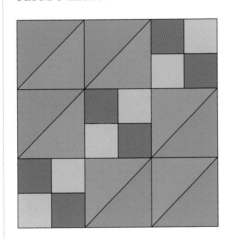

Log Cabin

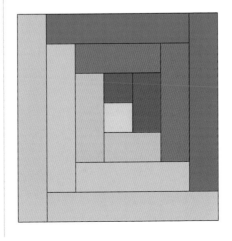

Lone Star

Maple Leaf

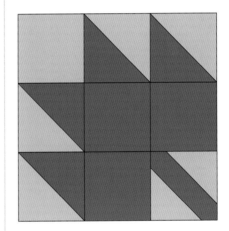

Mariner's Compass

New Mexico

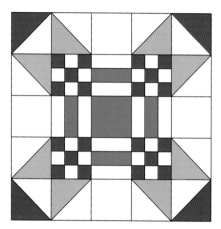

North Wind

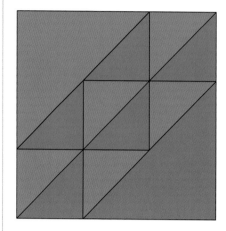

Ohio Star

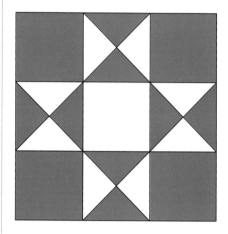

New York Beauty

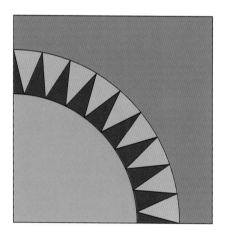

Northumberland Star

Overall Bill

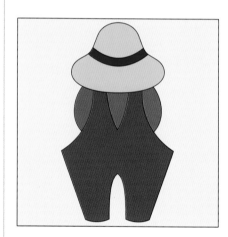

Nine-Patch

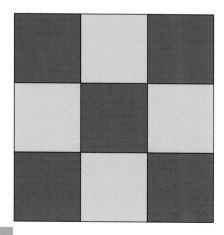

Ohio Rose

Pineapple

Pinwheel

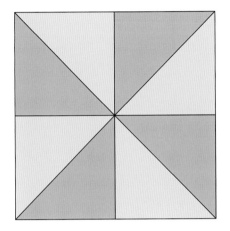

Schoolhouse

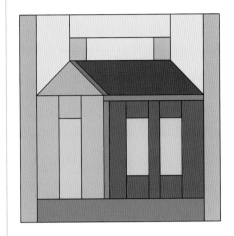

Snowball

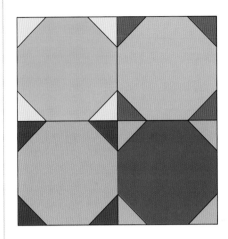

Rail Fence

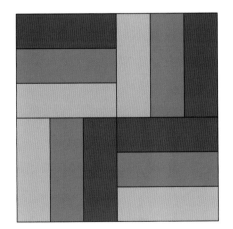

Shoofly

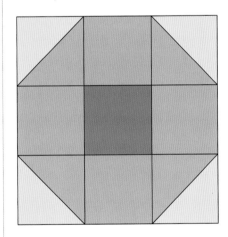

Storm at Sea

Sawtooth

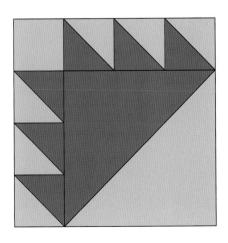

Snail's Trail

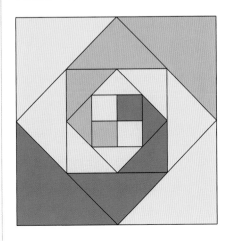

Sunbonnet Sue

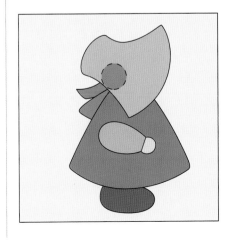

Trip Around the World

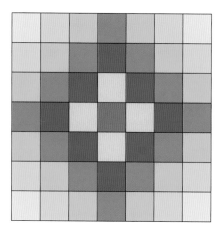

Windmill

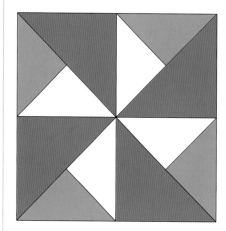

Triple Four-Patch

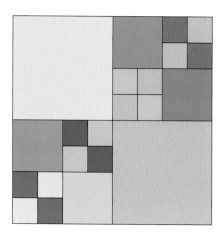

Tumbling Blocks

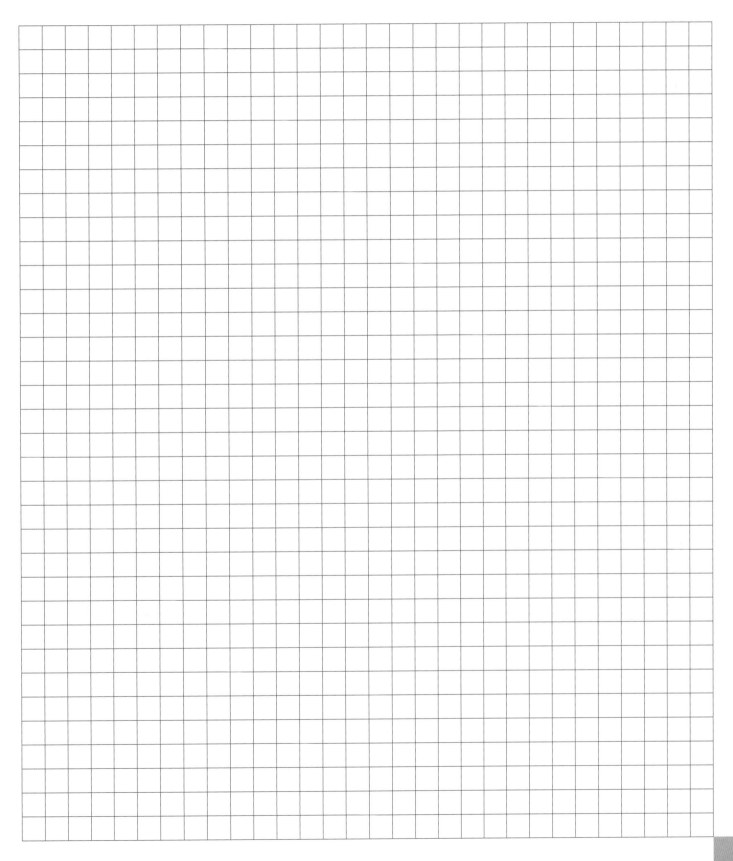

My Ideas for Planning Pieced Blocks

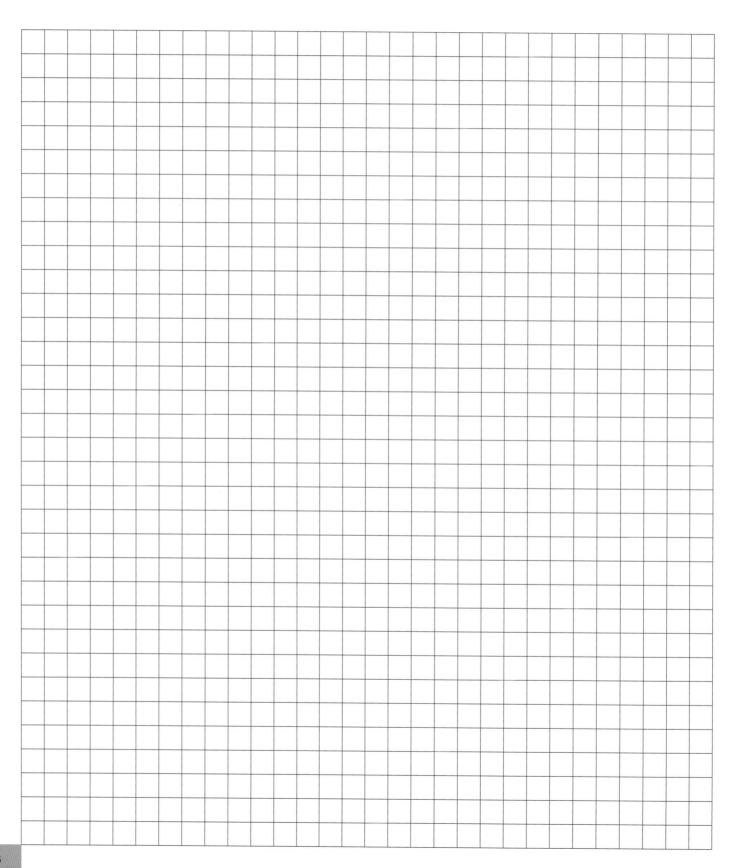

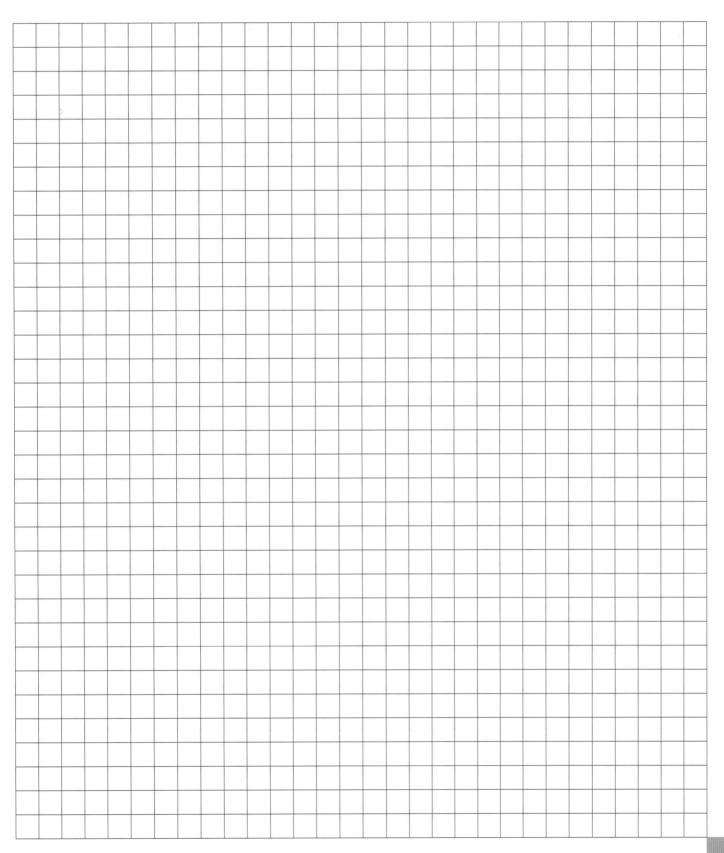

Planning Pieced Blocks

My Notes for Planning Pieced Blocks

My Notes for Planning Pieced Blocks

My Notes for Planning Pieced Blocks

Planning the Quilt Top

4

TABLE OF CONTENTS
Chapter 4—Planning the Quilt Top

UNDERSTANDING HOW THE ELEMENTS OF A QUILT TOP WORK TOGETHER will enable you to plan your quilt successfully. Sometimes you know exactly how you want your finished quilt to look before you cut the first piece of fabric. At other times, you've made or acquired blocks (maybe via an inheritance, a block exchange, or a purchase at an auction) without a specific project in mind. If you find yourself in the latter category, the information in this chapter will help you plan block arrangements that make an attractive and functional quilt top. It can also be used to alter a pattern and change its size or setting.

DETERMINING QUILT SIZE

If you use a pattern or kit and follow the instructions exactly, the finished measurements of the quilt are predetermined. However, if you choose to modify or design a pattern to make a quilt that fits a specific bed or display area, the finished size of the project is up to you. The first step in the planning process is to determine the desired finished size.

For a wall hanging, base the width and length on the space you have available for hanging the finished project. If you have a special quilt rack or hanger in mind, measure its width so your finished quilt will fit.

When making a throw, keep in mind who will be using it. Are they tall adults or small children? Will they want to lay it over their laps or

MEASURING A BED TO DETERMINE QUILT SIZE

Follow these instructions to measure a bed and determine the finished size of your quilt. When measuring, have the blankets, sheets, and pillows on the bed that will be used with the quilt. "Drop" is the part of the quilt that extends over the edge of the mattress. "Tuck" is the part of the quilt that folds under the pillows should you want your quilt to cover them. It can be shallow (10") or deep (20"). *Note:* The amount of quilting done and the type of batting used can result in a 3 to 5% loss in the overall size of the quilt; plan accordingly.

WIDTH

Measure the mattress width and add twice the drop length. For a comforter-size finished project, measure from the top of the mattress to slightly past its lower edge to figure the drop length. For a coverlet, measure from the top of the mattress to slightly past the bottom of the bed rail. For a bedspread, measure from the top of the mattress to just above the floor.

LENGTH

If you want the quilt to cover your pillows, measure the mattress length, then add one drop length plus 10" to 20" for the pillow tuck. The exact amount to add will depend on the size and fullness of your pillows and the depth of your tuck. If you do not want your quilt to go over your pillows, measure the mattress length and add one drop length.

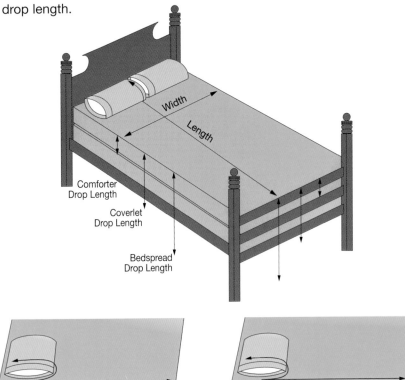

Comforter Drop Length

Coverlet Drop Length

Bedspread Drop Length

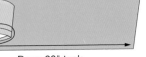

Deep 20" tuck

Shallow 10" tuck

wrap up in it? Your usage conclusions should provide you with the optimum finished size.

For bed-size quilts, see the Quick Reference Chart: Standard Bed and Batting Sizes *below*. For greater accuracy, you may wish to measure the bed you have in mind for the quilt you are making since mattress heights vary (see Measuring a Bed to Determine Quilt Size on *page 4–1*). You need to consider whether you want the quilt to fold under, then over the bed pillows or not and how far down on the bed you want it to hang (comforter, coverlet, or bedspread length).

QUICK REFERENCE CHART
STANDARD BED AND BATTING SIZES

Bed size	Mattress size	Batting size*
	W×L	W×L
Crib	23×46"	45×60"
Twin	39×75"	72×90"
Double (or Full)	54×75"	81×96"
Queen	60×80"	90×108"
King	76×80"	120×120"
California King	72×84"	

*Note: Batting sizes refer to commercially available, precut batts.

QUICK REFERENCE CHART
SAMPLE QUILT SIZES

Drops are on three sides	Twin mattress 39×75" W×L	Double mattress 54×75" W×L	Queen mattress 60×80" W×L	King mattress 76×80" W×L
With 10" drop	59×85"	74×85"	80×90"	96×90"
And 10" tuck	59×95"	74×95"	80×100"	96×100"
With 12" drop	63×87"	78×87"	84×92"	100×92"
And 10" tuck	63×97"	78×97"	84×102"	100×102"
With 14" drop	67×89"	82×89"	88×94"	104×94"
And 10" tuck	67×99"	82×99"	88×104"	104×104"
With 16" drop	71×91"	86×91"	92×96"	108×96"
And 10" tuck	71×101"	86×101"	92×106"	108×106"
With 18" drop	75×93"	90×93"	96×98"	112×98"
And 10" tuck	75×103"	90×103"	96×108"	112×108"
With 20" drop	79×95"	94×95"	100×100"	116×100"
And 10" tuck	79×105"	94×105"	100×110"	116×110"

ADJUSTING QUILT SIZE

If you know what size quilt you'd like to make, but following a particular pattern will result in a smaller or larger quilt than you want, there are several changes you can make. Keep in mind that when you are altering some parts of a quilt, you may also be changing the proportions of the elements in relationship to one another. (See Border Proportions on *page 4–6* for more information.) Sketch your ideas on graph paper first to see how the changes will affect the finished size and appearance of your quilt.

Sometimes you may not have the right number of blocks to complete a quilt center. If the quilt top will be too large because there are too many blocks, try rearranging the block layout. Or, eliminate blocks by changing the number of blocks in a row or the number of rows. Use any extra blocks in the quilt backing (see Chapter 10—Batting & Backing for more information).

If removing blocks makes the quilt top too small, regain some of the inches by adding sashing between rows. If reducing the number of blocks is not an option, consider using narrower sashing.

If the quilt top will be too small because you don't have enough blocks, make more blocks, or add setting squares to spread out the

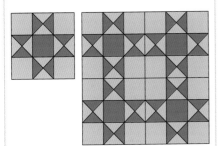

An asymmetrical block—one that does not have mirror-image halves—will look different when you rotate it. If you like having several possibilities for the way your quilt will look, use blocks that are asymmetrical, especially when the blocks are straight set, with no sashing.

blocks you have. Add or increase the width of the sashing between blocks, or try a diagonal (on point) block layout.

If you're still in the planning stages, consider changing the finished size of the blocks (see Chapter 3—Planning Pieced Blocks for more information on changing block size).

If you decide to alter the finished size by adjusting the border, consider not only reducing or enlarging the border width, but also creating an additional border. Again, keep the proportion of the borders to the finished quilt in mind.

ELEMENTS OF A QUILT TOP

All the elements of a quilt—blocks, borders, sashing, and binding—make a statement in the completed project. Whether that statement is subtle or bold is up to you, the quiltmaker.

Chapter 3—Planning Pieced Blocks outlines how you can achieve different designs by changing the placement and colors of shapes and units within blocks. Many of those same techniques can be used when planning a quilt top.

Blocks are the main visual element in the quilt center. They most commonly are square, but can also be other shapes, such as rectangular, triangular, or hexagonal. A single block style or several block styles may be used in a quilt top.

Setting squares or triangles are the secondary blocks or solid fabric pieces placed between the main

blocks. They give the eye a place to rest, setting off the main blocks.

Sashing refers to strips of fabric (or strips and squares) between blocks that give the blocks definition. Not all quilt tops have sashing.

Borders frame the quilt center, visually holding in the design. Borders also give the eye a stopping point. Some quilt tops do not have borders.

Binding can blend in or contrast with the border or blocks, depending on the design statement you wish to make.

BLOCK SETTING OPTIONS

Setting refers to how the blocks are arranged on the quilt top. The possibilities for combining blocks are nearly endless. The following setting options offer ideas. (See Chapter 9—Assembling the Quilt Top for specific information on joining the pieces together.)

STRAIGHT SET, BLOCK-TO-BLOCK

Lay out the blocks side by side in straight horizontal and vertical rows without sashing.

STRAIGHT SET, BLOCK-TO-BLOCK VARIATION

Change the direction of the asymmetrical blocks in a block-to-block layout and a new design will emerge.

STRAIGHT SET WITH ALTERNATE SQUARES OR BLOCKS

Lay out blocks with alternating setting (plain) squares or contrasting blocks in straight horizontal and vertical rows without sashing, alternating types.

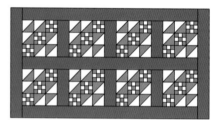

STRAIGHT SET WITH CONTINUOUS SASHING

Lay out the blocks in straight horizontal and vertical rows with strips for sashing between the blocks.

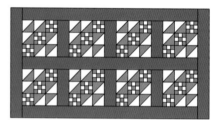

STRAIGHT SET WITH SASHING STRIPS AND SQUARES (CORNERSTONES)

Lay out the blocks in straight horizontal and vertical rows with alternating strips and squares for sashing between the blocks. *Note:* The blocks in the illustration *below* are composed of four smaller blocks.

SEE BEFORE YOU SEW

Experiment with block placement before you sew to produce the best design for your quilt center. Create a space where you can lay out all the blocks and any other elements, such as sashing or setting blocks and triangles.

One option is to place a bedsheet on a bed or floor. Arrange the blocks on the sheet, altering their positions until you're satisfied with the layout. Once you're pleased, pin them to the sheet. Roll up the sheet for temporary storage or to carry the quilt center to the sewing machine.

Or, place the blocks on a design wall. As you experiment with the layout, stand back from your work to see how the design is evolving.

DIAGONAL SET WITH ALTERNATE SQUARES OR BLOCKS

Lay out the blocks and setting (plain) squares or contrasting blocks in diagonal rows without sashing, alternating types. Cut or piece side and corner setting triangles to fill out the set (see Chapter 5—Cutting for information on cutting side and corner setting triangles).

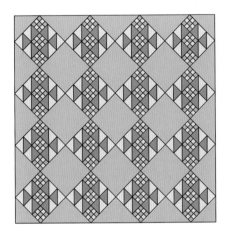

DIAGONAL SET WITH FLOATING BLOCKS

Lay out the blocks and setting (plain) squares in diagonal rows. To make it look as though the blocks are floating, cut the side and corner setting triangles up to 2" larger than the diagonal measurement of the block to fill out the set (see Chapter 5—Cutting for information on cutting side and corner setting triangles).

DIAGONAL SET WITH CONTINUOUS SASHING

Lay out the blocks in diagonal rows with strips for sashing between the blocks. Cut or piece side and corner setting triangles to fill out the set (see Chapter 5—Cutting for information on cutting side and corner setting triangles).

DIAGONAL SET WITH SASHING STRIPS AND SQUARES

Lay out the blocks in diagonal rows with alternating strips and squares for sashing between the blocks. Cut or piece side and corner setting triangles to fill out the set (see Chapter 5—Cutting for information on cutting side and corner setting triangles).

VERTICAL OR ZIGZAG SET

Lay out the blocks and setting triangles in diagonal rows for each vertical strip (see Chapter 5—Cutting for information on cutting side and corner setting triangles).

For a zigzag set, begin and end odd-numbered vertical rows with full blocks; begin and end even-numbered vertical rows with a trimmed block (a half block + seam allowance). *Note:* Because each half block needs a seam allowance, you cannot get two half blocks from one block. First join the pieces in each vertical row, then join the rows together.

To expand the size of your quilt top, you can add sashing strips between the vertical rows.

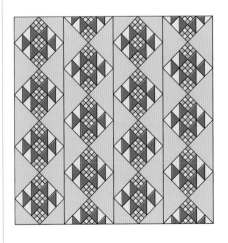

ROW-BY-ROW SET

Create a quilt top where each row is different from the others. Sashing can be added between the blocks and/or between the rows as desired.

FRAMED BLOCK SET

If you're beginning with a set of blocks that aren't all the same size, or if you're trying to unify blocks made in a variety of colors, consider framing the blocks with a single fabric. More frames in various widths can be added to each block to make them uniform. The blocks can then be organized in a straight block-to-block set (see *page 4–3*).

CONTEMPORARY SET

Not all quilts are square or rectangular. And at times, even traditional blocks are set in unusual ways. Blocks may vary in size and/or be staggered in creative arrangements. If you prefer a nontraditional setting, first sketch your design onto graph paper to determine the positions of blocks and sashing.

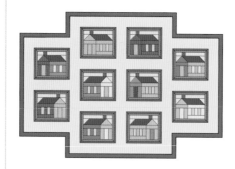

SINGLE-SHAPE SET

Create a quilt primarily from a single shape. The Lone Star and Grandmother's Flower Garden designs are two examples.

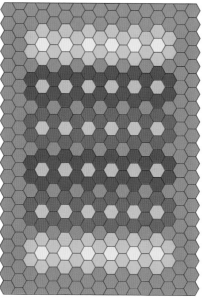

Borders frame a quilt center and can be as simple as single strips of complementary or contrasting fabric. A border also can be intricately pieced or elaborately appliquéd. When using a large-scale print in the quilt center's blocks, bring unity to the quilt by repeating it in the border.

BORDER PROPORTIONS

Borders should be in proportion to the size of the finished quilt. Generally, a small wall hanging should have a border of less than 6", whereas a quilt for a king-size bed could handle a 12–14" border. Borders that are too small can make a quilt seem out of balance. Borders that are too wide diminish the quilt center design. To decide how wide to make a border, begin with your finished block size. If your quilt center is made of 4" blocks, try a 4"-wide border.

If the quilt top needs to be enlarged, consider adding sashing, pieced borders, or multiple borders. Unless the difference is minimal, avoid adjusting only the border, as widening it can make the quilt look out of proportion.

TIP: Border strips should be cut on the lengthwise grain of the fabric. If the same fabric is used for the blocks and the borders, be sure to cut the borders before cutting the pieces for the blocks.

When trying to determine what type of border to add to your quilt center, look at quilting books and magazines for border and block combinations that appeal to you. Study the proportion of the border to the block size and the amount of piecing or detail in the border as compared to the blocks.

See Chapter 9—Assembling the Quilt Top for specific information on measuring and assembling the border elements.

STRAIGHT BORDERS

The simplest border uses a single fabric in strips around all four sides of the quilt center. Add the border strips in pairs to opposite edges. For example, first sew strips to the side edges, then add them to the top and bottom edges.

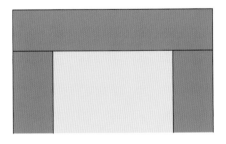

For added interest, inset rectangles at the center of each edge.

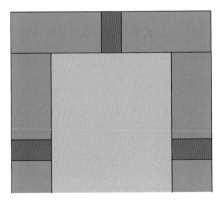

Or, add a solid square to each end of the top and bottom border strips before sewing the strips to the quilt center.

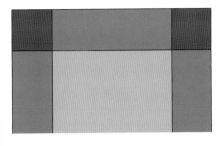

Using pieced blocks instead of solid squares adds even more interest.

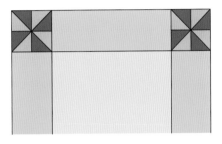

MITERED BORDERS

Mitering the corners of a straight border is another possible variation. You need to decide whether to use this method before you cut the border strips as mitering requires extra length.

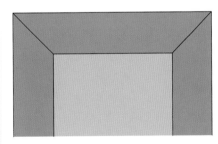

You may wish to add multiple border strips to your quilt top. They may be added one at a time or first joined into a unit that is then sewn to the quilt center. If you plan to miter the corners, joining the strips into a single unit first works best.

APPLIQUÉ BORDERS

The appliqué work on a border, whether by hand or machine, may be done before or after the border strips are joined to the quilt center.

You may wish to cut the border strips slightly larger than needed, trimming them after the appliqué work is complete, to give yourself room to work. Any appliqué pieces that cross over a seam will need to be sewn in place after the border strips are added to the quilt center.

Plan how your design will turn the corners by sketching out the complete border design before you begin appliquéing.

SCALLOPED BORDERS

A scalloped border edge softens the look of a quilt and adds another element of interest.

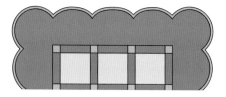

Mark scallops on borders after the border strips are sewn to the quilt center, then cut the scallops after the hand or machine quilting is complete. You will need to determine an appropriate width for your scallops so they will fit evenly along the edges and around the corners (see Chapter 9—Assembling the Quilt Top for more information on making scalloped borders).

PIECED BORDERS WITH STRAIGHT-SET BLOCKS

From a strip of pieced rectangles to a checkerboard of Four-Patch blocks, the options for pieced borders are many.

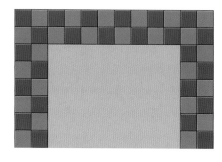

Pay special attention to the layout of the pieced blocks and, if the units are directional, how they turn the corners. It is best to have all four corners match.

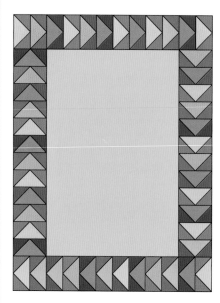

If this isn't possible, plan to use corner squares to avoid taking the focus off the center of your quilt.

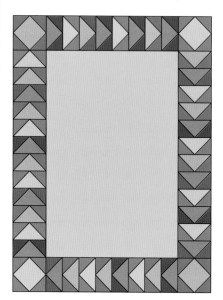

Make sure that the finished size of your block divides evenly into the finished measurement of your quilt center's edges. This will prevent you from having to use partial blocks in the border.

In cases where you cannot evenly divide the block size into the quilt center's edge measurements, your options may include resizing the pieced border blocks to fit, adding a spacer border (see *opposite*), or, if the difference is not too large, insetting a rectangle at the center of each border strip.

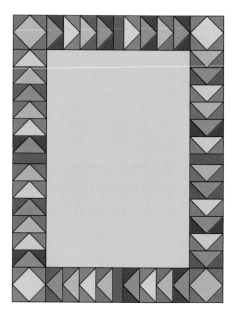

PIECED BORDERS WITH DIAGONALLY SET BLOCKS

Borders that contain blocks or units set diagonally, or on point, are easiest to use on a plain quilt center or a quilt center with blocks set on point. Refer to the Quick Reference Chart for Diagonal Measurements of Squares in Chapter 5—Cutting for mathematical help in planning a diagonally set border.

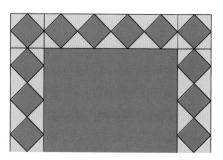

Make sure that the finished diagonal measurement of your block divides evenly into the finished measurements of your quilt center's edges. This will prevent you from having to use partial blocks in the border. In cases where you can't evenly divide the block size into the quilt center's edge measurements, add a spacer border (see Spacer Borders at *right*).

DIRECTIONAL BORDERS

Directional borders are those that have designs running in a particular sequence or order (such as triangle-squares combining into a sawtooth border). Because it is best for a border to appear to be the same along all four sides, you need to plan carefully in order to turn corners smoothly. Sketch your border on paper before proceeding with assembly.

Occasionally directional borders require a special corner unit or block to make the transition from side to side with visual ease. Again, draw your border on paper before proceeding with assembly to determine how and where the corner units will need to be rotated.

UNBALANCED BORDERS

For contemporary designs try borders of differing sizes along each side of the quilt center. For an asymmetrical look, sew border strips to only two or three sides of the quilt center.

SPACER BORDERS

Spacer borders are plain borders that are sewn between the quilt center and outer pieced borders. Think of a spacer border as a mat on a framed picture. They are a good solution when the dimensions of the pieced border and the quilt center are not compatible or whenever you'd like to have some visual "breathing room" between the pieced or appliquéd quilt center and the outer border.

Spacer borders can be the same width along all quilt center edges or they can be one width along the sides and another along the top and bottom.

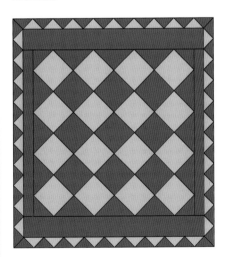

When the same fabric used for the pieced quilt center is used for a spacer border, the center blocks appear to float within the outer border.

A spacer border of contrasting fabric calls attention to the separation between the quilt center and the outer border.

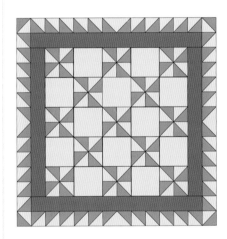

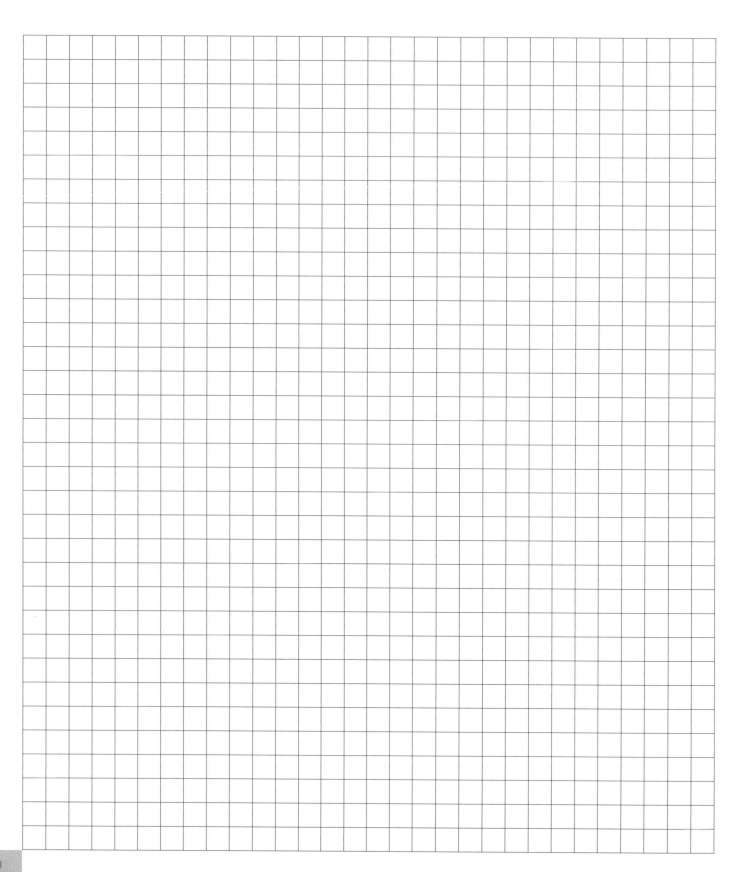

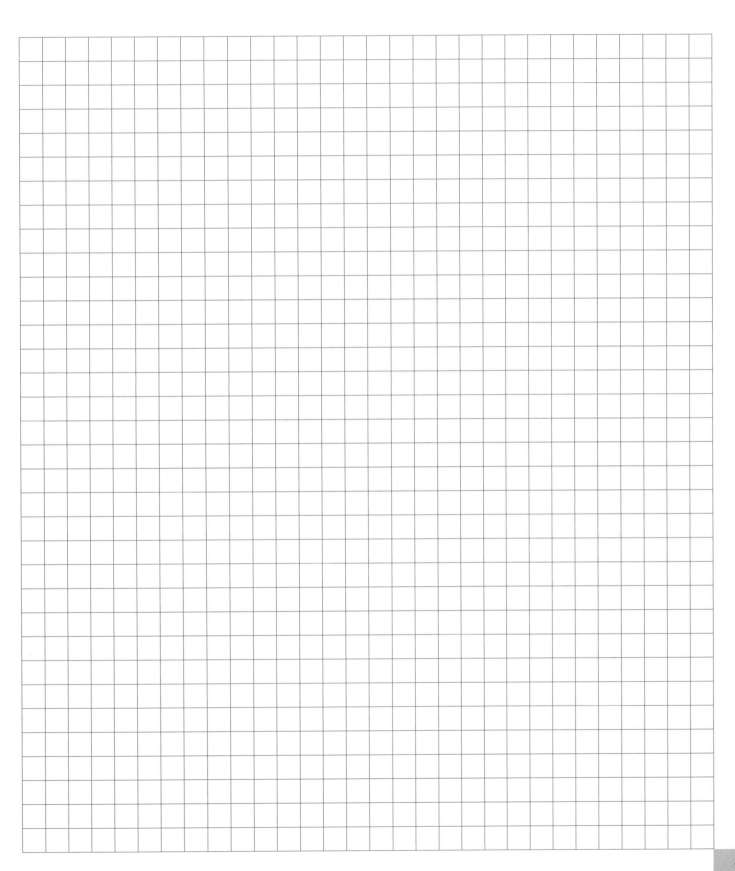

My Notes for Planning the Quilt Top

My Notes for Planning the Quilt Top

Cutting

5

TABLE OF CONTENTS
Chapter 5—Cutting

A SUCCESSFUL QUILT REQUIRES PRECISE CUTTING. With accurately cut pieces, even a beginning quiltmaker can assemble a quilt with ease. Gaining mastery in a variety of cutting techniques and knowing which one to use when can make all the difference in your quiltmaking experience.

CUTTING TOOLS

For a review of both traditional and rotary cutting tools, see Chapter 1— Tools, Notions, & Supplies.

> **TIP:** Many quilt patterns list pieces in the order in which they should be cut to avoid either waste or shortage of fabric.

FABRIC GRAIN

Always consider the fabric grain before cutting. The arrow on the pattern piece or template indicates which direction the fabric grain should run. Because one or more straight sides of every fabric piece should follow the lengthwise or crosswise grain, it is important that the line on the pattern or template runs parallel to the grain.

The *lengthwise grain* runs parallel to the tightly woven finished edge, or selvage, and is sometimes referred to as the *straight grain*. It has the least amount of stretch and is the strongest and smoothest grain. Do not use the selvage edge in a quilt. When washed, the selvage, because

it is so tightly woven, may shrink more than the rest of the fabric.

The *crosswise grain* runs perpendicular to the selvage. It is sometimes referred to as the *cross grain*. The crosswise grain is usually looser and has slightly more stretch than the lengthwise grain.

True bias intersects the lengthwise grain and crosswise grain at a 45° angle, but any line that runs diagonally between the two grain lines is called the bias. It has more stretch and flexibility than either the crosswise or lengthwise grain.

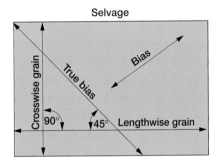

When the lengthwise grain and the crosswise grain intersect at a perfect right angle, the fabric is said to be on grain, or *grain perfect*. If the grains don't intersect at a perfect right angle, they are considered off grain and the threads are distorted.

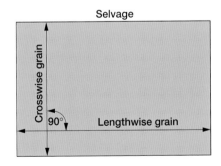

A fabric that is slightly off grain is still usable. However, significantly off-grain fabric will require careful handling during assembly and heavy quilting to stabilize it in a finished quilt.

MARKING WITH TEMPLATES

A template is a thin, firm pattern that aids quilters as they cut the various fabric pieces needed for patchwork and appliqué work. The centuries-old process of cutting patchwork or appliqué pieces employs scissors and templates. Using a template may still be the best way to mark and cut curved or irregular-shape pieces, and many quilters use templates for traditional shapes, too. Commercially available acrylic templates are helpful for quick rotary cutting of specialty shapes and patterns, especially those that need to be cut in large multiples.

This section addresses templates made for both hand and machine piecing. For information on cutting appliqué templates, see Chapter 8— Appliqué.

Templates can be made from different materials. What you choose depends on how often they will be used. Make sure that your choice of template material will hold up to the wear that it receives from multiple tracings without wearing away at the edges.

Sturdy, durable material such as template plastic, available at quilt and crafts supply stores, is suitable for making your own permanent templates for scissors-cut pieces.

MAKING TEMPLATES FOR HAND PIECING

(For information on appliqué templates, see Chapter 8—Appliqué.)

1. Lay template plastic over a printed quilt pattern and trace the pattern onto the plastic using a permanent marker and straightedge. Because it is for hand piecing, make the template the exact size of the finished piece; do not include seam allowances. Mark the template with its letter designation, grain line, and block name.

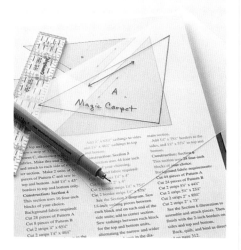

2. Cut out the template and check it against the original pattern for accuracy.

USING TEMPLATES IN HAND PIECING

1. Place the template facedown on wrong side of the fabric and trace around outside edges with a pencil, chalk, or special quilt marker that makes a thin, accurate line. *Note:* Place 220-grit sandpaper beneath the fabric to prevent stretching it as you trace around the template. Position tracings at least ½" apart. The lines drawn on the fabric are the sewing lines.

2. Mark cutting lines ¼" away from the sewing lines or estimate by eye a ¼" seam allowance around each piece as you cut out the fabric shapes with sharp scissors.

MAKING TEMPLATES FOR MACHINE PIECING

1. Lay template plastic over a printed quilt pattern and trace the pattern onto the plastic using a permanent marker and straightedge. Because it is for machine piecing, make the template the exact size of the finished piece plus the ¼" seam allowance. Mark the template with its block name, letter designation, grain line, and the matching point of each corner on the seam line.

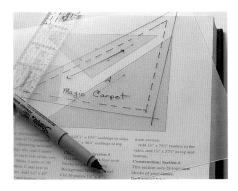

2. Cut out the template. Check the template against the original pattern for accuracy.

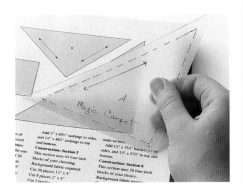

3. Using a pushpin, make a hole in the template at each corner matching point. The hole must be large enough for the point of a pencil or marking pen to mark through.

USING TEMPLATES IN MACHINE PIECING

1. Place the template facedown on the wrong side of the fabric and trace around outside edges with a pencil, chalk, or special quilt marker that makes a thin, accurate line.

Note: Place 220-grit sandpaper beneath the fabric to prevent stretching it as you trace around the template. Mark the corner matching points through the holes in the template; they should be right on the seam line. Position tracings without space between them as the lines drawn on the fabric are the cutting lines.

WHAT ABOUT DOG-EARS?

Long points that will extend beyond the seam allowance line after the pieces are stitched together—"dog-ears" in quilter's terms—can be eliminated when making a template. Why bother? It makes aligning the pieces for sewing easier.

As a general rule, you can blunt points of less than 90° at the ¼" seam line so they will match neighboring pieces. Trim points from templates on regularly shaped pieces when the right side of the piece is the same as the left side.

Angles other than 90° are trickier. When in doubt as to when and where to trim a template point, make your

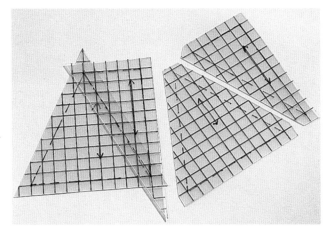

templates with the points left on. Then match the seam lines of adjoining pieces and decide whether you want to remove any points that stick out beyond both layers.

The untrimmed templates shown in the photo above overlap on the seam lines as they would if sewn together. The top and side points of the bottom triangle extend beyond both layers, so they could be trimmed off. Likewise, the left and bottom points of the upper triangle extend beyond both layers, so they, too, could be trimmed off. Once trimmed, the templates ready for use are shown to the right.

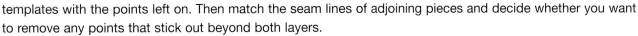

2. Using sharp scissors or a rotary cutter and ruler, cut precisely on the drawn lines.

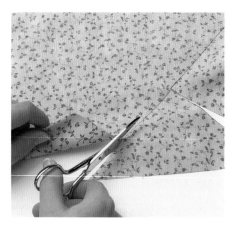

USING TEMPLATES FOR ROTARY CUTTING

Premade templates of thick plastic or acrylic material are often available at quilt shops in a variety of commonly used shapes. These templates are durable enough to be used with a rotary cutter, which speeds the cutting process.

1. Place the template faceup on the right side of an appropriately sized fabric strip.

2. Cut precisely around edges of template with a rotary cutter.

OTHER TEMPLATE TYPES
Printed Paper Patterns

To eliminate the tracing step, sandwich a printed paper pattern between two pieces of template plastic, or one piece of template plastic and tag board or sandpaper. Use rubber cement or a glue stick to adhere the template plastic to the top of the pattern piece and the template plastic, tag board, or sandpaper to the back of the pattern piece. Let the adhesive dry before cutting through all layers at once to make an accurate template.

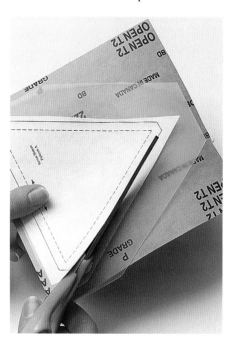

> **TIP:** Avoid the temptation to photocopy a printed pattern. Some photocopy machines may distort the image, and a slight difference in a pattern piece will result in a big difference in the overall quilt top.

Flexible, See-Through Plastic Sheeting

Available at quilt shops, this special-purpose, colored plastic uses static electricity to stick to the rotary-cutting ruler. It is used for do-it-yourself rotary-cutting template making. Cut the plastic to size and place on the rotary-cutting ruler as an aid in speedy cutting.

Graph Paper Templates

You can use the printed lines on graph paper to draw a pattern piece. Glue the graph-paper pattern to template plastic, tag board, or cardboard. Allow the adhesive to dry before cutting through all layers at once to make an accurate template.

ROTARY CUTTING

With a rotary cutter you can make accurate cuts through multiple layers of fabric. One of the strongest appeals of rotary cutting is the precision and speed with which you can cut multiple strips, squares, triangles, and diamonds, thus enhancing your enjoyment of the quiltmaking process.

As with many techniques, the more you practice the easier and more natural the process will become. Practice rotary cutting on fabric scraps until you develop confidence in your cutting accuracy.

TOOL BASICS

To rotary-cut fabrics you need three basic pieces of equipment—a rotary cutter, acrylic ruler, and cutting mat.

A rotary cutter should always be used with a cutting mat designed specifically for rotary cutting. The mat protects the cutting surface and keeps the fabric from shifting while it's being cut.

Cutting mats usually have one side printed with a grid and one side that's plain. To avoid confusion when lining up fabric with the lines printed on the ruler, some quilters prefer to use the plain side of the mat. Others prefer to use the mat's grid.

The round blade of a rotary cutter is razor sharp. Because of this, be sure to use a cutter with a safety guard and keep the guard over the blade whenever you're not cutting. Rotary cutters are commonly available in three sizes; a good all-purpose blade is a 45 mm.

For more information on the tools needed for rotary cutting and their care, see Chapter 1—Tools, Notions, & Supplies.

CARING FOR YOUR ROTARY CUTTER

- Always store your rotary cutter with the blade closed. Keep it out of the reach of children. Be certain to cut on a clean cutting mat; pins and other hard objects will make nicks in the blade.

- Periodically remove the blade from the cutter and carefully wipe away any lint and residue. Take the cutter apart, one piece at a time, laying out the parts in order. Add one drop of sewing machine oil around center of blade before reassembling the cutter.

- Replace blades as needed. Take the cutter apart one piece at a time, laying out the parts in order. Reassemble with a new blade. Dispose of the old blade using the new blade's packaging.

- High humidity can cause the rotary cutter blade to rust. To prevent this, store your rotary cutter in a cool, dry place.

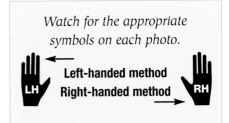

Watch for the appropriate symbols on each photo.

**Left-handed method
Right-handed method**

SQUARING UP THE FABRIC EDGE

Before rotary-cutting fabric into strips, it is imperative that one edge of the fabric be straightened, or squared up. Since the accuracy of all subsequent cuts depends on this first cut, squaring up the fabric edge is a critical step. There are several ways to square up fabric, but here we show two common ways: the single-ruler technique and the double-ruler technique. Instructions are given for both right-handed and left-handed cutting.

Squaring Up With The Single-Ruler Technique (right-handed)

This method requires just one ruler, but you must turn the mat or move to the opposite side of your cutting surface after squaring up the fabric before you can begin cutting strips.

1. Lay the fabric right side down on your cutting mat with one selvage edge away from you.

Cutting

2. Fold the fabric in half with the wrong side inside and selvages together.

3. Fold the fabric in half again, aligning the folded edge with the selvage edges. Lightly hand-crease all folds.

4. Position the folded fabric on the cutting mat with selvage edges away from you and the bulk of the fabric to your left.

5. With ruler on top of fabric, align a horizontal grid line on the ruler with the lower folded fabric edge, leaving about 1" of fabric exposed along the right-hand edge of ruler.

Do not try to align the uneven raw edges along the other side of the fabric. If the grid lines on the cutting mat interfere with your ability to focus on the ruler grid lines, turn your cutting mat over and work on the unmarked side.

6. Hold ruler firmly in place with your left hand, spreading your fingers apart slightly and keeping them away from the right-hand edge of the ruler. Apply pressure to the ruler with fingertips. (Some quilters keep their little finger just off the ruler edge, pressing it on the cutting mat to stabilize the ruler.) With the

ruler firmly in place, hold the rotary cutter with the handle at an angle to the cutting mat and the blade abutted against the ruler's right-hand edge. Roll the blade along the ruler's edge, starting your cut just off the folded edge and pushing the cutter away from you, toward the selvage edges.

7. The fabric strip to the right of the ruler's edge should be cut cleanly away, leaving you with a straight edge from which you can measure all subsequent cuts. Do not pick up the fabric once the edge has been squared; instead, turn the cutting mat to rotate the fabric.

8. Begin cutting strips, measuring from the cut edge.

Squaring Up With The Single-Ruler Technique (left-handed)

This method requires just one ruler, but you must turn the mat or move to the opposite side of your cutting surface after squaring up the fabric before you can begin cutting strips.

1. Lay the fabric right side down on your cutting mat with one selvage edge away from you.

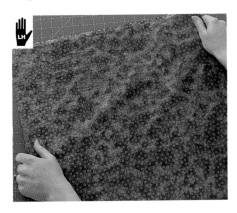

2. Fold the fabric in half with the wrong side inside and selvages together.

3. Fold the fabric in half again, aligning the folded edge with the selvage edges. Lightly hand-crease all folds.

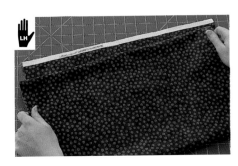

4. Position the folded fabric on the cutting mat with selvage edges away from you and the bulk of the fabric to your right.

5. With ruler on top of fabric, align a horizontal grid line on the ruler with the lower folded fabric edge, leaving about 1" of fabric exposed along the left-hand edge of ruler.

Do not try to align the uneven raw edges along the other side of the fabric. If the grid lines on the cutting mat interfere with your ability to focus on the ruler grid lines, turn your cutting mat over and work on the unmarked side.

6. Hold ruler firmly in place with your right hand, spreading your fingers apart slightly and keeping them away from the left-hand edge

TIP: When cutting several fabric strips in succession, it is possible for your ruler to get slightly askew, causing your strips to be crooked. How will you know? When you open a strip, there will be a slight swerve or bump at the center fold line.

To avoid cutting multiple crooked strips, stop every few strips when you're cutting and open them up. If you discover a bump in the middle, square up your fabric again before cutting any more strips.

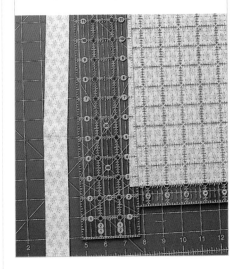

TIP: Bending at the hip rather than at the waist when rotary-cutting is easier and puts less stress on your back and arms. To facilitate this, place your cutting mat on an appropriate height table or countertop.

of the ruler. Apply pressure to the ruler with fingertips. (Some quilters keep their little finger just off the ruler edge, pressing it on the cutting mat to stabilize the ruler.) With the ruler firmly in place, hold the rotary cutter with the handle at an angle to the cutting mat and the blade abutted against the ruler's left-hand edge. Roll the blade along the ruler's edge, starting your cut just off the folded edge and pushing the cutter away from you, toward the selvage edges.

7. The fabric strip to the left of the ruler's edge should be cut cleanly away, leaving you with a straight edge from which you can measure all subsequent cuts. Do not pick up the fabric once the edge has been squared; instead, turn the cutting mat to rotate the fabric.

8. Begin cutting strips, measuring from the cut edge.

Squaring Up With The Two-Ruler Technique (right-handed)

This method requires two rulers, but you can begin cutting strips as soon as the fabric is squared up; turning the mat is not necessary.

1. Lay the fabric right side down on your cutting mat with one selvage edge away from you.

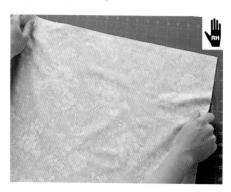

2. Fold the fabric in half with the wrong side inside and selvages together.

3. Fold the fabric in half again, aligning the folded edge with the selvage edges. Lightly hand-crease all the folds.

4. Position the folded fabric on the cutting mat with selvage edges away from you and the bulk of the fabric to your right.

5. With a large square ruler on top of the fabric, align a horizontal grid line on the ruler with the lower folded fabric edge. Leave a small amount of fabric exposed along the

> **TIP:** If your ruler is slipping when you put pressure on it, adhere small sandpaper dots to the underside of the ruler. They're available at quilt shops or you can make your own with a hole punch and fine-grain sandpaper.

left-hand edge of the ruler. Abut a rectangular ruler against the square ruler along left-hand edge.

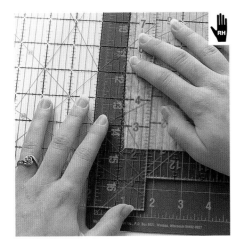

6. Carefully remove the large square ruler, leaving the rectangular ruler in place.

7. Trim away the edge of the fabric to square up fabric. Do not pick up the fabric once the edge has been squared.

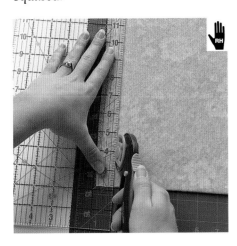

8. Reposition the rectangular ruler and you're ready to begin cutting strips, measuring from the cut edge without rotating the cutting mat.

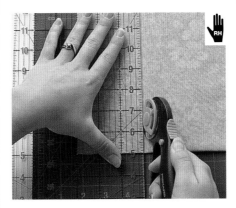

Squaring Up With The Two-Ruler Technique (left-handed)

This method requires two rulers, but you can begin cutting strips as soon as the fabric is squared up; turning the mat is not necessary.

1. Lay the fabric right side down on your cutting mat with one selvage edge away from you.

2. Fold the fabric in half with the wrong side inside and selvages together.

ROTARY-CUTTER TROUBLESHOOTING

Is your cutter not cutting through all the layers? Check the following:

- Is the blade dull? If so, replace it and carefully dispose of the used one. Some blades may be successfully sharpened with a special tool.

- Is there a nick in the blade? You'll know if you discover evenly spaced uncut threads, the result of a blade section not touching the fabric during each rotation. Replace the blade. In the future, avoid cutting over pins and/or dropping the rotary cutter.

- Did you use enough pressure? If you don't have a dull blade but still find large areas where fabric layers weren't cut through cleanly, or where only the uppermost layers were cut, you may not be putting enough muscle behind the cutter. If the problem persists, try cutting fewer fabric layers at a time.

- Is your mat worn out? With extended use, grooves can be worn into your cutting mat, leaving the blade with not enough resistance to make clear cuts through the fabric.

3. Fold the fabric in half again, aligning the folded edge with the selvage edges. Lightly hand-crease all the folds.

4. Position the folded fabric on the cutting mat with selvage edges away from you and the bulk of the fabric to your left.

5. With a large square ruler on top of the fabric, align a horizontal grid line on the ruler with the lower folded fabric edge. Leave a small

amount of fabric exposed along the right-hand edge of the ruler. Abut a rectangular ruler against the square ruler along right-hand edge.

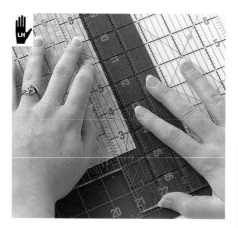

6. Carefully remove the large square ruler, leaving the rectangular ruler in place.

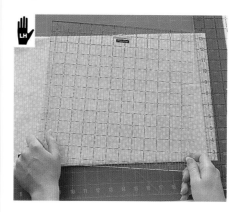

7. Trim away the edge of the fabric to square up fabric. Do not pick up the fabric once the edge has been squared.

8. Reposition your rectangular ruler and you're ready to begin cutting strips, measuring from the cut edge without rotating the cutting mat.

TIP: Keep even, firm pressure on the rotary cutter while pushing it away from your body. Never cut with the blade moving toward you.

ROTARY-CUTTING TIPS

• You can rotary-cut more than one large piece of fabric at a time. For best results, layer only up to four pieces. More than four layers may mean less precision.

• Before rotary-cutting, use spray sizing or spray starch to stabilize the large fabric pieces.

• Press to temporarily hold the fabric layers together.

CUTTING FABRIC WIDER THAN THE RULER

Occasionally you'll need to cut fabric that is wider than the ruler is long. Cutting border strips from the lengthwise grain is one example.

1. After squaring up the fabric, align the ruler and cut to the end of the ruler (see *page 5–5* for instructions on squaring up the fabric edge).

2. Leaving rotary cutter in place on the fabric, slide the ruler ahead to the uncut area. Align ruler edge with the fabric's cut edge.

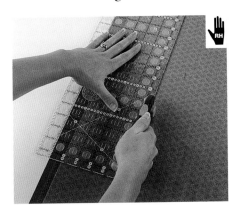

3. Continue cutting and moving the ruler ahead as needed until the desired length of fabric has been cut.

QUICK REFERENCE CHART
YARDAGE ESTIMATOR: SQUARES FROM STRIPS

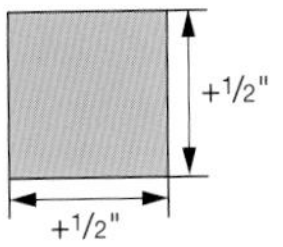

Use this chart to determine the number of squares that can be cut from various yardages. The figures on this chart are mathematically accurate. You may want to purchase extra fabric to allow for errors.

Yardage figures include ¼" seam allowances and are based on 42"-long strips.

SIZE OF SQUARE		YARDAGE (44/45"-wide fabric)							
Finished	Cut Strip Width	¼	½	¾	1	1¼	1½	1¾	2
1"	1½"	168	336	504	672	840	1008	1176	1344
1½"	2"	84	189	273	378	462	567	651	756
2"	2½"	48	112	160	224	288	336	400	448
2½"	3"	42	84	126	168	210	252	294	336
3"	3½"	24	60	84	120	144	180	216	240
3½"	4"	20	40	60	90	110	130	150	180
4"	4½"	18	36	54	72	90	108	126	144
4½"	5"	8	24	40	56	72	80	96	112
5"	5½"	7	21	28	42	56	63	77	91
5½"	6"	7	21	28	42	49	63	70	84
6"	6½"	6	12	24	30	36	48	54	66
6½"	7"	6	12	18	30	36	42	54	60
7"	7½"	5	10	15	20	30	35	40	45
7½"	8"	5	10	15	20	25	30	35	45
8"	8½"	4	8	12	16	20	24	28	32
8½"	9"	4	8	12	16	20	24	28	32
9"	9½"	-	4	8	12	16	20	24	28
9½"	10"	-	4	8	12	16	20	24	28
10"	10½"	-	4	8	12	16	20	24	24
10½"	11"	-	3	6	9	12	12	15	18
11"	11½"	-	3	6	9	9	12	15	18
11½"	12"	-	3	6	9	9	12	15	18
12"	12½"	-	3	6	6	9	12	15	15
12½"	13"	-	3	6	6	9	12	12	15
13"	13½"	-	3	6	6	9	12	12	15
13½"	14"	-	3	3	6	9	9	12	15
14"	14½"	-	2	2	4	6	6	8	8
14½"	15"	-	2	2	4	6	6	8	8
15"	15½"	-	2	2	4	4	6	8	8
15½"	16"	-	2	2	4	4	6	6	8
16"	16½"	-	2	2	4	4	6	6	8
16½"	17"	-	2	2	4	4	6	6	8
17"	17½"	-	2	2	4	4	6	6	8
18"	18½"	-	-	2	2	4	4	6	6

CUTTING SQUARES OR RECTANGLES FROM STRIPS (right-handed)

Use a rotary cutter and strips of fabric to cut multiple squares and rectangles accurately and quickly.

1. To cut squares, cut fabric strips that are the desired finished measurement of the square, plus ½" for seam allowances. For example, for 3" finished squares, cut 3½"-wide fabric strips.

2. Square up one end of each strip (see *page 5–5* for instructions).

3. Using a ruler, align a vertical grid line with the cut edge of a fabric strip. Align the top and bottom edges of fabric strip with horizontal lines on ruler.

To cut squares, cut fabric into lengths equal to the strip width.

For example, for 3" finished squares, cut the 3½"-wide fabric strips into 3½"-long pieces.

4. To cut rectangles, cut fabric strips that are the desired finished length, plus ½" for seam allowances. For example, for 3×5" finished rectangles, cut 3½"-wide fabric strips into 5½" lengths.

CUTTING SQUARES OR RECTANGLES FROM STRIPS (left-handed)

Use a rotary cutter and strips of fabric to cut multiple squares and rectangles accurately and quickly.

1. To cut squares, cut fabric strips that are the desired finished measurement of the square, plus ½" for seam allowances. For example, for 3" finished squares, cut 3½"-wide fabric strips.

2. Square up one end of each strip (see *page 5–5* for instructions).

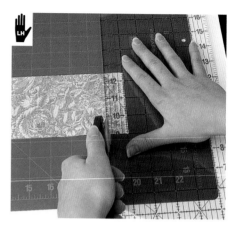

3. Using a ruler, align a vertical grid line with the cut edge of a fabric strip. Align the top and bottom edges of fabric strip with horizontal lines on ruler.

To cut squares, cut fabric into lengths equal to the strip width. For example, for 3" finished squares, cut the 3½"-wide fabric strips into 3½"-long pieces.

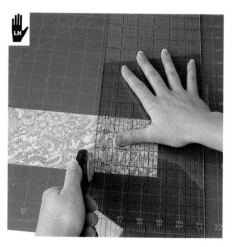

4. To cut rectangles, cut fabric strips that are the desired finished length, plus ½" for seam allowances. For example, for 3×5" finished rectangles, cut 3½"-wide fabric strips into 5½" lengths.

QUICK REFERENCE CHART
YARDAGE ESTIMATOR: RECTANGLES FROM STRIPS

Use this chart to determine the number of rectangles that can be cut from various yardages (see note below on cutting strip width for rectangles).

Yardage figures include ¼" seam allowances and are based on 42"-long strips.

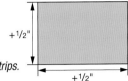

SIZE OF RECTANGLES		YARDAGE (44/45"-wide fabric)							
Finished	Cut Strip Width	¼	½	¾	1	1¼	1½	1¾	2
1×2"	1½×2½"	96	*196	288	*392	*504	*588	*700	*784
1×3"	1½×3½"	72	144	216	288	360	432	504	576
1½×3"	2×3½"	48	108	156	216	264	324	*378	432
1½×4½"	2×5"	32	72	*105	*147	*189	216	*252	*294
1½×8"	2×8½"	*21	*42	*63	*84	*105	*126	*147	*168
1½×9"	2×9½"	16	36	52	72	88	108	*126	*147
1½×10"	2×10½"	16	36	52	72	88	108	*126	144
1½×12"	2×12½"	12	27	*42	54	66	*84	*105	108
2×4"	2½×4½"	*32	*64	*96	*128	162	*192	225	*256
2×6"	2½×6½"	18	42	*64	84	108	*128	150	*176
2×8"	2½×8½"	*16	*32	*48	*64	*80	*96	*112	*128
2×9"	2½×9½"	12	28	40	56	72	84	100	112
2×10"	2½×10½"	12	28	40	56	72	84	100	112
2×12"	2½×12½"	9	21	*32	42	54	*64	*80	84
2½×5"	3×5½"	21	42	63	84	*112	126	*154	*182
2½×7½"	3×8"	15	30	45	60	75	90	105	*126
2½×8"	3×8½"	*14	*28	*42	*56	*70	*84	*98	*112
2½×9"	3×9½"	12	24	36	48	60	72	84	*98
2½×10"	3×10½"	12	24	36	48	60	72	84	96
2½×12"	3×12½"	9	18	*28	36	45	*56	*70	72
3×6"	3½×6½"	12	30	*48	60	72	*96	108	*132
3×8"	3½×8½"	*12	*24	*36	*48	*60	*72	*84	*96
3×9"	3½×9½"	8	20	28	40	48	60	72	*84
3×10"	3½×10½"	8	20	28	40	48	60	72	80
3×12"	3½×12½"	6	15	*24	30	36	*48	*60	60

*Note: Unless otherwise noted, always cut your initial strip from the smallest width of the rectangle. Sometimes you will reap more pieces from your yardage if you cut the first strip at the larger width. These exceptions have been denoted with an asterisk (*). For example, follow the line to the right of "Finished 1×2", Cut Strip Width 1½×2½"." With ½ yard of fabric, you will get more rectangles if you first cut strips 2½", then cross-cut the strips into 1½" segments.

CUTTING A SINGLE SQUARE OR RECTANGLE

1. Align a ruler in a fabric corner. Make two cuts along the ruler's edges to separate the section from remainder of fabric. Make sure the section is slightly larger than the square or rectangle you need.

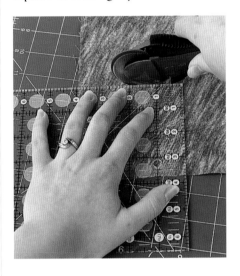

2. Rotate the section of fabric and align the cut edges of fabric with the desired measurements on the ruler. Make two more cuts along the ruler's edges to complete the square or rectangle.

QUICK REFERENCE CHART
YARDAGE ESTIMATOR: FLYING GEESE AND SQUARES FROM STRIPS

If you're using the one rectangle and two squares method of making Flying Geese units, use this chart to determine the number of rectangles and squares that can be cut from various yardages (see note below on cutting strip width for rectangles). For more information on making Flying Geese, see Flying Geese Method 1 in Chapter 7—Machine Piecing. *Yardage figures include ¼" seam allowances and are based on 42"-long strips.*

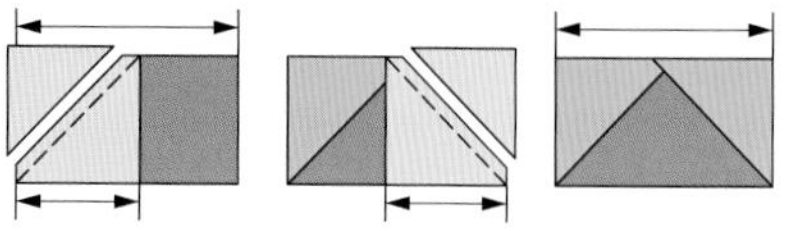

SIZE OF RECTANGLES AND SQUARES				YARDAGE (44/45"-wide fabric)							
Finished Unit Size	Rectangle Size	Square Size	Cut Strip Width	¼	½	¾	1	1¼	1½	1¾	2
½×1"	1×1½"		1"*	252	504	756	1,008	1,260	1,512	1,764	2,016
		1"	1"	378	756	1,134	1,512	1,890	2,268	2,646	3,024
¾×1½"	1¼×2"		1¼"*	147	*297	441	*594	756	903	1,050	1,197
		1¼"	1¼"	231	462	693	924	1,188	1,419	1,650	1,881
1×2"	1½×2½"		1½"*	96	*196	288	*392	480	*588	*700	*784
		1½"	1½"	168	336	504	672	840	1,008	1,176	1,344
1¼×2½"	1¾×3"		1¾"*	*72	*144	*216	*288	*360	*432	504	*576
		1¾"	1¾"	120	240	360	480	600	720	864	984
1½×3"	2×3½"		2"*	48	108	156	216	264	324	*378	432
		2"	2"	84	189	273	378	462	567	651	756
1¾×3½"	2¼×4"		2¼"*	40	80	120	*162	200	240	280	*324
		2¼"	2¼"	72	144	216	288	360	432	504	576
2×4"	2½×4½"		2½"*	*32	*64	*96	*128	162	*192	225	*256
		2½"	2½"	48	112	160	224	288	336	400	448
2¼×4½"	2¾×5"		2¾"*	24	48	*75	*105	*135	152	*180	*210
		2¾"	2¾"	45	90	135	195	240	285	330	390
2½×5"	3×5½"		3"*	21	42	63	84	*112	126	*154	*182
		3"	3"	42	84	126	168	210	252	294	336
2¾×5½"	3¼×6"		3¼"*	14	*36	56	77	91	112	133	154
		3¼"	3¼"	24	60	96	132	156	192	228	264
3×6"	3½×6½"		3½"*	12	30	*48	60	72	*96	108	*132
		3½"	3½"	24	60	84	120	144	180	216	240
3¼×6½"	3¾×7"		3¾"*	12	24	42	*55	72	84	*99	114
		3¾"	3¾"	22	44	77	99	132	154	176	209
3½×7"	4×7½"		4"*	10	20	30	45	*60	*70	*80	90
		4"	4"	20	40	60	90	110	130	150	180
3¾×7½"	4¼×8"		4¼"*	10	20	30	40	50	60	70	*81
		4¼"	4¼"	18	36	54	72	90	108	126	144
4×8"	4½×8½"		4½"*	8	*18	*27	*36	*45	*54	*63	*72
		4½"	4½"	18	36	54	72	90	108	126	144

*Note: Unless otherwise noted, always cut your initial strip from the smallest width of the rectangle. Sometimes you'll reap more pieces from yardage if you cut the first strip at the larger width. These exceptions are denoted with an asterisk (*). For example, follow the line to the right of "Finished Unit Size 1×2", Rectangle Size 1½×2½", Cut Strip Width 1½"." With ½ yard of fabric, you'll get more rectangles if you first cut strips 2½", then cross-cut the strips into 1½" segments.

FUSSY CUTTING

Isolating and cutting out a specific print or pattern is referred to as fussy cutting.

1. Trace finished-size shape on a piece of frosted template plastic that is at least 2" larger on all sides than desired shape.

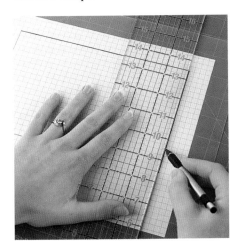

2. Using a crafts knife and ruler, cut away the interior of the shape to make a viewing window.

3. Move the viewing window over the fabric to isolate the desired portion of the print. Mark position with pins or chalk.

4. Remove the viewing window and re-mark as needed. Add seam allowances and cut out the print portion with scissors or a rotary cutter and ruler.

CUTTING HALF-SQUARE TRIANGLES (right-handed)

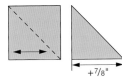

1. Square up the fabric (see *page 5–5* for instructions).

2. Cut the fabric in strips as wide as the desired finished width of the triangle-squares, plus ⅞" for seam allowances. For example, for a 3" finished half-square triangle, cut a 3⅞"-wide fabric strip.

3. Square up one end of each strip.

4. Using a ruler, cut the strip into lengths equal to the strip's width. In this example, the strip would be cut into 3⅞"-long pieces.

5. Position the ruler diagonally across a square and cut the square in half to make two equal-size right triangles.

QUICK REFERENCE CHART
YARDAGE ESTIMATOR: HALF-SQUARE (RIGHT) TRIANGLES FROM STRIPS

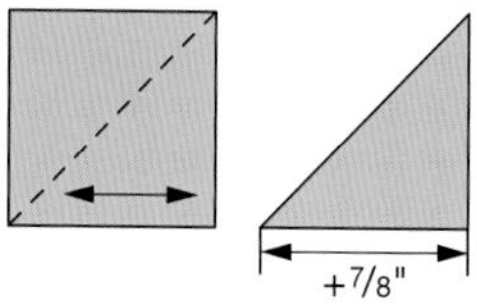

Use this chart to determine the number of half-square triangles that can be cut from various yardages.

Yardage figures include ¼" seam allowances and are based on 42"-long strips.

SIZE OF TRIANGLE		YARDAGE (44/45"-wide fabric)							
Finished	Cut Strip Width	¼	½	¾	1	1¼	1½	1¾	2
1"	1⅞"	176	396	616	836	1056	1232	1452	1672
1½"	2⅜"	102	238	374	510	612	748	884	1020
2"	2⅞"	84	168	252	336	420	504	588	700
2½"	3⅜"	48	120	192	240	312	384	432	504
3"	3⅞"	40	80	120	180	220	260	320	360
3½"	4⅜"	36	72	108	144	180	216	252	288
4"	4⅞"	16	48	80	112	144	176	192	224
4½"	5⅜"	14	42	70	84	112	140	154	182
5"	5⅞"	14	42	56	84	98	126	140	168
5½"	6⅜"	12	24	48	60	84	96	108	132
6"	6⅞"	12	24	36	60	72	84	108	120
6½"	7⅜"	10	20	30	40	60	70	80	90
7"	7⅞"	10	20	30	40	50	60	80	90
7½"	8⅜"	10	20	30	40	50	60	70	80
8"	8⅞"	8	16	24	32	40	48	56	64
8½"	9⅜"	-	8	16	24	32	40	48	56
9"	9⅞"	-	8	16	24	32	40	48	56
9½"	10⅜"	-	8	16	24	32	40	48	48
10"	10⅞"	-	6	12	18	24	24	30	36
10½"	11⅜"	-	6	12	18	18	24	30	36
11"	11⅞"	-	6	12	18	18	24	30	36
11½"	12⅜"	-	6	12	12	18	24	30	30
12"	12⅞"	-	6	12	12	18	24	24	30
12½"	13⅜"	-	6	12	12	18	24	24	30
13"	13⅞"	-	6	6	12	18	18	24	30
13½"	14⅜"	-	4	4	8	12	12	16	20
14"	14⅞"	-	4	4	8	12	12	16	16
14½"	15⅜"	-	4	4	8	8	12	16	16
15"	15⅞"	-	4	4	8	8	12	12	16
15½"	16⅜"	-	4	4	8	8	12	12	16
16"	16⅞"	-	4	4	8	8	12	12	16
16½"	17⅜"	-	4	4	8	8	12	12	16
17"	17⅞"	-	4	4	8	8	12	12	16
17½"	18⅜"	-	-	4	4	8	8	12	12
18"	18⅞"	-	-	4	4	8	8	12	12

CUTTING HALF-SQUARE TRIANGLES (left-handed)

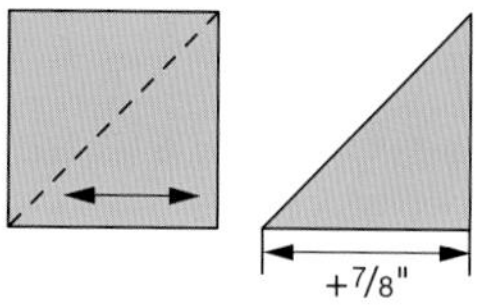

1. Square up the fabric (see *page 5–5* for instructions).

2. Cut the fabric in strips as wide as the desired finished width of the triangle-squares, plus ⅞" for seam allowances. For example, for a 3" finished half-square triangle, cut a 3⅞"-wide fabric strip.

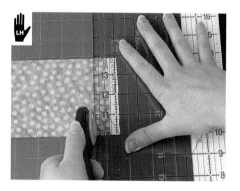

3. Square up one end of each strip.

TIP: Hold your cutter with the handle at a comfortable angle to the cutting surface and the exposed silver side of the blade snug against the edge of the ruler.

4. Using a ruler, cut the strip into lengths equal to the strip's width. In this example, the strip would be cut into 3⅞"-long pieces.

5. Position the ruler diagonally across the square and cut the square in half to make two equal-size right triangles.

TIP: Do not use the first ½" of fabric near each selvage edge. The selvages are more tightly woven. Using them in your quilt may cause puckering or distortion.

CUTTING QUARTER-SQUARE TRIANGLES (right-handed)

1. Square up the fabric (see *page 5–5* for instructions).

2. Cut the fabric in strips as wide as the desired finished width of the quarter-square triangle, plus 1¼" for seam allowances. For example, for a 3" finished quarter-square triangle, cut a 4¼"-wide fabric strip.

3. Square up one end of each strip.

4. Using a ruler, cut the strip into lengths equal to the strip's width. In this example, the strip would be cut into 4¼"-long pieces.

5. Position the ruler diagonally across square and cut the square in half to make two equal-size right triangles. Do not move or pick up the triangles.

6. Position the ruler diagonally across the cut square in the opposite direction and cut the square in half again to make a total of four equal-size triangles.

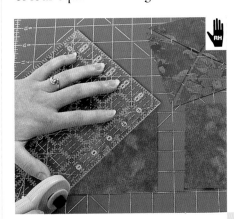

QUICK REFERENCE CHART
YARDAGE ESTIMATOR: QUARTER-SQUARE (RIGHT) TRIANGLES FROM STRIPS

Use this chart to determine the number of quarter-square triangles that can be cut from various yardages.

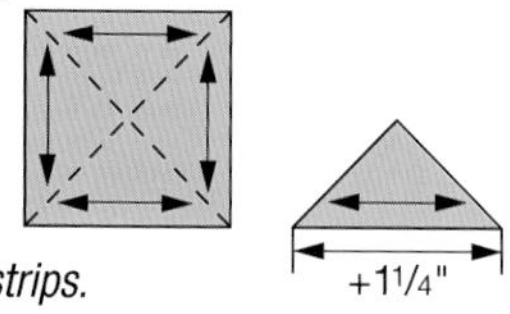

Yardage figures include ¼" seam allowances and are based on 42"-long strips.

SIZE OF TRIANGLE		YARDAGE (44/45"-wide fabric)							
Finished	Cut Strip Width	¼	½	¾	1	1¼	1½	1¾	2
1"	2¼"	288	576	864	1,152	1,440	1,728	2,016	2,304
1½"	2¾"	180	360	540	780	960	1,140	1,320	1,560
2"	3¼"	96	240	384	528	624	768	912	1,056
2½"	3¾"	88	176	308	396	528	616	704	836
3"	4¼"	72	144	216	288	360	432	504	576
3½"	4¾"	32	96	160	224	288	352	416	480
4"	5¼"	32	96	160	192	256	320	384	416
4½"	5¾"	28	84	112	168	196	252	280	336
5"	6¼"	24	48	96	120	168	192	240	264
5½"	6¾"	24	48	96	120	144	192	216	240
6"	7¼"	20	40	60	80	120	140	160	180
6½"	7¾"	20	40	60	80	100	120	160	180
7"	8¼"	20	40	60	80	100	120	140	160
7½"	8¾"	16	32	48	64	80	96	112	128
8"	9¼"	-	16	32	48	64	80	96	112
8½"	9¾"	-	16	32	48	64	80	96	112
9"	10¼"	-	16	32	48	64	80	96	112
9½"	10¾"	-	12	24	36	48	60	60	72
10"	11¼"	-	12	24	36	48	48	60	72
10½"	11¾"	-	12	24	36	36	48	60	72
11"	12¼"	-	12	24	24	36	48	60	60
11½"	12¾"	-	12	24	24	36	48	48	60
12"	13¼"	-	12	24	24	36	48	48	60
12½"	13¾"	-	12	12	24	36	36	48	60
13"	14¼"	-	8	8	16	24	24	32	40
13½"	14¾"	-	8	8	16	24	24	32	32
14"	15¼"	-	8	8	16	16	24	32	32
14½"	15¾"	-	8	8	16	16	24	32	32
15"	16¼"	-	8	8	16	16	24	24	32
15½"	16¾"	-	8	8	16	16	24	24	32
16"	17¼"	-	8	8	16	16	24	24	32
16½"	17¾"	-	8	8	16	16	24	24	32
17"	18¼"	-	-	8	8	16	16	24	24
18"	19¼"	-	-	8	8	16	16	24	24

CUTTING QUARTER-SQUARE TRIANGLES (left-handed)

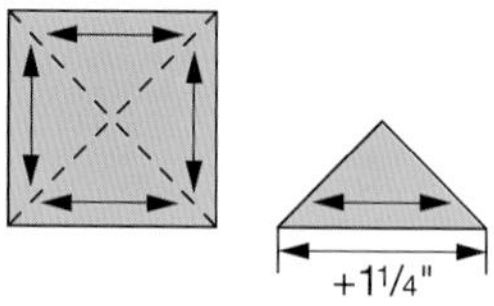

1. Square up the fabric (see *page 5–5* for instructions).

2. Cut the fabric in strips as wide as the desired finished width of the quarter-square triangle, plus 1¼" for seam allowances. For example, for a 3" finished quarter-square triangle, cut a 4¼"-wide fabric strip.

3. Square up one end of each strip.

4. Using a ruler, cut the strip into lengths equal to the strip's width.

In this example, the strip would be cut into 4¼"-long pieces.

5. Position the ruler diagonally across the square from corner to corner and cut the square in half to make two equal triangles. Do not move or pick up the triangles.

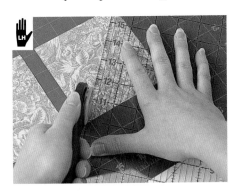

6. Position the ruler diagonally across the square from corner to corner in the opposite direction and cut the square in half again to make a total of four equal triangles.

CUTTING 60° EQUILATERAL TRIANGLES— STRIP METHOD

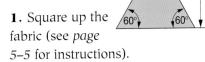

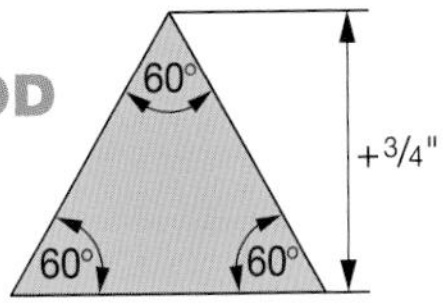

1. Square up the fabric (see *page 5–5* for instructions).

2. Cut the fabric in strips as wide as the desired finished height of the triangle, plus ¾" for seam allowances. For example, to make a finished equilateral triangle that is 3" high, cut a 3¾"-wide fabric strip.

3. Align a ruler's 60° line with the long, lower edge of the strip and cut.

4. Rotate the ruler so the opposing 60° line is aligned with the same long, lower edge of the strip and cut.

QUICK REFERENCE CHART
YARDAGE ESTIMATOR: 60° EQUILATERAL TRIANGLES FROM STRIPS

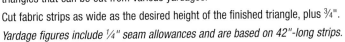

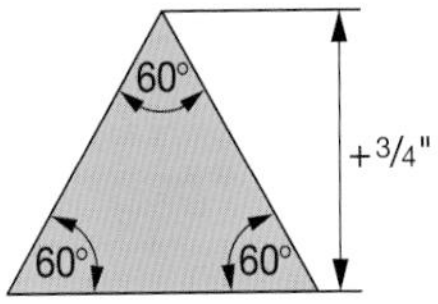

Use this chart to determine the number of 60° equilateral triangles that can be cut from various yardages.

Cut fabric strips as wide as the desired height of the finished triangle, plus ¾".

Yardage figures include ¼" seam allowances and are based on 42"-long strips.

HEIGHT OF TRIANGLE		YARDAGE (44/45"-wide fabric)							
Finished	Cut Strip Width	¼	½	¾	1	1¼	1½	1¾	2
1"	1¾"	180	360	540	720	900	1,080	1,296	1,476
1½"	2¼"	120	240	360	480	600	720	840	960
2"	2¾"	66	132	198	286	352	418	484	572
2½"	3¼"	36	90	144	198	234	288	342	396
3"	3¾"	32	64	112	144	192	224	256	304
3½"	4¼"	28	56	84	112	140	168	196	224
4"	4¾"	12	36	60	84	108	132	156	180

5. Repeat steps 3 and 4 to work your way across the fabric strip and cut additional equilateral triangles.

CUTTING CENTER TRIANGLES FOR ISOSCELES TRIANGLE-IN-A-SQUARE BLOCKS

+7/8"

The center triangle in a triangle-in-a-square block is an isosceles triangle, which means it has two sides of equal length.

1. Square up the fabric (see *page 5–5* for instructions).

2. Cut the fabric in strips as wide as the desired finished width of the triangle, plus ⅞". For example, to

make an isosceles triangle for a 3" finished triangle-in-a-square, cut a 3⅞"-wide fabric strip.

3. Square up one end of each strip.

4. Position the ruler over the strip and cut a square. In this example, cut a 3⅞" square from the 3⅞"-wide strip.

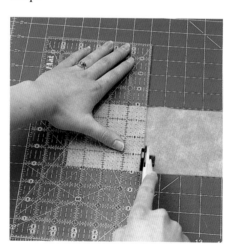

TIP: When cutting an equilateral triangle, note that the ruler sometimes covers the shape you are cutting. It's easier and more efficient to move the ruler from one side of the shape to the other than to move the fabric strip or rotate the cutting mat.

5. Fold the square in half to find top center and lightly finger-crease.

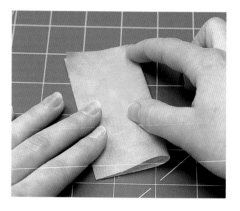

6. Position ruler diagonally across the square from a bottom corner to the creased top center mark and cut. Do not pick up the fabric pieces.

7. Rotate the ruler only and align it diagonally from the other bottom corner to the creased top center mark and cut.

CUTTING SIDE TRIANGLES FOR ISOSCELES TRIANGLE-IN-A-SQUARE BLOCKS

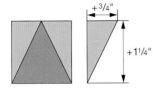

The side triangles in a triangle-in-a-square block are long triangles with a 90° corner.

1. Square up the fabric (see *page 5–5* for instructions).

2. Cut the fabric in strips as wide as the desired finished width of the side triangle plus ¾". For example, for a 3" finished triangle-in-a-square, the finished width of the side triangle is 1½", so you would cut a 2¼"-wide fabric strip (1½" + ¾").

3. Position two layers of strips, stacked with like sides together, parallel to one of the mat's grid lines and square up one end.

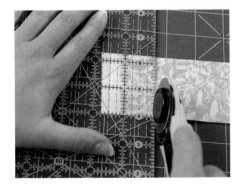

4. Position the ruler over the stacked strips and measure the desired finished height of the side triangle, plus 1¼" for seam allowances, and cut the rectangle. In this example, make one cut in the stacked 2¼"-wide strips to make two rectangles each 2¼×4¼".

Note: The isosceles triangle-in-a-square has two side triangles that are mirror images of each other. Always cut in double layers to make the mirror-image shapes. Two rectangles yield two left-hand side triangles and two right-hand side triangles.

5. Position the ruler diagonally across the stacked rectangles and cut the rectangles in half to make two each of the left-hand and right-hand side triangles.

CUTTING 45° TRAPEZOIDS

1. Square up the fabric (see *page 5–5* for instructions).

2. Cut the fabric in strips as wide as the desired finished height of the trapezoid, plus ½" for seam allowances. For example, for a 3"-high trapezoid, cut a 3½"-wide fabric strip.

3. Square up one end of each strip.

TIP: When aligning the pieces to sew together an isosceles triangle-in-a-square block, the side triangles must be even with the top point of the center triangle. The dog-ears extend at the base of the center triangle.

Once sewn together, this overlap at the top of the triangle is what creates the seam allowance along the upper edge of the block. When you sew it to another block, this seam allowance will be taken in, leaving the tip of your center triangle intact at the seam line.

4. Position the ruler over a strip and measure the desired finished length of the trapezoid, plus 1¼" for seam allowances, and cut a rectangle. For example, for a 10¼"-long finished trapezoid, cut an 11½" length from the strip to make a 3½×11½" rectangle.

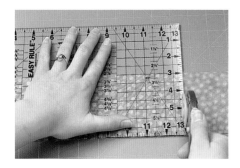

5. Align a ruler's 45° line with the horizontal edge of the rectangle. Cut a 45° angle from the bottom corner to the top edge. Do not pick up the fabric rectangle.

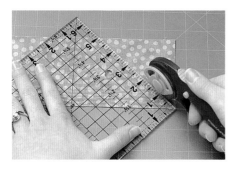

6. Pick up and rotate the ruler only. Position it on the opposite rectangle end and align the 45° line with the opposite edge of the fabric. Cut a 45° angle from the bottom corner to the top edge.

CUTTING 45° DIAMONDS

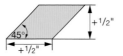

1. Square up the fabric (see *page 5–5* for instructions).

2. Cut the fabric in strips as wide as the desired finished width of the diamond, plus ½" for seam allowances. For example, for a 3"-wide diamond, cut a 3½"-wide fabric strip.

3. Square up one end of each strip.

4. Position the ruler on the strip, aligning the 45° line with the horizontal edge of the strip. Cut a 45° angle from the bottom edge to the top edge.

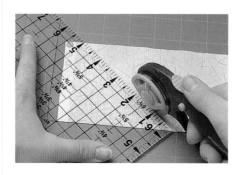

5. Aligning the ruler with the first cut edge, reposition the ruler on the strip at the desired width measurement, plus ½" for seam allowances. Cut a second 45° angle parallel to the first from the bottom edge to the top edge.

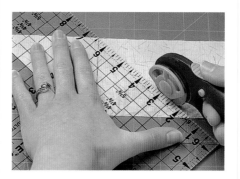

CUTTING SETTING TRIANGLES AND BLOCKS

Quilt blocks set on the diagonal (or "on point") may require setting triangles to fill out

the design. These setting triangles are often called filler triangles. When quilt blocks are turned on the diagonal it often means that the straight grain of the block is on the diagonal also (for more information see Chapter 9—Assembling the Quilt Top).

To stabilize the fabric and control its natural tendency to sag, it is critical that the setting triangles are cut so that the straight grain runs up and down.

Some quilters prefer to cut triangles ½ to 1" larger than required and trim away the excess fabric after piecing the top. The measurements given in the chart *opposite* are mathematically correct and do not allow for any excess fabric. *Note:* To "float" the blocks in a diagonal set, cut the side and corner setting triangles up to 2" larger than the diagonal measurement of the block (see Chapter 4—Planning the Quilt Top for more information on a Diagonal Set with Floating Blocks).

Side Triangles
Side setting triangles are quarter-square triangles; one square produces four side triangles.

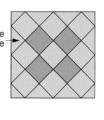

Side Triangle

To calculate the size to cut a square for setting triangles, multiply the finished block size by 1.414 and add 1¼" for seam allowances. (For example, 10" block × 1.414 = 14.14 + 1.25" = 15.39"; rounded up the measurement would be 15½".) Side triangle measurements for several standard block sizes are shown in the chart at *right*.

Corner Triangles

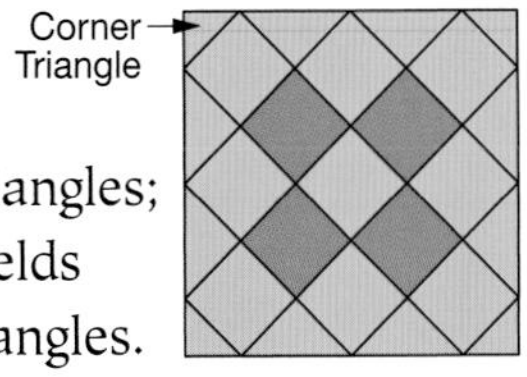

Corner triangles are half-square triangles; one square yields two corner triangles.

To calculate the size to cut a square for corner setting triangles, divide the finished block size by 1.414 and add .875" for seam allowances. (For example, 10" block divided by 1.414 = 7.07 + .875" = 7.945"; rounded up the measurement would be 8".) Shown at *right* are corner triangle measurements for several standard block sizes.

Setting Squares

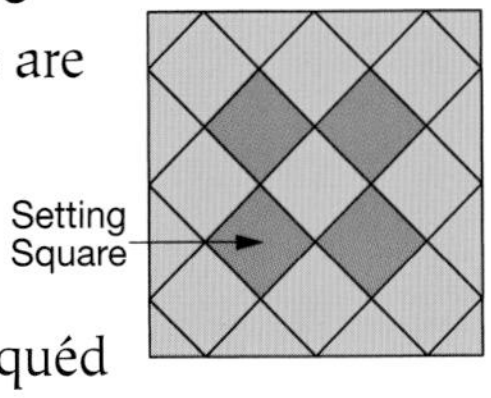

Setting squares are generally solid squares cut to place between pieced or appliquéd blocks to set off a design.

To calculate the size to cut a square for setting squares, add ½" to the finished block size to allow for seam allowances. (For example, 10" block + ½" = 10½".) Shown at *right* are setting square measurements for several standard block sizes.

QUICK REFERENCE CHART
SETTING TRIANGLES AND SETTING SQUARES

Use this chart to determine the correct size to cut side and corner setting triangles and setting squares based on the size of your finished block.

Finished Block Size	Size to cut square for side setting triangles *Formula A 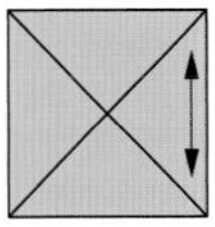	Size to cut square for corner setting triangles *Formula B 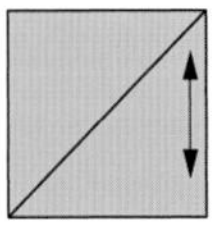	Size to cut setting squares *Formula C 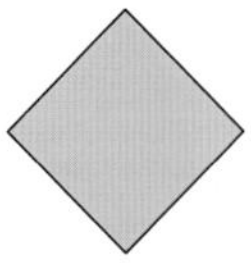
1"	2¾"	1⅝"	1½"
2"	4⅛"	2⅜"	2½"
3"	5½"	3"	3½"
4"	7"	3¾"	4½"
5"	8⅜"	4½"	5½"
6"	9¾"	5⅛"	6½"
7"	11¼"	5⅞"	7½"
8"	12⅝"	6⅝"	8½"
9"	14"	7¼"	9½"
10"	15½"	8"	10½"
11"	16⅞"	8¾"	11½"
12"	18¼"	9⅜"	12½"
13"	19¾"	10⅛"	13½"
14"	21⅛"	10⅞"	14½"
15"	22½"	11½"	15½"
16"	23⅞"	12¼"	16½"
17"	25⅜"	13"	17½"
18"	26¾"	13⅝"	18½"
19"	28⅛"	14⅜"	19½"
20"	29⅝"	15⅛"	20½"

• A—To calculate the size to cut a square for side setting triangles, multiply the finished block size by 1.414 and add 1.25" for seam allowances. (For example, 10" block × 1.414 = 14.14 + 1.25" = 15.39"; rounded up the measurement would be 15½".)

• B—To calculate the size to cut a square for corner setting triangles, divide the finished block size by 1.414 and add .875" for seam allowances. (For example, 10" block divided by 1.414 = 7.07 + .875" = 7.945"; rounded up the measurement would be 8".)

• C—To calculate the size to cut a setting square, add ½" to the finished block size to allow for seam allowances. (For example, 10" block + ½" = 10½".)

QUICK REFERENCE CHART
DIAGONAL MEASUREMENTS OF SQUARES

Use this chart to determine quilt center size of a diagonally set quilt.

For example, if blocks finish 12" and are set on point, quilt center size =

(17" × number of blocks horizontally) + (17" × number of blocks vertically).

To calculate the finished diagonal measurement of a block, multiply finished block measurement (without seam allowances) by 1.414.

Shown below are diagonal measurements for several standard block sizes. Figures are rounded up to the nearest ⅛" (.125").

Finished Block Size	Finished Diagonal Measurement	Decimal Equivalent of Diagonal Measurement
1"	1½"	1.5"
1½"	2⅛"	2.125"
2"	2⅞"	2.875"
2½"	3⅝"	3.625"
3"	4¼"	4.25"
3½"	5"	5.0"
4"	5⅝"	5.625"
4½"	6⅜"	6.375"
5"	7⅛"	7.125"
5½"	7⅞"	7.875"
6"	8½"	8.5"
6½"	9¼"	9.25"
7"	10"	10.0"
7½"	10⅝"	10.625"
8"	11⅜"	11.375"
8½"	12⅛"	12.125"
9"	12¾"	12.75"
9½"	13½"	13.5"
10"	14¼"	14.25"
10½"	14⅞"	14.875"
11"	15⅝"	15.625"
11½"	16⅜"	16.375"
12"	17"	17.0"
12½"	17¾"	17.75"
13"	18½"	18.5"
14"	19⅞"	19.875"
15"	21¼"	21.25"
16"	22⅝"	22.625"
17"	24⅛"	24.125"
18"	25½"	25.5"
19"	26⅞"	26.875"
20"	28⅜"	28.375"

TIPS FOR CUTTING BORDERS

See Chapter 9–Assembling the Quilt Top for more information.

- Always cut on the straight grain of the fabric, never on the bias, because the bias has give and borders with give will cause the quilt to stretch out of shape over time.

- Cut the borders on the lengthwise grain (parallel to the selvage) if you have enough fabric. If cut from a single piece of fabric they will not need to be seamed and will rarely stretch.

- If you must cut the borders on the crosswise grain (perpendicular to the selvage) and seam them, sew them together with diagonal seams, which will be less visible. Borders cut on the crosswise grain have a bit more give and stretch than those cut on the lengthwise grain, and may stretch or sag over time.

QUICK REFERENCE CHART
MAGIC NUMBERS FOR ROTARY CUTTING

To determine the cutting size of a variety of shapes when rotary-cutting, use this chart.

All measurements assume a ¼" seam allowance is being used.

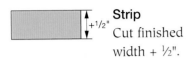

Strip
Cut finished width + ½".

Square and Rectangle
Cut finished size + ½".

Half-Square Triangle
Cut finished width + ⅞".

Quarter-Square Triangle
Cut finished width + 1¼".

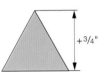

Equilateral Triangle
Cut finished height + ¾".

Isosceles Triangle-in-a-Square
Center Triangle
Cut finished width + ⅞".

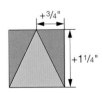

Isosceles Triangle-in-a-Square
Side Triangle
Cut finished width + ¾", finished height + 1¼" (must be made in mirror images).

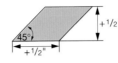

45° Diamond
Cut finished height + ½", finished width + ½".

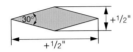

30° Diamond
Cut finished height + ½", finished width + ½".

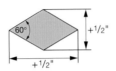

60° Diamond
Cut finished height + ½", finished width + ½".

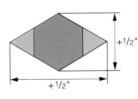

Hexagon
From a 60° diamond, cut finished height + ½", finished width + ½".

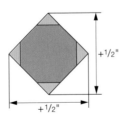

Octagon
From a square, cut finished height + ½", finished width + ½".

QUICK REFERENCE CHART
RULER AND CALCULATOR EQUIVALENTS

If you're trying to convert a calculated yardage or measurement into the nearest ruler equivalent, use this at-a-glance reference chart.

Ruler Fraction	Calculator Decimal
1/64	.016
1/32	.031
1/16	.0625
1/8	.125
3/16	.1875
1/4	.25
5/16	.3125
3/8	.375
7/16	.4375
1/2	.50
9/16	.5625
5/8	.625
11/16	.6875
3/4	.75
13/16	.8125
7/8	.875
15/16	.9375

Cutting

QUICK REFERENCE CHART
YARDAGE AND METRIC EQUIVALENTS

If you need to convert a pattern's units of measurement, use this chart to determine the quantities needed.

Equivalents are for inches, yardage in eighths and decimals, and meters.

INCHES	YARDS (fractions)	YARDS (decimals)	METERS	INCHES	YARDS (fractions)	YARDS (decimals)	METERS
4½"	⅛ yd.	.125 yd.	.144 m	157½"	4⅜ yd.	4.375 yd.	4.001 m
9"	¼ yd.	.25 yd.	.229 m	162"	4½ yd.	4.5 yd.	4.115 m
12"	⅓ yd.	.333 yd.	.304 m	166½"	4⅝ yd.	4.625 yd.	4.229 m
13½"	⅜ yd.	.375 yd.	.343 m	171"	4¾ yd.	4.75 yd.	4.343 m
18"	½ yd.	.5 yd.	.457 m	180"	5 yd.	5.0 yd.	4.572 m
22½"	⅝ yd.	.625 yd.	.572 m	184½"	5⅛ yd.	5.125 yd.	4.686 m
24"	⅔ yd.	.667 yd.	.610 m	189"	5¼ yd.	5.25 yd.	4.801 m
27"	¾ yd.	.75 yd.	.686 m	193½"	5⅜ yd.	5.375 yd.	4.915 m
31½"	⅞ yd.	.875 yd.	.8 m	198"	5½ yd.	5.5 yd.	5.029 m
36"	1 yd.	1.0 yd.	.914 m	202½"	5⅝ yd.	5.625 yd.	5.144 m
40½"	1⅛ yd.	1.125 yd.	1.029 m	207"	5¾ yd.	5.75 yd.	5.258 m
45"	1¼ yd.	1.25 yd.	1.143 m	216"	6 yd.	6.0 yd.	5.486 m
48"	1⅓ yd.	1.333 yd.	1.219 m	220½"	6⅛ yd.	6.125 yd.	5.601 m
49½"	1⅜ yd.	1.375 yd.	1.257 m	225"	6¼ yd.	6.25 yd.	5.715 m
54"	1½ yd.	1.5 yd.	1.372 m	229½"	6⅜ yd.	6.375 yd.	5.829 m
58½"	1⅝ yd.	1.625 yd.	1.486 m	234"	6½ yd.	6.5 yd.	5.944 m
60"	1⅔ yd.	1.667 yd.	1.524 m	238½"	6⅝ yd.	6.625 yd.	6.058 m
63"	1¾ yd.	1.75 yd.	1.6 m	243"	6¾ yd.	6.75 yd.	6.172 m
67½"	1⅞ yd.	1.875 yd.	1.715 m	252"	7 yd.	7.0 yd.	6.401 m
72"	2 yd.	2.0 yd.	1.829 m	256½"	7⅛ yd.	7.125 yd.	6.515 m
76½"	2⅛ yd.	2.125 yd.	1.943 m	261"	7¼ yd.	7.25 yd.	6.629 m
81"	2¼ yd.	2.25 yd.	2.057 m	265½"	7⅜ yd.	7.375 yd.	6.744 m
84"	2⅓ yd.	2.333 yd.	2.134 m	270"	7½ yd.	7.5 yd.	6.858 m
85½"	2⅜ yd.	2.375 yd.	2.172 m	274½"	7⅝ yd.	7.625 yd.	6.972 m
90"	2½ yd.	2.5 yd.	2.286 m	279"	7¾ yd.	7.75 yd.	7.087 m
94½"	2⅝ yd.	2.625 yd.	2.4 m	288"	8 yd.	8.0 yd.	7.315 m
96"	2⅔ yd.	2.667 yd.	2.438 m	292½"	8⅛ yd.	8.125 yd.	7.43 m
99"	2¾ yd.	2.75 yd.	2.515 m	297"	8¼ yd.	8.25 yd.	7.544 m
108"	3 yd.	3.0 yd.	2.743 m	301½"	8⅜ yd.	8.375 yd.	7.658 m
112½"	3⅛ yd.	3.125 yd.	2.858 m	306"	8½ yd.	8.5 yd.	7.772 m
117"	3¼ yd.	3.25 yd.	2.972 m	310½"	8⅝ yd.	8.625 yd.	7.887 m
120"	3⅓ yd.	3.333 yd.	3.048 m	315"	8¾ yd.	8.75 yd.	8.001 m
121½"	3⅜ yd.	3.375 yd.	3.086 m	324"	9 yd.	9.0 yd.	8.23 m
126"	3½ yd.	3.5 yd.	3.2 m	328½"	9⅛ yd.	9.125 yd.	8.344 m
130½"	3⅝ yd.	3.625 yd.	3.315 m	333"	9¼ yd.	9.25 yd.	8.458 m
132"	3⅔ yd.	3.667 yd.	3.353 m	337½"	9⅜ yd.	9.375 yd.	8.573 m
135"	3¾ yd.	3.75 yd.	3.429 m	342"	9½ yd.	9.5 yd.	8.687 m
144"	4 yd.	4.0 yd.	3.658 m	346½"	9⅝ yd.	9.625 yd.	8.801 m
148½"	4⅛ yd.	4.125 yd.	3.772 m	351"	9¾ yd.	9.75 yd.	8.915 m
153"	4¼ yd.	4.25 yd.	3.886 m	360"	10 yd.	10.0 yd.	9.144 m

QUICK REFERENCE CHART
YARDAGE WIDTH CONVERSION

If the width of your fabric is different than what the pattern calls for, use this chart to determine the yardage needed.

Yardage conversions are from 44/45"-wide fabric to 36"- or 58/60"-wide fabrics.

44/45"-wide	36"-wide	58/60"-wide	44/45"-wide	36"-wide	58/60"-wide
1/8 yd.	1/4 yd.	1/8 yd.	4 3/8 yd.	5 1/2 yd.	3 1/3 yd.
1/4 yd.	1/3 yd.	1/4 yd.	4 1/2 yd.	5 5/8 yd.	3 1/2 yd.
1/3 yd.	1/2 yd.	1/3 yd.	4 5/8 yd.	5 7/8 yd.	3 5/8 yd.
3/8 yd.	1/2 yd.	1/3 yd.	4 3/4 yd.	6 yd.	3 5/8 yd.
1/2 yd.	5/8 yd.	1/2 yd.	5 yd.	6 1/4 yd.	3 7/8 yd.
5/8 yd.	7/8 yd.	1/2 yd.	5 1/8 yd.	6 1/2 yd.	4 yd.
2/3 yd.	7/8 yd.	5/8 yd.	5 1/4 yd.	6 5/8 yd.	4 yd.
3/4 yd.	1 yd.	5/8 yd.	5 3/8 yd.	6 3/4 yd.	4 1/8 yd.
7/8 yd.	1 1/8 yd.	2/3 yd.	5 1/2 yd.	6 7/8 yd.	4 1/4 yd.
1 yd.	1 1/4 yd.	7/8 yd.	5 5/8 yd.	7 1/8 yd.	4 1/3 yd.
1 1/8 yd.	1 1/2 yd.	7/8 yd.	5 3/4 yd.	7 1/4 yd.	4 3/8 yd.
1 1/4 yd.	1 5/8 yd.	1 yd.	6 yd.	7 1/2 yd.	4 5/8 yd.
1 1/3 yd.	1 2/3 yd.	1 1/8 yd.	6 1/8 yd.	7 2/3 yd.	4 3/4 yd.
1 3/8 yd.	1 3/4 yd.	1 1/8 yd.	6 1/4 yd.	7 3/4 yd.	4 7/8 yd.
1 1/2 yd.	1 7/8 yd.	1 1/4 yd.	6 3/8 yd.	8 yd.	4 7/8 yd.
1 5/8 yd.	2 1/8 yd.	1 1/4 yd.	6 1/2 yd.	8 1/8 yd.	5 yd.
1 2/3 yd.	2 1/8 yd.	1 1/3 yd.	6 5/8 yd.	8 1/3 yd.	5 1/8 yd.
1 3/4 yd.	2 1/4 yd.	1 1/3 yd.	6 3/4 yd.	8 1/2 yd.	5 1/8 yd.
1 7/8 yd.	2 3/8 yd.	1 1/2 yd.	7 yd.	8 3/4 yd.	5 1/3 yd.
2 yd.	2 1/2 yd.	1 5/8 yd.	7 1/8 yd.	9 yd.	5 1/2 yd.
2 1/8 yd.	2 2/3 yd.	1 5/8 yd.	7 1/4 yd.	9 1/8 yd.	5 1/2 yd.
2 1/4 yd.	2 7/8 yd.	1 3/4 yd.	7 3/8 yd.	9 1/4 yd.	5 5/8 yd.
2 1/3 yd.	3 yd.	1 7/8 yd.	7 1/2 yd.	9 3/8 yd.	5 3/4 yd.
2 3/8 yd.	3 yd.	1 7/8 yd.	7 5/8 yd.	9 5/8 yd.	5 7/8 yd.
2 1/2 yd.	3 1/8 yd.	2 yd.	7 3/4 yd.	9 3/4 yd.	6 yd.
2 5/8 yd.	3 1/4 yd.	2 yd.	8 yd.	10 yd.	6 1/8 yd.
2 2/3 yd.	3 1/3 yd.	2 1/8 yd.	8 1/8 yd.	10 1/4 yd.	6 1/4 yd.
2 3/4 yd.	3 1/2 yd.	2 1/8 yd.	8 1/4 yd.	10 1/3 yd.	6 1/3 yd.
2 7/8 yd.	3 5/8 yd.	2 1/4 yd.	8 3/8 yd.	10 1/2 yd.	6 3/8 yd.
3 yd.	3 3/4 yd.	2 1/3 yd.	8 1/2 yd.	10 5/8 yd.	6 1/2 yd.
3 1/8 yd.	4 yd.	2 3/8 yd.	8 5/8 yd.	10 7/8 yd.	6 5/8 yd.
3 1/4 yd.	4 1/8 yd.	2 1/2 yd.	8 3/4 yd.	11 yd.	6 3/4 yd.
3 3/8 yd.	4 1/4 yd.	2 5/8 yd.	9 yd.	11 1/4 yd.	6 7/8 yd.
3 1/2 yd.	4 3/8 yd.	2 2/3 yd.	9 1/8 yd.	11 1/2 yd.	7 yd.
3 5/8 yd.	4 5/8 yd.	2 3/4 yd.	9 1/4 yd.	11 5/8 yd.	7 1/8 yd.
3 3/4 yd.	4 3/4 yd.	2 7/8 yd.	9 3/8 yd.	11 3/4 yd.	7 1/8 yd.
3 7/8 yd.	4 7/8 yd.	3 yd.	9 1/2 yd.	11 7/8 yd.	7 1/4 yd.
4 yd.	5 yd.	3 1/8 yd.	9 5/8 yd.	12 yd.	7 1/3 yd.
4 1/8 yd.	5 1/4 yd.	3 1/4 yd.	9 3/4 yd.	12 1/4 yd.	7 1/2 yd.
4 1/4 yd.	5 1/3 yd.	3 1/4 yd.	10 yd.	12 1/2 yd.	7 5/8 yd.

My Notes for Cutting

My Notes for Cutting

Hand Piecing

TABLE OF CONTENTS
Chapter 6—Hand Piecing

QUILTER TESTED FOR ACCURACY

TRADITIONAL HAND PIECING produces seams with "soft," or rounded, edges. Edges are rounded because you can press the seam allowances in any direction since you don't sew into them. For some quilters, hand sewing means one has more control than with machine sewing. Those who enjoy hand piecing will tell you it's a relaxing, portable pursuit.

THE IMPORTANCE OF ACCURATE SEAMS

Quilting depends upon accuracy in workmanship at every step. Hand-sew along accurately marked lines throughout quilt construction to make certain all the pieces fit together smoothly and accurately.

Make certain to use a template that is the exact desired size. Take the time to test your template periodically during use to be sure all fabric pieces and blocks are the correct size. Even a slight deviation from the marked seam line will multiply quickly considering the number of pieces that are sewn together to make a quilt top (see Chapter 5—Cutting for more information on making templates).

SUPPLIES

See Chapter 1—Tools, Notions, & Supplies for complete information on marking tools, thread choices, and needle options for hand piecing. The following items are the basic necessities to get started.

Marking Pencil: Use a sharp quilter's pencil to draw around templates onto fabric. (Place 220-grit sandpaper beneath your fabric pieces to prevent stretching them as you mark lines.)

Thread: Use high-quality cotton or cotton-wrapped polyester thread for hand piecing. Don't be tempted to purchase bargain-basement thread. These short-staple threads fray easily and are difficult to needle. Economize elsewhere, but splurge on the best available thread to make hand-piecing an enjoyable process.

Use a neutral-color thread, such as gray, taupe, or beige, throughout assembly if your fabrics have many colors; otherwise, match your thread to the lighter fabric. Because you use relatively short lengths of thread when hand piecing, you can change colors with ease.

> **TIP: What does "difficult to needle" mean?** This phrase refers to the ease (or lack thereof) with which the needle glides through fabric.

Needles: Treat yourself to a new packet of "sharps" or "betweens" needles as you begin a project. These thin, sharp, all-purpose needles glide in and out of fabrics with ease. Which size and type you use depends on personal preference and comfort. Start with a multisize packet, trying the size 10 needle first. Replace needles as needed. A blunt needle will weaken your fabric and an older needle with a burr may snag your fabric.

STITCH LENGTH

Experienced hand piecers use ⅛"-long stitches (or eight stitches per inch) as their goal. Begin and end a row of stitching at the indicated matching points with a knot or a few backstitches.

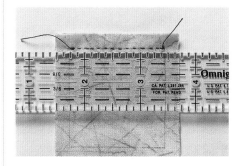

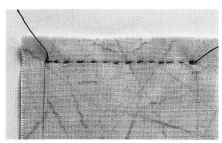

HAND PIECING SETUP

Seam: Sew only on marked lines, beginning and ending at matching points.

Thread: Use an 18" length of top quality, 50-weight, 100% cotton or cotton-polyester thread.

Needle: Thin needles such as "sharps" or "betweens" are best; choose a size you can thread with ease.

Stitch length: About ⅛" or 8 stitches per inch; strive for evenly spaced stitches.

Thimble: Use one if desired.

Hand Piecing

More important than achieving a set number of stitches per inch is achieving consistency in your stitch length and spacing. Six uniform stitches per inch spaced an equal distance apart will result in a more desirable finished appearance than eight uneven stitches per inch. Rather than focusing on the quantity of stitches per inch, focus on the quality of your stitching.

PINNING

Because seam lines of patchwork pieces must line up perfectly, you need to pin before sewing. Use extra-fine pins as large-diameter pins can leave holes in your fabric and distort seaming. Use as many pins as needed to hold the fabric pieces securely.

With right sides together, align the seam lines of two pieces. *Note:* Seam lines should be marked on the wrong side of both pieces (see

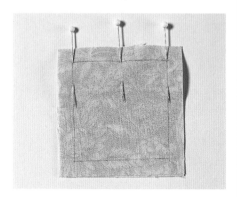

Chapter 5—Cutting for information on marking your fabric pieces). Push a pin through both fabric layers at each matching point, first at the ends, then at the center. Add pins along the length of the seam line as needed.

KNOTS TO KNOW

There are times when you'll want to use more than a backstitch to secure a thread tail. Below are the steps for tying three different knots—knot on the needle, two-loop backstitch knot, and one-loop backstitch knot.

The knot on the needle, also known as the quilter's knot, is a good knot for most hand sewing, including hand piecing, appliqué, and quilting.

The two-loop backstitch knot and the one-loop backstitch knot are good choices when you want to end a line of sewing.

Choose the knot that works best for your situation.

KNOT ON THE NEEDLE
1. With your needle threaded, hold the thread tail on top of the needle, extending it about ½" above.

> **TIP:** To avoid eye strain, invest in a fine-wire needle threader available at quilt shops and sewing stores.

2. Holding the thread tail against the needle with one hand, use your other hand to wrap the thread around the needle clockwise three times.

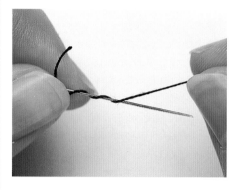

3. Pinching the thread tail and thread wraps with your thumb and forefinger, grasp the needle near the point and gently pull it through the thread wraps.

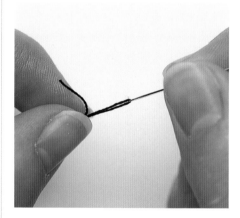

4. Continue pinching the thread wraps until the thread is pulled completely through and forms a small, firm knot near the end of the thread tail.

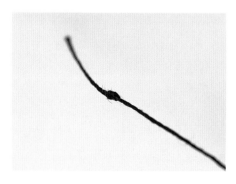

TWO-LOOP BACKSTITCH KNOT

1. Take a small backstitch close to where your last stitch ended, making a loop.

2. Draw the needle through the loop, making a second loop.

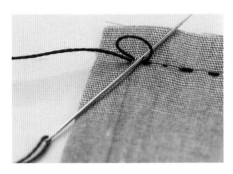

3. Then draw the needle through the second loop.

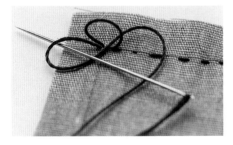

4. Pull gently on the needle to make a figure eight.

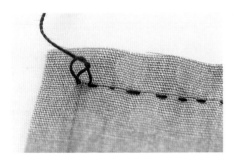

5. Pull the thread up tightly to close the figure eight and make a knot. Clip the thread end.

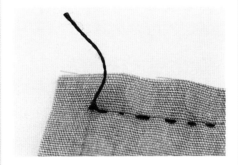

ONE-LOOP BACKSTITCH KNOT

1. Take a small backstitch on top of your last stitch, making a small loop.

2. Draw the needle through the loop.

3. Pull the thread tightly to close the loop and make a knot.

4. Make a second knot, if necessary. Clip the thread end.

TIP: Having trouble threading a needle?

• Moisten the needle *eye* instead of the thread. The capillary action of the saliva draws the thread right into the needle's eye.

• Try putting the needle on the thread instead of the thread through the needle. Hold the thread between your thumb and forefinger, with the thread extending slightly above your fingers. Slide the needle's eye onto the thread.

SEWING A STRAIGHT SEAM

1. With right sides together, align the seam lines of two pieces. *Note:* Seam lines should be marked on the wrong side of both pieces (see Chapter 5—Cutting for information on marking your fabric pieces).

Push a pin through both fabric layers at each matching point, first at the ends, then at the center. Add pins along the length of the seam line as needed.

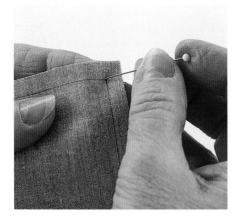

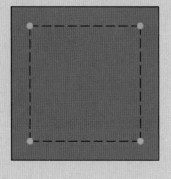

2. To begin sewing, remove the pin at one end and insert your needle through both layers of fabric at the matching points. Make a backstitch or two, leaving a 1" tail.

Or, make a small knot at the end of the thread and insert your needle through both layers of fabric at the matching points. *Note:* Keep seam allowances free of stitching. They are not sewn down as they are in machine piecing.

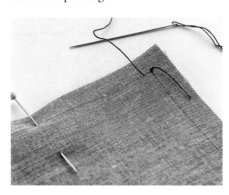

3. Weave your needle in and out of the fabrics along the seam line using a short running stitch. Take four to six stitches before pulling the thread taut. To add stability to the seam,

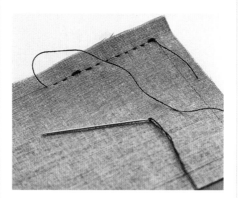

take a backstitch every ¾ to 1" along the length of the seam.

4. Remove pins as you sew, and turn the piece over frequently to make certain your stitches are on the marked seam line of the underside piece. Do not sew past the matching points at the other end where the future seams will intersect.

5. At the opposite matching points, remove the final pin and take a final stitch. Make a backstitch or two at the matching points. Trim the thread, leaving a short tail.

TIP: The fabric strength should be greater than that of the thread used for piecing. Then, if the seams are under stress, the thread will break before the fabric tears. For this reason, stronger polyester threads shouldn't be used for piecing cotton fabrics.

JOINING ROWS OF PATCHWORK

1. With right sides together, align the seam lines of two pieces. *Note:* Seam lines should be marked on the wrong side of both pieces (see Chapter 5—Cutting for information on marking your fabric pieces). Push a pin through both fabric layers at each matching point, first at the ends, then at the center. Add pins along the length of the seam line as needed.

2. Remove the pin at one end and insert your needle through both layers of fabric at the matching points. Make a backstitch or two, leaving a 1" tail. Or, make a small knot at the end of the thread and insert your needle through both layers of fabric at the matching points. *Note:* Keep seam allowances free of stitching. They are not sewn down as they are in machine piecing.

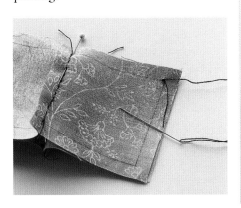

3. Weave your needle in and out of the fabrics along the seam line using a short running stitch. When you reach a seam allowance, take a backstitch.

4. Insert your needle at the matching points, coming out on the opposite side. *Note:* The seam allowance itself should be free from stitching.

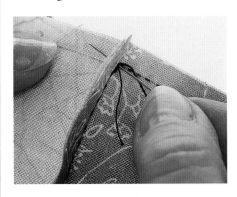

5. Take a stitch, then a backstitch.

6. Remove the pins as you sew, and turn the pieces over frequently to check that your stitches are on the marked seam line of the underside piece.

7. Continue sewing to the end of the patchwork row, joining at the seams as described and backstitching at the final matching points to complete the seam. Leave a short thread tail.

8. Press the seams to one side as they are completed using your finger, a hardwood hand ironing tool, mini iron, or iron.

SEWING DIAMOND SHAPES

Because diamond shapes have at least two sides cut on the bias grain, they can be tricky to handle. (Remember that bias means stretch.) Handle bias-cut pieces carefully as they can easily stretch out of shape.

To control the stretchiness of diamond shapes, cut them facing the same direction on the fabric with the straight of grain along two edges (see Chapter 5—Cutting for more information). As with other hand piecing, do not stitch into the seam allowances.

1. With right sides together, align the seam lines of two pieces. *Note: Seam lines should be marked on the wrong side of both pieces (see Chapter 5—Cutting for information on marking your fabric pieces).* Push a pin through both fabric layers at each matching point, first at the ends, then at the center. Add pins along the seam line as needed.

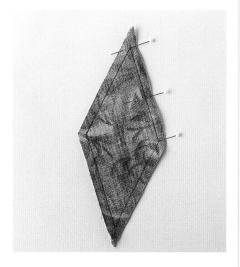

2. To begin sewing, remove the pin at one end and insert your needle through both layers of fabric at the matching points. Make a backstitch or two, leaving a 1" tail. *Note: Keep seam allowances free of stitching.*

They are not sewn down as they are in machine piecing.

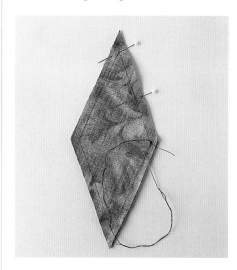

3. Weave your needle in and out of the fabrics along the seam line using a short running stitch. Take four to six stitches before pulling the thread taut. To add stability to the seam, take a backstitch every ¾ to 1" along the length of the seam. Remove pins as you sew.

> **TIP:** A loop knot can be substituted for a backstitch to secure pieces at each seam allowance intersection (see page 6–3). The knot or backstitch gives the intersection strength.

4. Turn the piece over frequently to make certain your stitches are on the marked seam line of the underside piece.

5. Sew to the opposite matching point; do not sew past it, where future seams will intersect. Make a backstitch or two at the matching points. Trim the thread, leaving a short tail.

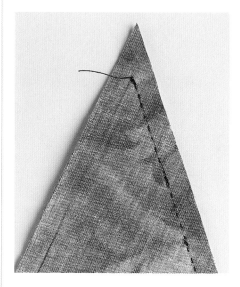

SET-IN SEAMS

Blocks composed of diamond shapes frequently contain set-in squares and triangles. Setting in such pieces requires negotiating multiple seam allowances. The following instructions describe a square being set into the opening left by two pieced-together diamonds.

1. With right sides together, pin one edge of the diamond unit to one edge of the square, aligning matching points. Hand-stitch the seam from the open end of the diamond into the corner, beginning and ending at the matching points and removing pins as you sew.

Backstitch at the inside corner to secure, but do not cut the thread. *Note:* Keep seam allowances free of stitching. They are not sewn down as they are in machine piecing.

2. Bring the adjacent edge of the square up and align it with the adjacent edge of the diamond unit. Insert a pin at aligned matching points, then pin the remainder of the seam line. Hand-stitch the seam from the corner to the open end of the angle, removing pins as you sew. Do not sew past the matching points at the end. Backstitch to secure the seam. Leave a short thread tail.

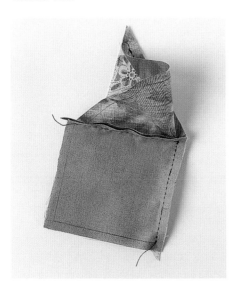

3. Press both seam allowances of the set-in square toward the diamonds; press the diamonds' joining seam to one side.

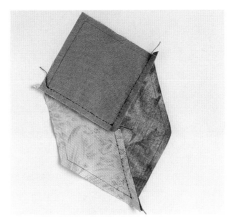

Sew a set-in triangle in the same manner as a set-in square.

DIAMONDS AND CENTER-INTERSECTING BLOCKS

The eight-pointed star represents one of the more challenging blocks because it's tricky to achieve a smooth, unpuckered center. Understanding the direction to sew and press these multiple seams can make a big difference in your finished block.

1. Lay out eight diamonds in a star shape.

2. Layer the diamonds in pairs with right sides together. Align marked seam lines and matching points exactly; pin together. Sew from matching point to matching point, backstitching at each seam end as described in Sewing Diamond Shapes, *opposite. Note:* Keep seam allowances free of stitching. They are not sewn down as they are in machine piecing.

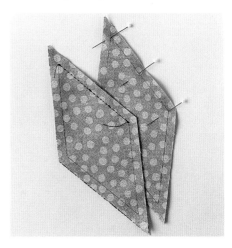

3. Finger-press the seam allowances to one side, pressing all seams in the same direction (clockwise or counterclockwise).

4. Layer two diamond pairs with right sides together. Where the points intersect, push pins straight down. Beginning at the outer corner with a backstitch, stitch toward the intersection, adjusting the stitch length as needed for the needle to come up at the matching points pinhole; backstitch to make a star half. Repeat to make a second star half.

5. Pin the star halves with right sides together, aligning the matching points at each end. Secure the center point by positioning a pin straight down through the intersection. Add pins as needed to keep the star halves aligned.

6. Beginning at the outer matching points with a backstitch, sew up to the intersection, adjusting stitch length as needed for the needle to come up at the center matching points pinhole; backstitch.

7. Stitching through the top seam allowance only, nudge the seam allowance to the right. Make a backstitch on the opposite side of the seam. Carefully align the points on both sides of the seam as you sew to the opposite outer matching points.

8. At the end of the seam, remove the final pin and stitch in the matching points pinhole; make a backstitch or two.

9. Press the seam allowances to one side in a circular fashion, causing them to swirl neatly in the center, which reduces the bulk where the star points are joined.

CURVED SEAMS

Curved shapes add gentle ease and a sense of motion to pieced designs. Stitching curves by hand is easy to do because you can maintain precise control of the fabric pieces.

Typically with curved pieces you'll be joining two separate shapes: a convex curve with a concave curve.

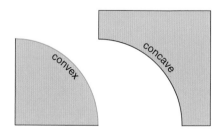

As with other hand piecing, transfer the seam lines, matching points, and center points from the templates to the fabric pieces, and do not stitch into seam allowances.

The following example shows the piecing sequence of curved pieces.

1. Trace around the templates, making sure the seam lines, matching points, and center points are clearly marked on the wrong side.

2. If the template doesn't have a center mark, fold the concave piece in half and gently finger-crease the center of the curved edge. Repeat folding and creasing the convex piece.

3. Layer the pieces with right sides together and center points aligned; the convex piece should be facing you. Pin the pieces together perpendicular to the seam line at the center points.

4. Pinning perpendicular to the seam line and curling the pieces

> **TIP:** To avoid confusion when you're piecing, keep like units pinned together with a label or in a labeled storage bag or container. This will prevent you from inadvertently grabbing the wrong-size piece.

around your thumb, insert a pin at each end matching point, aligning the seam lines. Add pins about every ½" between the ends and the center. Keeping the convex piece against your thumbs and gently curling the fabric over them will allow you to ease in any excess fabric without creating folds or tucks.

5. To begin sewing, remove the pin at one end and insert your needle through both layers of fabric at the matching points. Make a backstitch or two, leaving a 1" tail. *Note:* Keep seam allowances free of stitching. They are not sewn down as they are in machine piecing.

6. Weave your needle in and out of the fabrics along the seam line using a short running stitch. Take four to six stitches before pulling the thread taut. To add stability to the seam, take a backstitch every ¾ to 1" along the length of the seam.

7. Remove pins as you sew and ease the fabric into the curves, gently curving the pieces around your thumb to keep the seam lines aligned. Turn the piece over frequently to make certain your stitches are on the marked seam line.

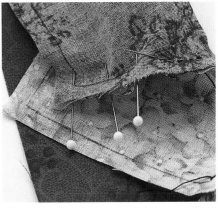

It is not necessary to clip seam allowances when hand-piecing since you are able to ease the fabric into the curves as you stitch.

8. Stop sewing at the opposite matching points and make a backstitch or two. Trim the thread, leaving a short tail.

9. Press the seam allowance toward the convex piece.

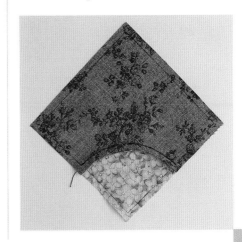

ENGLISH PAPER PIECING

This technique of stabilizing fabric with a paper template is a sure way to guarantee accuracy. English paper piecing is most effective for designs that don't have long straight sides but do have numerous set-in corners, such as the hexagon shapes in a Grandmother's Flower Garden quilt.

Many precut paper templates are available through quilt shops and by mail order. If you wish to make your own templates, trace the pattern on a sturdy paper multiple times and cut out carefully and accurately.

1. Pin a paper template to one or more layers of fabric. Cut out around the template with a ¼" seam allowance. Your seam allowance does not have to be exact because the template will be an accurate guide.

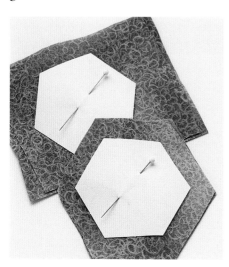

2. Place a template right side down on the wrong side of a fabric piece and fold the seam allowance over one edge. Beginning with a knot on the right side of the fabric, baste the seam allowance in place; stitch

through the fabric and the paper template with ¼"-long stitches. Finger-press the basted edge.

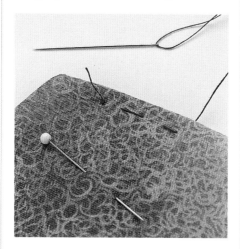

3. As you approach a corner, fold the seam allowance of the next edge over the template and continue stitching. Stitch all edges in the same manner. Don't knot the thread as you finish, but do leave a thread tail of about ½" or so on the fabric's right side.

4. Repeat steps 2 and 3 until all fabric pieces have been basted to paper templates.

5. Place two fabric-covered templates with right sides together, aligning the edges to be joined. Pin the pieces together at the center.

6. With a single strand of quilting thread, begin stitching about ⅛" from one corner using tiny whipstitches and catching a thread of both fabric folds. You'll feel the paper templates with your needle, but do not stitch through them.

7. Backstitch to the nearest corner.

8. Once you reach the corner, reverse the direction of your stitching and sew across the edges to the opposite corner. Take a backstitch, and knot the thread with the knot in the fabric using a backstitch loop knot (see *page 6–3*).

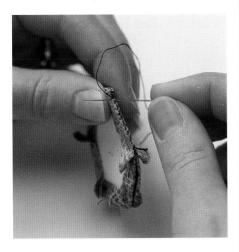

9. Lightly press open the joined pieces and check the seam from the right side. Stitches should not show. If they do, take smaller whipstitches through less of the fabric folds as you sew.

10. To set in a piece, pin and sew the seam on one side. Reposition the stitched pieces so the next seam is aligned and continue sewing.

11. When all edges of a piece have been stitched to adjoining pieces, remove the paper template, pulling the basting threads and templates out from the back.

My Notes for Hand Piecing

Machine Piecing

7

TABLE OF CONTENTS
Chapter 7—Machine Piecing

PIECING BY MACHINE makes it possible for many quilters to complete a large patchwork quilt in far less time than it would take to do by hand. For some, machine piecing also allows for greater accuracy in seaming together individual pieces, as well as larger units and blocks.

THE IMPORTANCE OF EXACT ¼" SEAMS

Quilting depends upon accuracy in workmanship at every step. Use exact ¼" seams throughout quilt construction to make certain all the pieces fit together smoothly and accurately. Once you've selected a seam guide, take the time to test it to make sure you will be sewing seams that are ¼" wide. Even a slight deviation will multiply quickly considering the number of pieces that are sewn together to make a quilt top.

CHOOSING A SEAM GUIDE

¼" presser foot: On many machines the distance between the needle and the right edge of the presser foot is ¼". If this is not the

case with your machine, consider purchasing a special ¼" presser foot for use in patchwork and quilting.

Most sewing machine companies offer this specialty foot for their machines. In addition, several generic ¼" feet are available for use on a variety of models. Be sure to note what type of shank or by what means the presser foot is attached to your machine before purchasing.

Masking tape or adhesive moleskin: Layers of masking tape or moleskin placed on your machine bed in front of the throat plate act as a guide for the fabric, feeding it straight into the presser foot and needle.

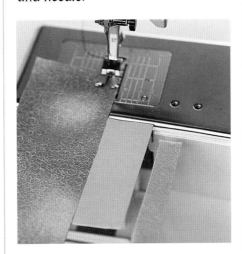

TESTING YOUR PRESSER FOOT

Test your presser foot by aligning the raw fabric edges with the right edge of the presser foot and sewing a sample seam. Measure the resulting seam allowance using a

> **Sew patchwork pieces together with ¼" seam allowances unless otherwise specified.**

ruler or graph paper that has a ¼" grid as a guide.

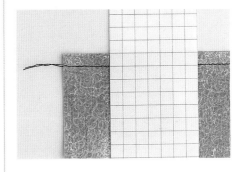

Your sewing machine may allow you to move the needle position to the left or right to create a perfect ¼" seam allowance. If so, note the needle position in your machine's manual or on a self-stick note placed near your machine so you can quickly reset your machine each time you piece patchwork.

If your presser foot is not a perfect ¼" and your needle cannot be repositioned, you can mark a ¼" seam guide on the throat plate with masking tape or moleskin using ¼" graph paper as a measuring tool. Carefully trim the graph paper along a grid line. Place the graph paper under the needle. Slowly lower the

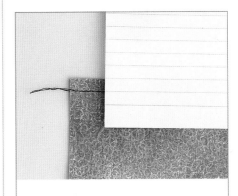

TIP: Use a lined index card to measure your seam allowances when you don't have a ruler or graph paper available. The lines are exactly ¼" apart.

needle into the grid one line from the newly trimmed edge. Use masking tape or moleskin to mark the new seam guide's location ahead of the needle.

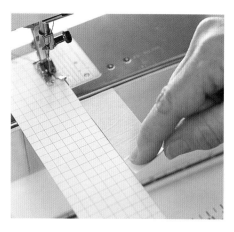

PRACTICE SEWING EXACT ¼" SEAMS

1. Cut three 1½"-wide strips of contrasting fabrics.

2. Sew together two of the strips using a ¼" seam allowance. Join the third strip to the first two, again using a ¼" seam allowance.

3. Press the seam allowances away from the center strip.

4. On the right side of the fabric, measure the width of the center strip. If your seam allowances are ¼", the center strip should measure 1" wide.

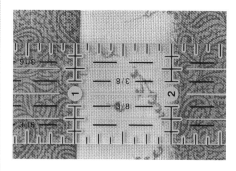

If your center strip does not measure 1" wide, you did not sew ¼" seams. Repeat steps 1 through 4 until you get a 1"-wide center strip. Retest your seam guide as necessary.

MACHINE PIECING SETUP

Seam gauge: ¼"

Thread: Top-quality, 50-weight, 100% cotton or cotton/polyester

Needle: 75/11 or 80/12

Stitch length: 10 to 12 stitches per inch (2.0- to 2.5-mm setting)

Tension: Balanced

Stitch length: If in doubt about the length of your stitches, sew a sample, then use a ruler to check the number of stitches per inch.

Machine tension: Adjust the tension, if necessary, to produce balanced stitches. If the tension is too tight, seams can pucker and pull; if the tension is too loose, stitches can pull apart and/or show on the fabric right side. (See Chapter 1—Tools, Notions, & Supplies and your machine's manual for making needed adjustments to tension.)

SUPPLIES

Thread: Use top-quality, 100% cotton or cotton-wrapped polyester thread for best results. It's tempting to purchase cheap thread because large quantities are needed for patchwork and quilting. However, substandard threads break and fray, adding needless frustration to an otherwise enjoyable experience.

Many seasoned quilters keep just three shades of thread in their stash for sewing patchwork: light (beige, light gray), medium (taupe, gray, gray-green) and dark (navy, black, dark green).

When piecing with high-contrast fabrics, use thread in two different colors—one in the needle and one in the bobbin—matching thread colors to fabric colors. Make sure the threads are of the same type and weight.

If your quilt has fabrics in many colors, use thread in a neutral color, such as gray, taupe, or beige, throughout the assembly.

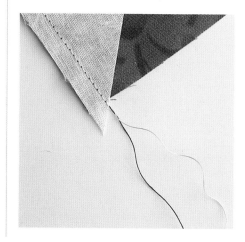

Needles: Begin every project with a new sewing machine needle. Change it after every eight hours of sewing, as a blunt needle will weaken fabric; a needle with a burr may snag the fabric. Most often, a sharp point 75/11 or 80/12 needle is best for machine piecing (use a 90/14 needle for flannel). Often if stitches are not forming correctly or you're having trouble getting your machine to produce even stitches, the problem can be corrected by simply changing your machine needle.

PINNING

When you want the seam lines of patchwork pieces to line up perfectly or when you are piecing complicated blocks, you need to pin pieces together before sewing. There are times when you can skip this step. For instance, when sewing together long strips in a strip-piecing project, there's no need to pin the pieces together before assembling (see Strip Piecing on *page 7-12*). Some pinning guidelines follow.

Use extra-fine pins: Do not use pins labeled "quilting" as they often are thick and long and can leave holes in your fabric and distort the seams you're trying to match. Some quilters prefer glass-head pins because they are easy to see and they stand up to the heat of an iron. Avoid plastic-head pins as they may melt when ironed. (See Chapter 1—Tools, Notions, & Supplies for additional information.)

Abut seams when possible: When aligning two pieced units, press the seam allowances in opposite directions and place them with right

sides together. First insert a pin through both layers at the seam intersection to hold the pieces in place. Bring the pin back up through the seam intersection from the opposite side.

Then pin pieces together with the pins no more than ⅛" away from either side of the seam.

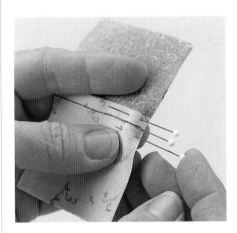

TIP: If the seam allowances were inconsistent and you're sewing together one pieced unit that is slightly longer than the second, place the longer unit on the bottom, against the machine bed. The feed dogs will ease in a bit of extra fullness.

Place pins perpendicular to the seam with heads toward the right edge for easy removal (left-handed quilters may want to place pins with heads facing left).

An alternative to this method is to place a single pin diagonally through the pieces, catching both the top and bottom seam allowances.

Use as many pins as needed to get the job done: Three pins can hold some pieced blocks together. Others require more. Pin longer pieces at the ends first, then at the center; pin along the length as needed.

Avoid sewing over pins: Remove each pin right before the machine needle gets to it so the pinhole can be filled by the machine needle and so your machine needle doesn't strike a pin.

When a machine needle hits a pin it can, at best, nick, bend or break the needle, or worse, alter the machine's timing.

SEWING A STRAIGHT SEAM THAT WILL BE INTERSECTED

It is not necessary to backstitch the beginning of a seam that will be intersected with another seam later in the quiltmaking process.

Begin stitching at the edge of the fabric. Hold the top and bobbin threads together in your left hand as you begin a seam to avoid catching the threads in the stitching. Stitch slowly and evenly.

Guide the fabric with one hand on the fabric in front of the presser foot and the other hand on the fabric to the left of the presser foot. Let the machine walk the fabric through to the opposite edge. Pushing or pulling the fabric will result in uneven, puckered seams.

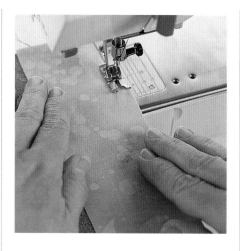

If the fabric is "swallowed" by the machine, replace the throat plate with a small-holed, straight-stitch throat plate (see tip box *below*).

TIP: Advice on Throat Plates
A standard throat plate, *above,* has an oval-shape opening for the needle to pass through. A straight-stitch throat plate, *below,* has a small round hole for the needle to pass through, allowing less area for the machine to take in or "swallow" the fabric.

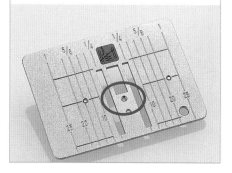

Or, cover the hole with masking tape. The needle will pierce a hole of the needed size in the tape as it goes up and down. *Note:* Make sure the masking tape does not cover the feed dogs.

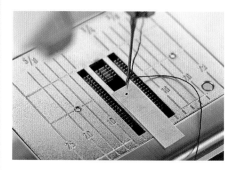

You may wish to sew on a small fabric scrap to begin the seam. Stitch on the fabric scrap first, then feed in patchwork fabrics. End the seam with a small scrap, too. Then, snip off the stitched scrap. This technique is particularly useful when you are joining small pieces and prevents the patchwork seam from puckering at the beginning or

TROUBLESHOOTING TIP: On most machines, the presser foot must be up when you're threading the sewing machine to ensure that the thread goes through the tension discs. If your stitch quality is poor, before making any other adjustment, lift the presser foot, unthread the machine and try rethreading it. Often, this is the only fix you'll need.

having incomplete stitches at the beginning or end.

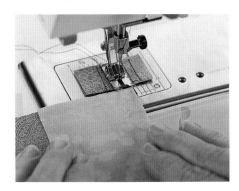

CHAIN PIECING

Patchwork pieces that are sewn together from edge to edge without backstitching can be sewn together in a single long chain to save time and thread. To chain-piece, feed pairs of pieces under the machine needle without lifting the presser foot or clipping the threads. Short lengths of thread will link the stitched pairs.

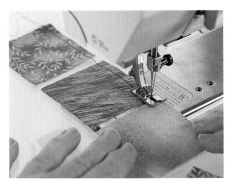

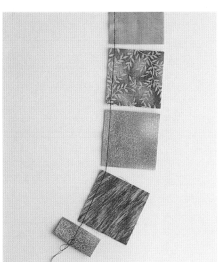

Blocks and rows of blocks can be chain-pieced also. Feed the pairs of blocks or rows under the machine needle to join them. Pay attention to the direction of the seam allowances, alternating them whenever possible.

SEWING A STRAIGHT SEAM THAT WILL NOT BE INTERSECTED

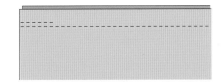

Secure seams that will not be sewn across again (such as those in border units) and seams that are not sewn to the edge of the fabric (as with inset seams) with a few backstitches on top of previous stitching at both the beginning and the end.

SET-IN SEAMS

Set-in seams are used to construct blocks that cannot be successfully assembled with continuous straight seams. The piece to be added is stitched into the unit in two steps. Diamond blocks frequently contain set-in squares and triangles. Joining stitches for these pieces run from marked dot to marked dot and do not extend into seam allowances.

TRANSFERRING DOTS TO FABRIC PIECES

To ensure that the pieces fit together accurately, the pattern templates should have dots marked on the ¼" seam line at the outer and inner corners. To transfer those dots to the fabric pieces, first pierce a small hole through the dots on the template with a large needle or awl. Make

> **TIP:** Having trouble with your thread not pulling off the spool properly? Check to see how the spool is situated on the machine's spool pin. Sometimes, if the thread is pulling out from the underside of the spool, simply turning the spool over so the thread feeds off over the top of the spool (or vice versa) can change the thread tension enough to make a difference in the stitch quality.

Machine Piecing

sure the hole is just large enough for the point of a marking pen or pencil. Align the template over the wrong side of the fabric piece and mark through the holes.

STARTING A SET-IN SEAM
Seams that begin away from the fabric edge need to be secured with a few backstitches.

Method 1:
Begin sewing forward at the dot for a couple of stitches, take a couple of backstitches, and continue sewing to the opposite edge or dot. Avoid the urge to backstitch too far. You do not want to go past the starting point. Too many layers of thread will add unnecessary bulk to the finished seam. Stitching forward, backstitching, and stitching forward again gives the beginning part of the seam three layers of thread.

Method 2:
1. Turn your work so the starting dot is ¼" in front of the needle. Stitch forward to the dot.

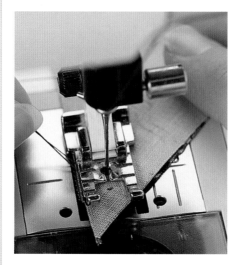

2. Leaving the needle in the fabric, pivot the work 180º and continue sewing the seam. With this method, there are only two layers of thread in the beginning part of the seam.

ENDING A SET-IN SEAM
Seams that end away from the fabric edge need to be secured with a few backstitches.

Method 1:
End sewing forward at the dot and take a few backstitches.

Method 2:
1. End sewing forward at the dot. Leave the needle in the fabric at the dot, pivot the work 180º.

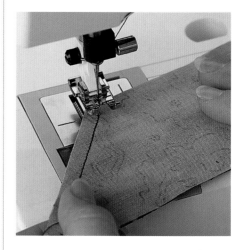

2. Take a couple of stitches forward on top of the previous stitching.

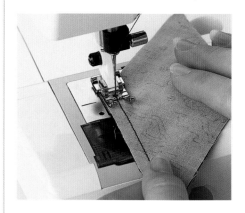

ASSEMBLING A SET-IN SEAM
1. Mark joining dots at the ¼" seam lines on the wrong side of pieces at the outer and inner corners (see Transferring Dots to Fabric Pieces on *page 7–5*).

2. Pin and sew together the first two pieces, starting and stopping at the dots. Press the pieces open.

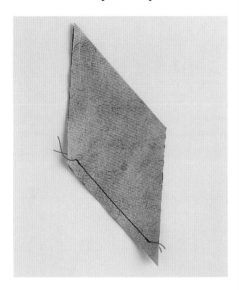

3. Matching the corners and dots of the first and third pieces, pin and sew from the dot at the inside corner to the dot at the outer edge.

4. Bring the edge of the second piece up and align it with the adjacent edge of the third piece, matching corners and dots, and sew from the dot at the inside corner to the dot at the outer edge.

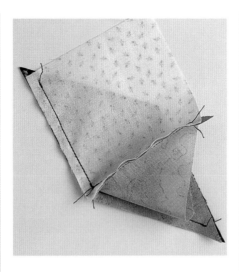

5. Press the unit open.

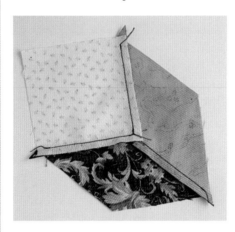

Sew a set-in triangle in the same manner as a set-in square.

DIAMONDS AND CENTER-INTERSECTING BLOCKS

An eight-pointed star represents one of the more challenging blocks because it's tricky to assemble with a smooth, unpuckered center. Directional stitching from joining dot to joining dot and directional pressing make the difference.

1. Mark joining dots at the ¼" seam lines on the wrong side of each diamond-shape piece in all corners.

2. Lay out the eight diamond shapes as they will be assembled.

TIP: When it's time to change threads, cut the thread at the spool and pull the remaining thread out through the needle. This prevents thread pieces from breaking off in the tension discs or getting stuck inside your machine.

3. With right sides together, pin the diamond shapes together in pairs along the adjoining seam, matching dots exactly. Sew from the center dots to the outer dots, backstitching at each end as described in Set-In Seams, which begins on *page 7-5*.

4. Press the seam allowances to one side, pressing them all in the same direction, either clockwise or counterclockwise.

5. Join the diamond pairs to make two star halves, sewing from the center dots to the outer dots. Trim fabric dog-ears that extend beyond the raw edges.

6. Pin the two star halves together. Secure the center point and add pins as needed to keep the star halves aligned.

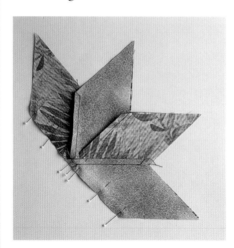

TIP: The fabric strength should be greater than that of the thread used for piecing. Then, if the seams are under stress, the thread will break before the fabric tears. For this reason, stronger polyester threads shouldn't be used for piecing cotton fabrics.

7. Stitch from the outer dot to the opposite outer dot to join the two star halves. Press the seam allowance to one side.

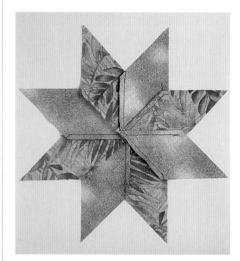

8. Set-in any remaining pieces as described in Assembling a Set-in Seam, which begins on page 7-6.

PARTIAL SEAMS

Some blocks have pieces surrounding a center shape that extend unequally beyond the center. These blocks can be constructed with a seam that appears to be set-in but is actually made in two steps. The key is to sew a partial seam.

1. Sew part of the first seam (about half the distance).

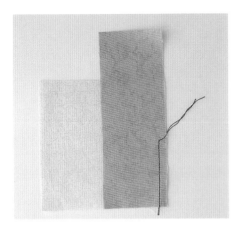

2. Add remaining pieces in the appropriate sequence.

3. Complete the stitching of the first, or partial, seam.

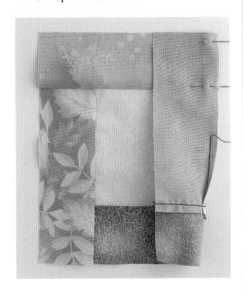

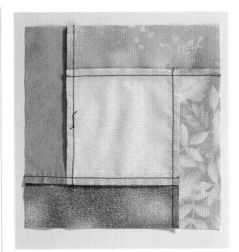

CURVED SEAMS

Joining pieces with curved edges presents challenges. Cutting a small notch in the center of a curved edge makes it easier.

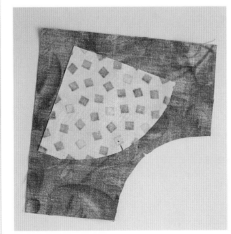

1. With right sides together match the center notches of curved edges. Pin together at the center point, at seam ends, and liberally in between, gently easing the edges as needed to align.

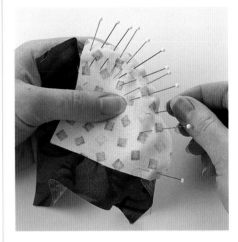

2. Sew together the curved edges. Clip into the seam allowance of the edge that curves in (concave) as needed, but do not cut into or beyond the seam lines. Do not clip the convex edge.

TIP: Some quilters prefer not to clip curved seams. Instead they use a longer stitch length and sew slowly which helps ease the fabric layers together (the center notch is still necessary).

3. Press the seam allowance toward the piece that has the inner (concave) curve.

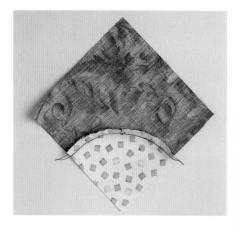

PRESSING

Good pressing is essential for accurate piecing (see Chapter 1— Tools, Notions, & Supplies for information on pressing equipment). In general, every seam needs to be pressed before another unit is added, and most seam allowances are pressed to one side (see Pressing Bias Seams and When to Press Seams Open *opposite*).

Press with an iron set on a temperature appropriate to the fabric on a flat, firm surface. (An ironing

TIP: Make a mini ironing surface by covering an empty cardboard fabric bolt with layers of cotton batting, then wrapping it with muslin.

board or pad with a heat-resistant cushion and cotton cover is fine. Avoid a Teflon-coated, heat-reflective ironing board cover. This coating reflects heat and steam upward, not allowing them to pass completely through the fabrics.)

To avoid distorting your quilt pieces, press only after pieces are stitched together.

PRESSING STRAIGHT SEAMS

Straight seams should be pressed with the iron parallel to the straight grain of the fabric.

1. First press the stitching flat with right sides together and the darker fabric on top. "Setting the seam" is the term for this critical first step that locks the threads together, smooths out any puckers, and evens out minor thread tension differences.

PRESS, DON'T IRON.
Don't know the difference?
IRONING involves moving
the iron while it has contact
with the fabric; this
stretches and distorts
fabrics and seams.
PRESSING means picking
up the iron (with or without
steam) off the surface of
the fabric and putting
it back down in
another location.

2. Beginning at one end of the seam, lift up the top piece and position the tip of the iron on the lighter color fabric. Glide the iron along the seam edge with the tip moving from the lighter color piece to the darker color piece. This method will both open up the unit and press the seam to one side in a single step. Pressing the unit from the right side helps avoid pressing tucks and pleats into the seams.

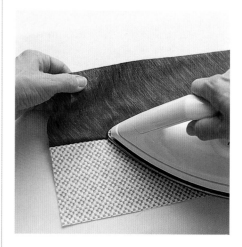

3. Some quilt patterns specify which direction to press the seam allowances. When in doubt, press seam allowances toward the darker fabric. This avoids creating a shadow on the lighter fabric. If pressing toward the lighter fabric is a must, trim the darker fabric seam allowance by 1/16" after the seam is sewn to prevent any shadows.

4. If a seam allowance has been pressed the wrong way, return it to its original unpressed state and press the unit flat to remove the crease. Allow the fabric to cool, then press the seam allowance in the desired direction.

PRESSING BIAS SEAMS

A bias seam should be pressed with the iron at a 45° angle to the seam and along the straight grain to avoid distortion.

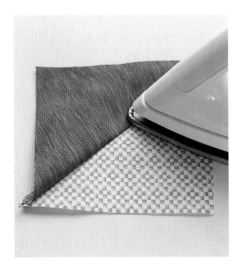

TIP: Once fabric pieces have been pressed, let them cool in place. It prevents distortion of bias edges.

FINGER-PRESSING

As a temporary measure, you can press short seam allowances with your finger.

1. Place a pieced unit on a hard surface. From the wrong side, spread the unit apart with the seam allowance folded toward the darker fabric. Press with your fingers along the length of the seam allowance.

2. Turning the unit right side up with the seam allowance still facing the darker side, finger-press again.

Finger pressing isn't a substitute for using an iron, but it does temporarily press seam allowances in one direction or another. It's a good method to use if you're unsure which way seams will eventually need to be pressed.

OPPOSING SEAMS

When two seams will be joined together, press the seam allowances in opposite directions. This helps distribute the bulk of the seam allowances evenly and ensures that the seam allowances can abut one another.

WHEN TO PRESS SEAMS OPEN

Seam allowances are pressed open when multiple seams come together in one area. This helps distribute the fabric bulk evenly in a small area, eliminating lumps and making the seam easier to quilt through.

When pressing seams open, press first from the wrong side of the fabric. Use your fingernail or a hardwood hand ironing tool to open up the seam ahead of the iron.

PLANNING TO PRESS

Eliminate ironing board guesswork by developing a plan for pressing. Look at a practice block that represents the block or blocks in your project. Divide the block into rows or units. Observe which seams will abut and know that the seam allowances in adjoining rows will be pressed in opposing directions in one of the following two ways.

Method 1:

Press seam allowances in odd-numbered rows in one direction and those in even-numbered rows in the opposite direction.

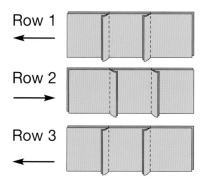

Method 2:

Press seam allowances in odd-numbered rows to the outside of block and those in even-numbered rows to the inside of the block.

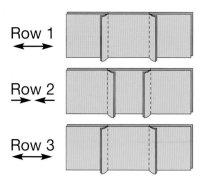

Choose a method based on how the blocks are set together. If pieced blocks are to be alternated with plain blocks, the direction of the seam allowances on outer edges will be of little consequence. If pieced blocks are to be positioned next to other pieced blocks, the direction to press the seams on alternating blocks may need to change from the original plan.

STRIP PIECING

This fast machine-piecing technique involves sewing together long fabric strips that then are cut into segments which are sewn together into blocks.

Four-Patch Strip Piecing

1. You need same-size strips of two different fabrics. With right sides together, sew together the two strips along a long edge to make a strip set. Press the seam allowance toward the darker fabric.

2. Use a ruler and rotary cutter to cut the strip set into segments that are the same width as a single strip before stitching. (For example, if the individual strips were 2½x42", you would cut the strip set into 2½"-wide segments.) Align the ruler's cross line with the seam line of the

strip to be sure your cuts are straight.

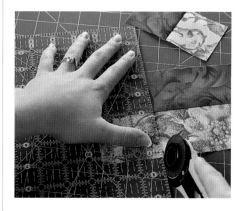

3. Rotate a segment 180°, pair it with another segment, match the seam lines, and sew together to make a Four-Patch block. Chain-piecing can be used if you wish to assemble multiple Four-Patch blocks. (See Chain Piecing on *page 7-5*.)

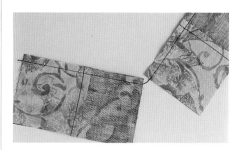

4. Press each Four-Patch block open, pressing the seam allowance to one side. Repeat with the remaining segments to make as many Four-Patch blocks as you need.

Nine-Patch Strip Piecing

1. You need three same-size strips each of two different fabrics. With right sides together, sew the strips together lengthwise in sets of three, alternating fabrics, to make two strip sets. Press the seam allowances toward the darker fabrics.

2. Use a ruler and rotary cutter to cut the strip sets into segments that are the same width as a single strip. (For example, if the strips were 2x42", you would cut the strip sets into 2"-wide segments.) Align the ruler's cross line with the seam line of the strip to be sure your cuts are straight.

3. Sew together two segments from one strip set and one segment from the other strip set to make a Nine-Patch block.

4. Press the Nine-Patch block open, pressing the seam allowances away from the center strip. Repeat with the remaining segments to make as many Nine-Patch blocks as you need.

FOUNDATION PIECING

To make precisely pieced, intricate blocks, you can sew together fabric scraps on a paper pattern, or foundation. Some quilters find this technique to be freeing because precise cutting isn't required and grain line direction is not a worry. However, because you add fabric from the reverse (underneath) side of the paper, it requires you to think about piecing in a different way.

1. Trace the desired pattern onto tissue paper, including all numbers and lines to make a paper foundation.

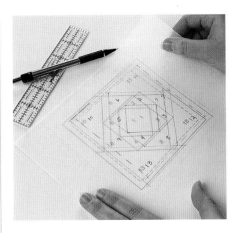

Repeat the tracing step for each block or staple the traced paper foundation onto multiple layers of tracing tissue paper. With no thread in your machine needle and a medium to long stitch length, sew precisely on the lines of the traced pattern. The needle will pierce holes in the tissue layers that will exactly match the pattern lines.

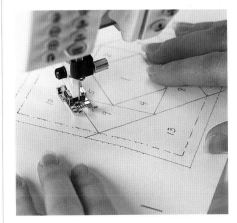

2. Cut out the traced or needle-pierced paper foundations beyond the outer lines.

Machine Piecing

3. Set your machine's stitch length on a short setting (18 to 20 stitches per inch). This will help perforate the foundation, making it easier to remove once the block is completed.

4. Fabric pieces need to be at least ¼" larger on all sides than the areas they are to cover. Cutting generous fabric pieces will reduce the chance for assembly errors. The fabric pieces are sewn directly to the foundation patterns. Because the foundation patterns provide support, there's no need to consider grain lines when cutting fabric pieces. The fabric pieces don't have to be cut perfectly, as the excess will be trimmed away after you've stitched the piece to the paper foundation.

Layer the fabric pieces for areas 1 and 2 with right sides together.

5. With the right side of the paper foundation facing up, place the layered fabric pieces under area 1. The fabric for piece 1 should be next to the foundation. To check fabric placement, pin through the foundation and the two layers of fabric at the seam line (the line where areas 1 and 2 join) and flip open piece 2. It should completely cover area 2 on the foundation and extend at least ¼" beyond it. If it doesn't, reposition your fabric and check again.

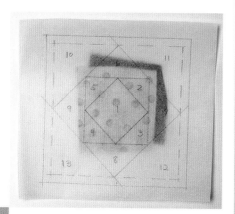

6. With the paper foundation still on top, stitch through the paper and the fabric on the shared line where pieces 1 and 2 join. Begin stitching ¼" before the seam line and continue, staying precisely on the line, until ¼" after it ends.

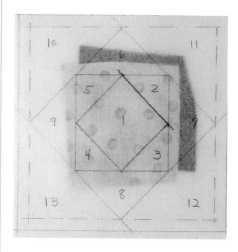

7. Trim the seam allowance to ¼". Be careful to trim away only the fabric, not the paper foundation.

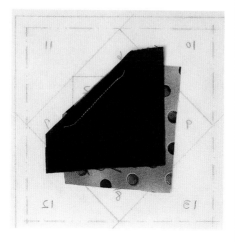

8. Press open piece 2 from the fabric side.

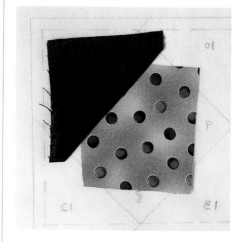

9. Add piece 3, following the same procedure and joining it on the shared line between areas 2 and 3.

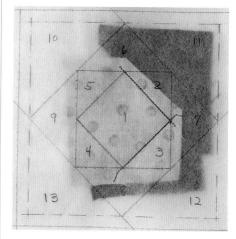

10. Join the remaining fabric pieces in numerical order, trimming and pressing after each addition.

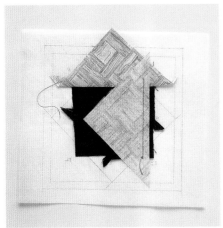

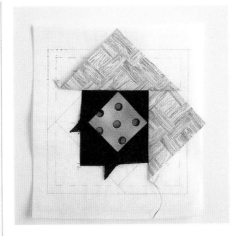

11. Trim on the outer foundation lines, leaving a ¼" seam allowance on all sides. It is not necessary to sew the seam allowance on the outer edges of the block to the foundation. Join the paper-pieced blocks together before removing the paper foundations.

PIECING BASIC QUILT BLOCK UNITS

TRIANGLE-SQUARE

The triangle-square is a basic unit used in making many quilts. Use this simply pieced unit on its own or as a part of a larger, more elaborately pieced quilt block. Five different methods of making triangle-squares are outlined here.

Choose the method that works best for you.

Method 1: Using Two Same-Size Triangles of Contrasting Fabrics

This method eliminates waste, but requires careful handling of the fabric to avoid distortion as you join bias edges. To determine what size half-square triangles to cut, add ⅞" to the desired finished size of the triangle-square. For example, for a 2" finished triangle-square, cut a 2⅞" square, cutting it diagonally in half to yield two triangles.

1. With right sides together, sew the triangles together along the long edges using a ¼" seam allowance.

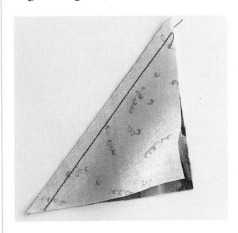

2. Press the seam allowance toward the darker fabric to make one triangle-square. *Note:* If the seam allowance must be pressed toward the lighter fabric, trim the edge of the darker seam by ¹⁄₁₆" so it won't show through on the right side of the block.

3. Trim the dog-ears of the seam allowance (the fabric that extends beyond the block edges) to make a square.

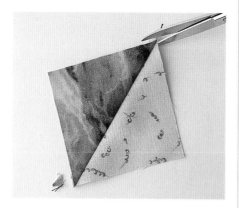

Method 2: Using Two Same-Size Squares of Contrasting Fabrics (to make two triangle-squares)

This method eliminates fabric waste but requires precise marking and stitching. To determine what size squares to cut, add ⅞" to the desired finished size of the triangle-square. For example, for a 3" finished triangle-square, cut 3⅞" squares.

1. Use a quilter's pencil to mark a diagonal line on the wrong side of one square. To prevent the fabric from stretching as you draw the lines, place 220-grit sandpaper under the square.

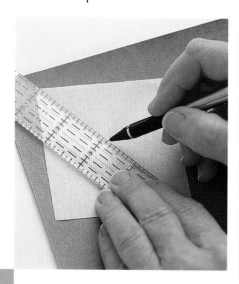

2. Layer the marked square atop the second square. Sew the squares together with two seams, stitching ¼" on each side of the drawn line.

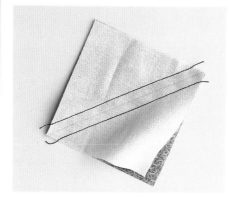

3. Cut the squares apart on the drawn line to make two triangle units.

4. Press each triangle unit open to make two triangle-squares.

5. Trim the dog-ears of the seam allowance to make a square.

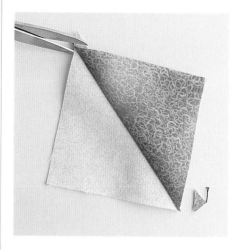

Method 3: Using Two Same-Size Squares of Contrasting Fabrics (to make one triangle-square)

With this method there is some waste as you trim off excess fabric; however, it is not necessary to mark directly onto the fabric. To determine what size squares to cut, add ½" to the desired finished size of the triangle-square. For example, for a 3" finished triangle-square, cut 3½" squares.

1. Using an iron, press one square in half diagonally with the wrong side inside.

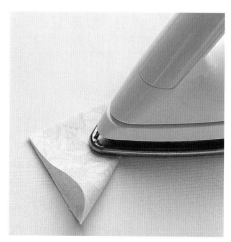

2. Open up the pressed square; layer it atop the second square with right sides together. Sew the squares together with one seam, stitching on the pressed crease line.

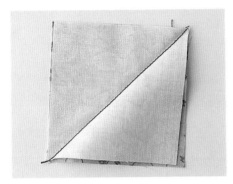

3. Align a ruler with the ¼" mark on top of the stitched seam line. Trim away the excess fabric.

4. Press the triangle unit open to make a triangle-square.

5. Trim the dog-ears of the seam allowance to make a square.

Method 4: Using Two Same-Size Rectangles of Contrasting Fabrics (to make multiple triangle-squares)
This method requires more preparation, but can minimize waste and ensure accuracy when you are making a large number of identical triangle-squares.

TIP: To prevent your fabric from stretching as you mark it, place it on 220-grit sandpaper.

1. Use a quilter's pencil to mark the desired number of squares on the wrong side of one rectangle of fabric. Draw squares at least ½" from the fabric edge and make them the desired size of a finished triangle-square plus ⅞".

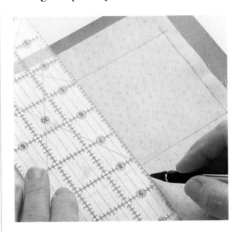

2. Draw a diagonal line through the center of each square. Diagonal lines in adjoining squares should oppose one another.

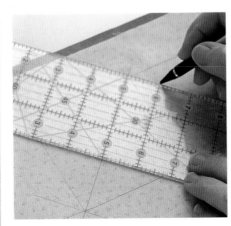

3. Layer the marked rectangle atop the unmarked rectangle with right sides together. Sew together the fabric rectangles by stitching

---

¼" on each side of the drawn diagonal lines.

4. Press the stitched rectangles to set the seams.

5. Using a rotary cutter and ruler, cut on the drawn lines to make triangle units.

6. Press each triangle unit open to make a triangle-square. Each drawn square yields two triangle-squares.

7. Trim the dog-ears of the seam allowance to make a square block.

Method 5: Using Two Bias Strips of Contrasting Fabrics
(to make multiple triangle-squares)
1. Cut bias strips 1" wider than the desired finished size of the triangle-squares.

2. With right sides together and ends matching, join two contrasting strips along the long edges with a ¼" seam allowance. (To get the most cuts from pieced bias strips, sew the strips together with a V at one end.)

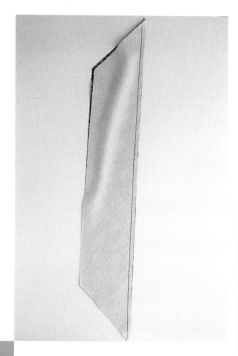

3. Press the seam allowance toward the darker fabric.

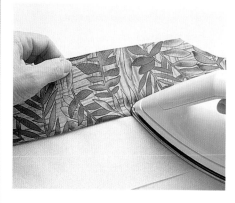

4. Using a square ruler marked with a 6" grid and a rotary cutter, cut squares ½" larger than the desired finished size of the triangle-squares. (For example, if you want the finished size of your triangle-square to be 2½", cut the triangle-square at 3".) Keep the diagonal line of the gridded square and the seam line of the sewn strips aligned.

FLYING GEESE
Method 1: Using a Rectangle of One Fabric and Two Squares of a Contrasting Fabric
To determine what size of rectangle to cut, add ½" to the finished height and width of the Flying Geese unit. Cut two squares the same size as the height of the cut rectangle. For example, for a 1½×3" finished Flying Geese unit, cut a 2×3½" rectangle and two 2" squares.

1. Use a quilter's pencil to mark a diagonal line on the wrong side of each square. To prevent the fabric from stretching as you draw the lines, place 220-grit sandpaper

TIP: When you're using the rectangle and two squares method to make Flying Geese, why do the squares overlap at the upper point of the center triangle?

Once sewn together, this overlap is what creates the seam allowance along the upper edge of the pieced Flying Geese unit.
  When you sew the Flying Geese unit into a block, this seam allowance will be taken in, leaving the tip of your triangle intact at the seam line. Without it, the tip of the triangle would be sewn into the seam and you'd have no sharp point at the top of the triangle.

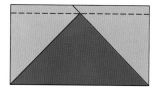

under the square. *Note:* Instead of drawing a line, you may press the squares in half diagonally as described in Method 3 of Triangle-Squares, which begins on *page 7–16.*

2. With right sides together, align a marked square with one end of a rectangle; note the placement of the marked diagonal line. Stitch on the marked line.

3. Trim the seam allowance to ¼".

4. Press the attached triangle open.

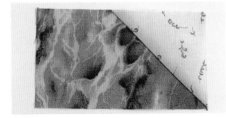

5. Align a second marked square with the opposite end of the rectangle, again noting the

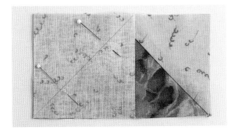

placement of the marked diagonal line. Stitch on the marked line; trim as before.

6. Press the attached triangle open to make a Flying Geese unit.

Method 2: Using One Large Triangle of One Fabric and Two Small Triangles of a Contrasting Fabric

To determine what size of quarter-square triangle to cut for the center of the Flying Geese unit, add 1¼" to the desired finished width of the Flying Geese unit. To determine what size half-square triangles to cut for the small triangles, add ⅞" to the desired finished height of the Flying Geese unit. For example, for a 1½×3" finished Flying Geese unit, cut a 4¼" square, cutting it diagonally twice in an X to yield four large triangles. Cut a 2⅜" square, cutting it diagonally in half to yield two small triangles.

1. With right sides together, sew a small triangle to a short edge of the large triangle using a ¼" seam allowance. *Note:* The corners of the small triangle will extend ¼" beyond each end of the large triangle.

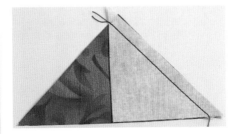

2. Press the attached small triangle open, pressing the seam allowance toward the small triangle.

3. In the same manner, join the remaining small triangle to the large triangle.

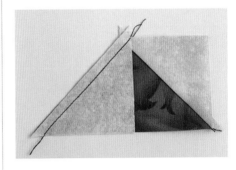

4. Press the small triangle open to make a Flying Geese unit.

5. Trim the dog-ears.

My Notes for Machine Piecing

My Notes for Machine Piecing

Appliqué

8

APPLIQUÉ

TABLE OF CONTENTS
Chapter 8—Appliqué

THE TIME-HONORED TRADITION OF APPLIQUÉ—adding fabric motifs to a foundation fabric—allows for freedom in design not always available with piecing. Styles range from simple to intricate, primitive to elegant. Appliqué can be done by hand or machine. Numerous appliqué methods have been developed giving quiltmakers choices when it comes to the finished appearance.

TEMPLATES

An appliqué template is a pattern used to trace the appliqué shape onto fabric. The template's material depends on how often the template will be used. Make sure that your template will hold up to the wear that it receives from multiple tracings without deteriorating at the edges. A sturdy, durable material such as template plastic, available at quilt and crafts supply stores, is suitable for making permanent templates for scissors-cut appliqué pieces. (For information on cutting templates for piecing, see Chapter 5—Cutting.)

MAKING APPLIQUÉ TEMPLATES

1. For most appliqué techniques you need to make your templates the exact size of the finished pieces with no seam allowances included. The seam allowances are added when you cut out the appliqué pieces. Trace the patterns onto template plastic using a permanent marker. Use a ruler for any straight lines.

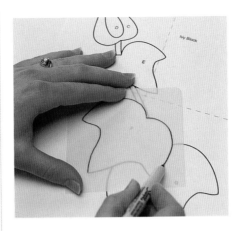

2. Mark each appliqué template with its letter designation, grain line (if indicated), block name, and appliqué sequence order. (See *page 8–2* for more information on Stitching Sequence.) Mark an X on edges that do not need to be turned under and transfer the Xs to the fabric shapes when you trace around the templates.

3. Cut out each template, then verify their accuracy by placing them over their printed patterns.

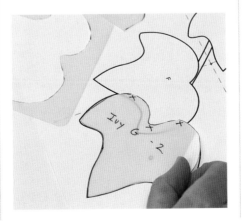

USING APPLIQUÉ TEMPLATES

1. Choose a marking tool to trace around the templates on fabric. A pencil works well on light-color fabric; a white, silver, or yellow dressmaker's pencil is a good choice on dark-color fabric. (See Chapter 1—Tools, Notions, & Supplies for complete information on marking tools.) If you're using a pencil, keep the point sharp to ensure accuracy. Do not use a ballpoint or ink pen; it may bleed when washed. Test all marking tools on a fabric scrap before using them.

2. Place templates on the fabric, positioning them at least ½" apart. (Whether you place them faceup or facedown on the fabric's right or wrong side depends on the appliqué method you choose.) Trace around each template with your selected marking tool. The drawn lines represent the sewing lines. The specific appliqué technique you choose will dictate how much,

> **TIP:** To prevent stretching the fabric as you draw around the template, place 220-grit sandpaper under the fabric.

if any, seam allowance you leave when cutting out the shape.

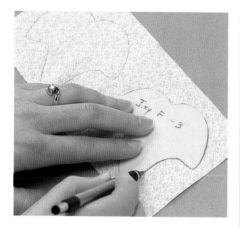

3. Cut out the appliqué shapes, including seam allowances if necessary for your chosen appliqué method.

STITCHING SEQUENCE

Edges of appliqué pieces that will be covered by other pieces do not need to be turned under before they are appliquéd. By preparing all your appliqué pieces at one time, you

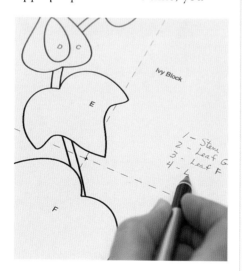

TIP: To create a mirror image of a template with fabric, flip the template over before tracing it onto the fabric.

can plan any overlaps, which will save stitching time and considerable bulk in the finished project.

If your pattern does not indicate a numerical stitching sequence, observe which piece is closest to the foundation fabric and farthest away from you. That is the first piece you should appliqué to the foundation. Appliqué the rest of the pieces to the foundation, working from the bottom layer to the top.

PREPARING APPLIQUÉ PIECES

Prepare your appliqué pieces according to the needs of your chosen appliqué method. Preparation options include basting, freezer paper, spray starch, double appliqué, and fusible web. Read the introduction to each method that follows to determine which one will work for your selected method.

BASTING METHOD

This method uses a reusable template, marking tool, and thread to prepare appliqué pieces for hand or machine appliqué.

1. Place your templates on the right side of the fabric, positioning them at least ½" apart; trace.

2. Cut out the appliqué shapes, adding a ³⁄₁₆" seam allowance to all edges. Clip inside curves and points to within a thread of the marked lines, making clips closer together in the curved areas. Try to make your clips on the bias grain of the seam allowance, which means your clips will be often diagonal, rather than perpendicular, lines. This directional clipping prevents fabric from raveling while you're working with the edges. *Note:* Some hand quilters who use the needle-turn appliqué method choose to stop their appliqué preparation with this step (for more information, see Needle-turn Appliqué, on *page 8–19*).

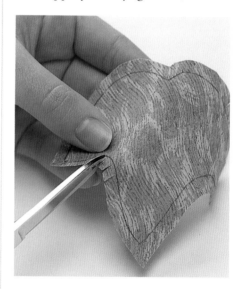

3. Working from the right side of the appliqué piece and beginning at an inner point, use a contrasting color thread to baste the seam allowance under following the marked lines. For easier removal of the thread later, begin and end your basting thread on the right side of appliqué piece.

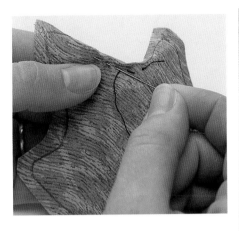

4. For a sharp outer point, fold the fabric straight over the point.

5. Then fold in an adjacent seam allowance, overlapping the folded point. Baste in place.

6. As you reach the outer point, fold over the remaining adjacent seam allowance and continue basting around the shape.

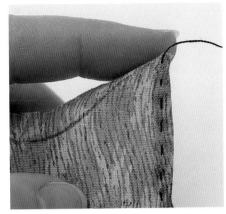

USING FREEZER PAPER

Many quilters choose to use freezer paper for appliqué. Available in grocery stores and some quilt shops, freezer paper has a shiny coating on one side that temporarily adheres to fabric when pressed with a warm iron. It is not necessary to consider the grain line of the fabric when utilizing freezer-paper templates.

FREEZER-PAPER METHOD 1

This method uses freezer-paper templates to hold the seam allowances of the appliqué pieces in place. (Refer to Using Freezer Paper *above* for additional information.) This technique may be used to prepare pieces for hand or machine appliqué.

1. Trace the appliqué patterns on the dull side of the freezer paper. Cut out the shapes on the traced lines to make freezer-paper templates.

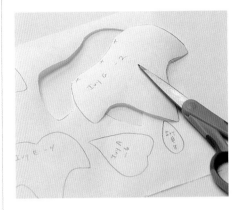

2. Place the freezer-paper templates dull side up on the right side of the fabric. While holding the freezer paper in place, cut the shapes from fabric, adding a 3/16" seam allowance to all edges.

3. Turn the freezer-paper templates shiny side up and place on the wrong side of the appliqué shape. Clip the inside curves or points on

the appliqué shapes. When clipping inside curves, clip halfway through the seam allowances. Try to make your clips on the bias grain of the seam allowance, which means your clips often will be diagonal, rather than perpendicular, lines. This directional clipping prevents fabric from raveling while you're working with the edges.

4. Beginning at an inner point of an appliqué shape, use the tip of a hot, dry iron to push the seam allowance over the edge of the freezer paper. The seam allowance will adhere to

TIP: Some appliqué techniques require you to make a reverse image of the shapes. To do so, tape the appliqué pattern facedown on a light box or sunny window. Secure a piece of tracing paper over the shape and trace with a fine-line marker or mechanical pencil.

Mark its name or number and the word reversed on the traced pattern. This will serve as a reminder when you're using the shape that you've already reversed the image.

the shiny side of the freezer paper. *Note:* Do not touch the iron soleplate to the freezer paper past the turned fabric edge.

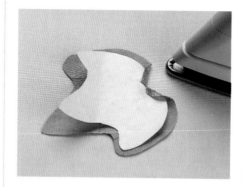

5. Continue working around the appliqué shape, turning one small area at a time and pressing the seam allowance up and over the freezer paper. Make certain the appliqué fabric is pressed taut against the freezer-paper template.

Small pleats in the fabric may appear as you round outer curves. If there is too much bulk in a seam allowance, make small V clips around outer curves to ease the fabric around the edge.

6. For a sharp outer point, fold the fabric straight over the point of the freezer-paper template; press to freezer paper.

7. With the tip of the iron, push an adjacent seam allowance over the edge of the freezer paper.

8. Repeat with the remaining adjacent seam allowance, pushing the seam allowance taut to ensure a sharp point.

9. After all edges are pressed, let the appliqué shape cool, then either remove the freezer-paper template before proceeding with the desired hand- or machine-appliqué technique or leave in to stitch (see tip box on *page 8–19* for information on removing templates after appliqué has been sewn in place).

FREEZER-PAPER METHOD 2

This technique involves pressing entire freezer-paper templates, shiny side down, to the appliqué fabric. The freezer paper is removed before the appliqué is sewn in place. (Refer to Using Freezer Paper on *page 8–3* for additional information.) This technique may be used to prepare pieces for hand or machine appliqué.

1. Trace a reverse image of the appliqué patterns on the dull side of the freezer paper. Cut out the shapes on the traced lines to make freezer-paper templates. *Note:* To create a reverse image, tape the appliqué pattern facedown on a light box or sunny window (see tip box *opposite).*

2. Place the appliqué fabric wrong side up on a pressing surface. With a dry iron on a cotton setting, press a freezer-paper shape, shiny side down, to the appliqué fabric. Leave the iron on the paper for a few

TIP: If you're placing multiple templates on a fabric piece, be sure to leave at least ½" between shapes to allow for the turn-under allowances.

seconds. Lift the iron to check that the template is completely adhered to the fabric. If the template is not completely adhered, press again.

3. Cut out the appliqué shape, adding a 3/16" seam allowance to all edges. Clip inside curves or points on the appliqué shape. When clipping inside curves, clip halfway through seam allowance. Try to make your clips on the bias grain of the seam allowance, which means clips often will be on diagonal, rather than perpendicular, lines. This directional clipping prevents fabric from raveling while you're working with the edges.

4. Beginning at one inner point of an appliqué shape, use the tip of a dry, hot iron to push the seam allowance over the edge of the freezer paper to create a sharp edge. *Note:* The seam allowance will not adhere to the dull side of the freezer paper.

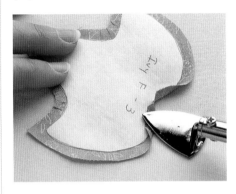

5. Continue working around the appliqué shape, turning one small area at a time and pressing the seam allowance up and over the freezer paper. Make certain the appliqué fabric is pressed taut against the edges of the freezer-paper template.

Small pleats in the fabric may appear as you round outer curves. If there is too much bulk in a seam allowance, make small V clips around outer curves to ease the fabric around the edge.

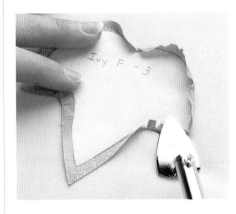

6. For a sharp outer point, fold the fabric straight over the point of the freezer-paper template; press.

7. With the tip of the iron, push an adjacent seam allowance over the edge of the freezer paper. Repeat with the remaining adjacent seam allowance, pushing the seam allowance taut to ensure a sharp point.

8. After all edges are pressed, let the appliqué shape cool, then remove the freezer-paper template.

FREEZER-PAPER METHOD 3

This method involves pressing entire freezer-paper templates, shiny side down, to the appliqué fabric. A water-soluble glue stick is used to hold the seam allowances in place. The freezer paper is not removed until after the appliqué is sewn in place. (Refer to Using Freezer Paper on *page 8–3* for additional information.) This technique may be used to prepare pieces for hand or machine appliqué.

1. Trace a reverse image of the appliqué patterns onto the dull side of the freezer paper. Cut out the shapes on the traced lines to make freezer-paper templates. *Note:* To create a reverse image, tape the appliqué pattern facedown on a light box or sunny window (see tip box on *page 8–4*).

2. Place the appliqué fabric wrong side up on a pressing surface. With a dry iron on a cotton setting, press a freezer-paper template, shiny side down, to the appliqué fabric. Leave the iron on the paper for a few seconds. Lift the iron to check that the template is completely adhered to the fabric. If the template is not completely adhered, press again.

3. Cut out the appliqué shape, adding a ³/₁₆" seam allowance to all edges. Clip inside curves or points on the appliqué shape. To make a sharp edge at a deep inside point, clip the seam allowance to within one thread of the freezer-paper template.

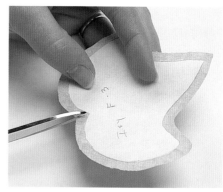

When clipping inside curves, clip halfway through seam allowance. Try to make your clips on the bias grain of the seam allowance, which means your clips will be diagonal, rather than perpendicular, lines. This directional clipping prevents fabric from raveling while you're working with the edges.

4. Using a water-soluble glue stick, apply glue to the exposed seam allowance and to the outer edge of the freezer-paper template.

5. At a deep inside point, use the tip of your thumb to press the seam allowance on both sides of the clip down against the freezer-paper template.

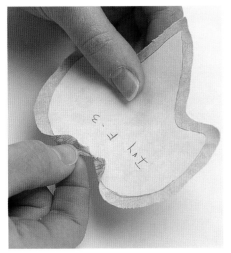

Small pleats in the fabric may appear as you round outer curves. If there is too much bulk in the seam allowance, make small V clips around outer curves to ease the fabric around the edge.

6. Using the tip of your thumb and index finger, continue working the seam allowance over the edge by pinching the fabric. Work in small areas at a time.

7. To make a sharp outer point, fold and glue the fabric point straight over the point of the freezer-paper template. Push one adjacent edge of

the seam allowance over the edge of the freezer paper; glue. Repeat with the remaining adjacent seam allowance.

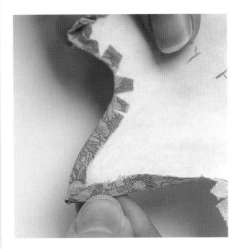

8. The freezer-paper template is not removed until after the appliqué is stitched in place (see tip box on *page 8–19* for information on removing templates after appliqué has been sewn in place).

> **TIP:** Store your glue sticks in the refrigerator. This keeps them firmer, making them easier to use and longer lasting.

FREEZER-PAPER METHOD 4

This technique involves pressing the shiny side of the freezer-paper templates to the right side of the appliqué fabric. The seam allowances are not turned under. (Refer to the Using Freezer-Paper on *page 8–3* for additional information.) This technique may be used to prepare pieces for needle-turn appliqué (see *page 8–19*).

1. Trace finished-size appliqué patterns onto the dull side of the freezer paper. Cut out the shapes on the traced lines to make freezer-paper templates.

2. Place the appliqué fabric right side up on a pressing surface. With a dry iron on a cotton setting, press a freezer-paper template, shiny side down, to the appliqué fabric. Leave the iron on the paper for a few seconds. Lift the iron to check that the template is completely adhered to the fabric. If the template is not completely adhered, press again.

3. Cut out the appliqué shape, adding a ³⁄₁₆" seam allowance to all edges. Clip inside curves or points on the appliqué shape. When clipping inside curves, clip halfway through seam allowance. Try to make your clips on the bias grain of the seam allowance, which means your clips will be diagonal, rather than perpendicular, lines. This directional clipping prevents fabric from raveling while you're working with the edges.

4. Do not remove the template until the appliqué piece is stitched in place.

SPRAY-STARCH METHOD

With this method spray starch holds the appliqué's seam allowances against a reusable, heat-resistant template, which is removed before the appliqué is sewn in place. This technique may be used to prepare pieces for hand or machine appliqué.

1. Make a heat-resistant, plastic template the exact finished size of the appliqué motif. Mark the template's right side.

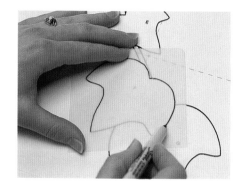

2. Place the template wrong side up on the wrong side of the appliqué fabric and trace. Cut around the shape, adding a ³⁄₁₆" seam allowance to all edges.

3. With wrong sides up, center the template on the appliqué fabric shape. Spray a small amount of starch into a dish. Working on a pressing surface covered with a tea towel or muslin, dip a cotton swab in the starch and moisten the outer edge of the seam allowance.

4. Clip all inside points. Beginning at an inside point, use the tip of a hot, dry iron to turn the seam allowance over the edge of the template and press it in place until the fabric is dry.

5. Continue pressing around the appliqué shape, clipping inside curves or points and adding starch as necessary. When clipping inside curves, clip halfway through the seam allowance. Try to make your clips on the bias grain of the seam allowance, which means your clips often will be diagonal, rather than perpendicular, lines. This directional clipping prevents fabric from raveling while you're working with the edges. Make certain the fabric is pressed taut against the appliqué template.

6. To make a sharp outer point, moisten the seam allowance and fold the fabric point straight over the point of the freezer-paper template. Push one adjacent edge of the seam allowance over the edge of the freezer paper. Repeat with the remaining adjacent seam allowance.

Small pleats in the fabric may appear as you round outer curves. If there is too much bulk in the seam allowance, make small V clips around outer curves to ease the fabric around the edge.

7. Press the appliqué from the right side, then remove template.

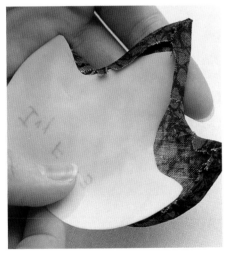

DOUBLE-APPLIQUÉ METHOD

This method eases the challenge of turning under seam allowances by facing the appliqué pieces with sheer, featherweight, nonfusible, nonwoven interfacing. This technique may be used to prepare pieces for hand or machine appliqué.

1. Place a rigid template wrong side up on the wrong side of the appliqué fabric; trace. The traced line is your stitching line.

2. With right sides together, layer your appliqué fabric with a like-size piece of sheer, featherweight, nonfusible, nonwoven interfacing.

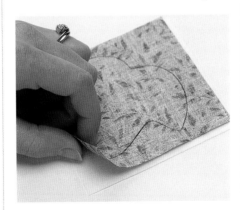

3. Sew the pieces together, stitching on the marked line. Cut out the appliqué shape, adding a 3/16" allowance to all edges.

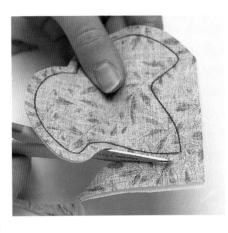

4. Trim the interfacing seam allowance slightly smaller than the appliqué fabric. This will enable the seam allowance to roll slightly to the back side of the appliqué once it is turned. Clip at the inner curves and points.

5. Clip a small slit in the center of the interfacing, being careful not to cut through the appliqué fabric.

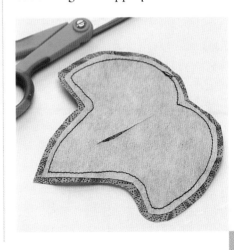

6. Turn the appliqué right side out through the slit.

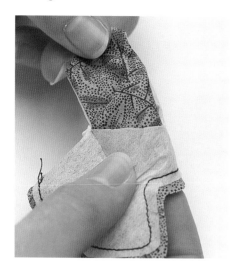

7. Press the appliqué piece from the right side.

FUSIBLE WEB METHOD
This method eliminates the need to turn under any seam allowances. Choose a lightweight, paper-backed fusible web that can be stitched through unless you plan to leave the appliqué edges unfinished. If the appliqué edges will not be sewn in place, you may wish to use a heavyweight, no-sew fusible web. (See Chapter 1—Tools, Notions, & Supplies for more information on fusible web.) This technique is commonly used for machine appliqué, but also can be used for hand appliqué.

1. Position the fusible web with the paper side up over the appliqué patterns and place on light box. Use a pencil to trace each pattern the specified number of times. If you are tracing multiple pieces at one time, leave at least ½" between tracings. *Note:* If you are not using an appliqué pattern designed especially for fusible web, you will need to create a mirror image of the pattern before tracing it. If you don't, your appliqués will be reversed once you cut them from fabric. To create a reverse image, tape the appliqué

Manufacturer's instructions for adhering fusible web vary by brand. Follow the instructions that come with your fusible web to ensure success. Factors such as the iron's temperature setting, a dry or steam iron, and the length of time you press are critical to attaining a secure bond between the fusible web and the fabric.

pattern facedown on a light box or sunny window (see tip box on *page 8–4*).

Cut out the traced appliqué patterns roughly ¼" outside the traced lines. Do not cut directly on the traced lines.

2. If you are working with multiple appliqué layers or want to reduce the stiffness of the finished project, consider cutting away the center of your fusible web shapes. To do this, cut ¼" inside the traced lines and discard the centers.

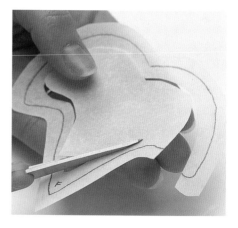

3. Place the fusible web shapes paper side up on the back of the designated appliqué fabrics. Press in place following the manufacturer's instructions. Do not slide the iron, but pick it up to move it from one area to the next. Let the appliqué shapes cool.

4. Cut out the fabric shapes on the drawn lines. Peel off the paper backings.

MAKING AND APPLYING BIAS STEMS AND VINES

Fabric strips needed to make curved appliqué stems and vines should be cut on the bias so that they are flexible enough to bend without wrinkles or puckers. (For information on cutting bias strips, see Chapter 5—Cutting.)

QUICK METHOD 1

1. Cut bias strip two times the desired finished width plus ½". For example, for a 1"-wide finished stem, cut a 2½"-wide bias strip. *Note:* Handle strips carefully to avoid stretching.

2. Fold the bias strip in half lengthwise with the wrong side inside and press to make an appliqué stem.

3. Trace the stem placement line on the appliqué foundation fabric as a seam guide.

4. Pin the appliqué stem to the appliqué foundation with the raw edge next to the marked seam guide. Sew the stem in place by machine or hand using a ¼" seam allowance.

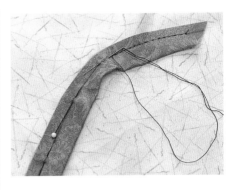

5. Fold the stem over the stitching line, covering the seam allowance and marked seam guide. Trim the seam allowance if necessary. Press in place.

TIP: If the finished width of your bias stem is extremely narrow, trim the excess seam allowance before folding the stem over the stitching line.

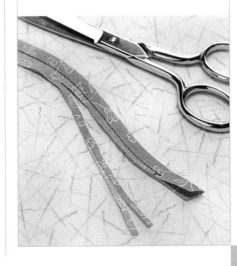

6. Secure the folded stem edge to the appliqué foundation using a machine blind hem stitch or slip-stitching by hand.

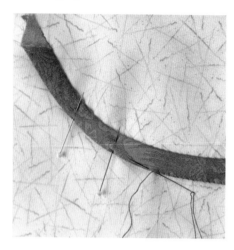

TIP: Since it always maintains a sharp point, a mechanical pencil is a good choice for marking placement lines on an appliqué foundation or to use when tracing around templates on fabric.

QUICK METHOD 2

1. Cut bias strip three times the desired finished width. For example, for a ¾"-wide finished stem, cut a 2¼"-wide bias strip. *Note:* Handle strips carefully to avoid stretching.

2. Fold the bias strip in thirds lengthwise with wrong side inside. The first fold should be a thread short of meeting the second fold.

3. Trace the stem placement line on the appliqué foundation fabric as a seam guide.

4. Unfold the bias strip, and place it on the appliqué foundation with the raw edge next to the marked seam line; machine- or hand-sew on the first fold line.

5. Fold the bias strip over the stitching line, covering the seam allowance and marked seam guide. Trim the seam allowance if necessary. Press in place.

6. Secure the second folded stem edge to the appliqué foundation using a machine blind hem stitch or slip-stitching by hand.

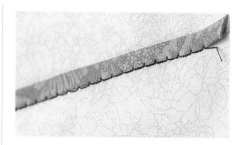

BIAS BAR METHOD

This method uses metal or heat-resistant plastic bias bars purchased in a size to match the desired finished width of the bias stem. (For more information on bias bars, see Chapter 1—Tools, Notions, & Supplies.) If instructions for strip width and seam allowance are provided with your bias bars, refer to them. If not, refer to the following.

1. Cut a bias strip twice the desired finished width plus ¾". For example, for a ½"-wide finished bias stem, cut a 1¾"-wide bias strip. Handle the strip's edges carefully to prevent stretching. Fold the strip in half lengthwise with the wrong side together; lightly press.

2. Stitch the length of the strip with the folded edge on the machine seam guide (to the right of the presser foot), the raw edges to the left, and a seam allowance equivalent to the desired finished width. For example, for a ½"-wide finished bias stem, stitch ½" away from the folded edge.

3. Trim away the seam allowance, leaving only enough fabric to hold the seam intact (about ¹⁄₁₆").

4. Slide the bias bar into the stem with the seam allowance centered on a flat side of the bar. Press the seam allowance to one side so that neither the seam nor the seam allowance is visible along the edges.

5. Remove the bar from the stem, and press the stem again.

6. Trace the stem placement line on the appliqué foundation fabric as a seam guide.

7. Pin the bias stem to the appliqué foundation covering the marked line and secure the stem in place using a machine blind hem stitch or slip-stitching by hand.

FINGER-PRESSING METHOD

1. Cut a bias strip to the desired finished width plus ½". For example, for a ¼"-wide finished bias stem, cut a ¾"-wide bias strip. Handle the strip's edges carefully to prevent stretching.

2. Finger-press under ¼" along both long edges.

3. Pin the bias stem to the appliqué foundation and secure the stem in place using a machine blind hem stitch or slip-stitching by hand.

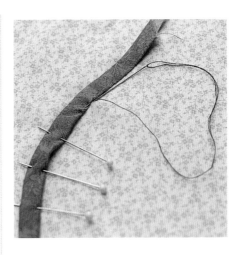

FUSIBLE WEB METHOD

Using lightweight fusible web eliminates the need to turn under a strip's seam allowances. It is often the preferred method for making stems when the appliqués also are prepared with fusible web.

1. Cut a piece of lightweight fusible web the finished length of the desired stems by the width of a stem times the number of stems desired. For example, if you need 13 stems that are each ¼" wide and 10" long, cut a piece of fusible web 3½×10". The extra ¼" allows you to make the first cut on the edge of the fusible web.

Cut a bias edge on your appliqué fabric. Following the manufacturer's directions, press the fusible web piece to the wrong side of the appliqué fabric along the bias edge.

2. Trim the fabric to the edge of the fusible web. Then cut bias strips the desired finished widths and lengths of the appliqué stems.

3. Trace the stem placement line on the appliqué foundation fabric as a guide.

4. Peel off the paper backings. Following the manufacturer's directions, press the stems in place on the appliqué foundation, covering the marked line. Sew the bias stems to the appliqué foundation using a machine blind hem stitch or slip-stitching by hand.

POSITIONING THE APPLIQUÉ PIECES

There are many ways to position pieces for appliqué. Some require more preparation than others. If you're new to appliqué, experiment with different positioning methods to select the one that's best for you.

FOLDED FOUNDATION METHOD

1. Cut the appliqué foundation fabric larger than the desired finished size to allow for any take-up in the fabric that might occur during the appliqué process. For example, for a 12" finished square, cut a 14"-square appliqué foundation. When the appliqué is complete, you'll trim the foundation to 12½" square. (The extra ¼" on each side will be used for seam allowances when assembling the quilt top.)

2. Fold the square appliqué foundation in half vertically and horizontally to find the center and divide the square into quarters. Lightly finger-press to create positioning guides for the appliqué pieces.

3. Then fold the square appliqué foundation diagonally in both directions and lightly finger-press to make additional positioning guidelines.

4. Draw corresponding vertical, horizontal, and diagonal positioning guidelines on your full-size appliqué pattern if they are not already marked.

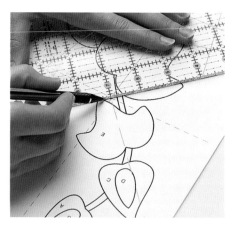

5. Prepare the appliqué pieces using the desired method. (See Preparing Appliqué Pieces beginning on *page 8–2.*) Referring to your appliqué pattern, pin and stitch the appliqué pieces to the foundation using your desired method; work from the bottom layer up.

TIP: When cutting appliqué foundations, stay at least ½" away from the selvage edge, which is tightly woven. It can cause your foundation to have a rippled edge if you cut too near it.

6. After the appliqué is complete, trim the appliqué foundation to the desired finished size plus seam allowances.

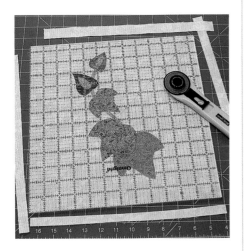

MARKED FOUNDATION METHOD

1. Cut the appliqué foundation fabric larger than the desired finished size to allow for any take-up in the fabric that might occur during the appliqué process. For example, for a 12" finished square, cut a 14"-square appliqué foundation. When the appliqué is complete, you'll trim the foundation square to 12½" square. (The extra ¼" on each side will be used for seam allowances when assembling the quilt top.)

2. Using a faint pencil line and your full-size appliqué pattern, trace the design onto the appliqué foundation fabric. To avoid having markings

show after the appliqué is complete, lightly mark just inside the design lines and just at critical points (for example, where two lines intersect or at the tips of leaves).

3. Prepare the appliqué pieces using the desired method. (See Preparing Appliqué Pieces beginning on *page 8–2.*) Referring to your appliqué pattern, pin and stitch the appliqué pieces to the foundation using your desired method; work from the bottom layer up.

4. After the appliqué is complete, trim the appliqué foundation to the desired size plus seam allowances.

LIGHT BOX METHOD

1. Cut the appliqué foundation fabric larger than the desired finished size to allow for any take-up in the fabric that might occur during the appliqué process. For example, for a 12" finished square, cut a 14"-square appliqué foundation. When the appliqué is complete, you'll trim the foundation square to 12½" square. (The extra ¼" on each side will be used for seam allowances when assembling the quilt top.)

2. Place your full-size appliqué pattern on a light box and secure it with tape. Center the appliqué foundation fabric atop the appliqué pattern.

> **TIP:** Numbers on appliqué pieces are important. They indicate the appliquéing sequence and designate the right sides of the templates.

3. Prepare the appliqué pieces using the desired method. (See Preparing Appliqué Pieces beginning on *page 8–2.*) Return to the light box and pin the bottom layer of appliqué pieces in place on the appliqué foundation. Stitch the appliqué pieces to the foundation using your desired method.

4. After stitching the bottom layer of appliqué pieces, return the appliqué foundation to the light box. Match the next layer of appliqué pieces with the pattern, pin, and stitch. Continue in this manner until all appliqué pieces are stitched to the foundation.

5. Trim the appliqué foundation to the desired size plus seam allowances.

OVERLAY METHOD

1. Cut the appliqué foundation fabric larger than the desired finished size to allow for any take-up in the fabric that might occur during the appliqué process. For example, for a 12" finished square, cut a 14"-square appliqué foundation. When the appliqué is complete, you'll trim the foundation square to 12½" square. (The extra ¼" on each side will be used for seam allowances when assembling the quilt top.)

2. Position clear upholstery vinyl (or other clear flexible plastic) over your full-size appliqué pattern and precisely trace the design with a permanent marker.

3. Center the vinyl overlay on the appliqué foundation fabric. Pin the top of the overlay to the foundation.

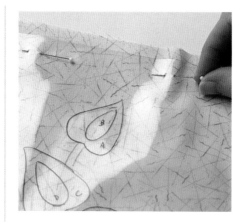

4. Prepare the appliqué pieces using the desired method. (See Preparing Appliqué Pieces beginning on *page 8–2.*) Once the appliqué pieces have been prepared, slide the bottommost appliqué piece right side up between the appliqué foundation and the overlay. When the piece is in place beneath its corresponding position on the vinyl overlay, remove the overlay and pin the appliqué piece to the foundation. Stitch the appliqué to the foundation using your desired method.

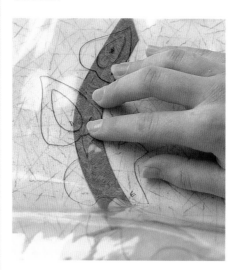

5. Pin the vinyl overlay on the foundation and position the next appliqué piece in the stitching sequence. Pin and stitch it to the foundation as before. Continue adding appliqué pieces in this manner until all appliqués have been stitched in place.

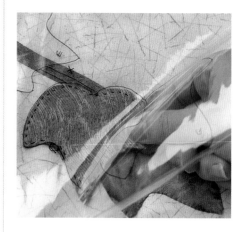

6. Trim the appliqué foundation to the desired size plus seam allowances.

HOLDING APPLIQUÉ PIECES IN POSITION

Once the appliqués and foundations have been prepared for stitching, the appliqué pieces can be held in place with pins, basting threads, spray adhesive, fusible web, or fabric glue stick. The number of appliqué layers you are working with may influence your choice.

Pins: Use as many straight pins as needed to hold each appliqué piece in place on the appliqué foundation for both machine and hand appliqué. Pins are generally used to hold no more than two layers at a

time and are pushed through from the top. Some hand appliquérs like to place pins on the back side of the work to prevent catching thread in pins as they work. Remove the pins as you stitch.

Basting: Sewing long stitches about ¼" from the turned-under edges is another way to secure prepared appliqué pieces to a foundation for both machine and hand appliqué. Begin and end the basting stitches on the right side of the appliqué for easier removal. You may wish to remove basting stitches when the entire appliqué work is complete or, if the basting threads impede stitching progress, remove them as you go. This is the preferred method of quilters who wish to hold multiple appliqué layers in position at once before permanently stitching them in place.

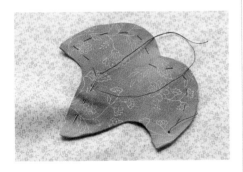

Fabric basting spray: When lightly sprayed on the wrong side of appliqué pieces, this adhesive

usually allows you to position and reposition appliqués while you work. It can hold appliqués in place for both machine and hand appliqué. Work in a well-ventilated area and cover your work surface with paper. Be careful to spray lightly, as overspraying can cause a gummy build-up that makes stitching difficult.

Fabric glue or glue stick: Apply these adhesives lightly to the wrong side of the prepared appliqué pieces along the outer edges or in the center. Press the appliqué piece to the appliqué foundation fabric. Be sure to apply the glue sparingly to avoid a build-up that would be difficult to stitch through. This method can be used for both machine and hand appliqué.

> **TIP:** If residue from basting spray or a glue stick builds up on your needle, wipe it off with rubbing alcohol.

Fusible web: This adhesive is most often used to hold pieces in position for machine appliqué. If you have an appliqué project with multiple layers of pieces that are prepared with fusible web, you may wish to hold them in position before adhering them to the foundation. To do so, place your full-size appliqué pattern beneath a clear, nonstick pressing sheet. Layer the prepared appliqué pieces in position right side up on the pressing sheet. Press lightly, just enough to fuse the pieces together, following the manufacturer's instructions. Do not slide the iron, but pick it up and

move it from one area to the next. Let the pieces cool, then remove the fused appliqués from the pressing sheet and fuse them to the appliqué foundation.

HAND APPLIQUÉ

There are many ways to hand-stitch pieces in place on an appliqué foundation. If you're new to hand appliqué, experiment with each to determine which method is most comfortable for you.

For most hand appliqué, use a sharp, between, straw, or milliners needle and the finest thread you can find that matches the appliqué pieces. The higher the number, the finer the thread, so look for silk or fine cotton machine-embroidery threads; they will make your appliqué stitches nearly invisible (for more information on thread and needle choices, see Chapter 1—Tools, Notions, & Supplies).

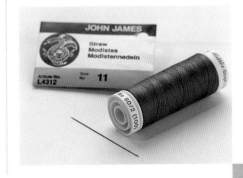

TRADITIONAL APPLIQUÉ STITCH

This technique uses appliqué pieces that have had the seam allowances turned under. (For more information, see Preparing Appliqué Pieces, which begins on *page 8–2.*)

For best results, use a sharp, between, straw, or milliners needle.

1. Prepare the appliqué pieces by turning the seam allowances under. Pin, baste, or glue an appliqué piece in place on the appliqué foundation.

2. Working with a length of thread no longer than 18", insert the needle into the wrong side of the appliqué foundation directly beneath the edge of the appliqué piece. Bring the needle up through the rolled edge of the appliqué piece.

TIP: If you're using appliqué pieces that have the freezer-paper template inside the appliqué shape while it's being stitched, be sure your stitching catches the fabric edge only. Keeping the paper template clear of stitching makes it easier to remove once the appliqué is stitched down.

3. Hold the needle parallel to the edge of the appliqué with the point of the needle next to the spot where the thread just exited.

4. Slide the point of the needle under the appliqué edge, into the appliqué foundation, and forward about ⅛" to ³⁄₁₆", bringing the needle point out through the rolled edge of the appliqué.

5. Give the thread a gentle tug to bury the stitch in the fabric and allow the appliqué shape to rise up

TIP: Match your thread color to the appliqué pieces. *Note:* Contrasting thread was used in the photos for illustration purposes only.

off the foundation. Continue stitching in the same manner around the shape along rolled edge.

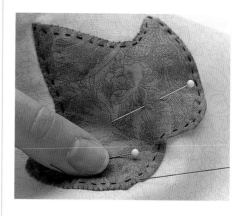

6. On the wrong side of the appliqué foundation, the stitches will be slightly angled.

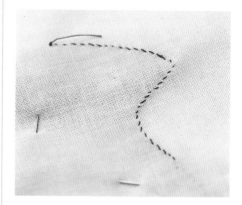

7. End the thread by knotting it on the wrong side of the foundation, beneath the appliqué piece.

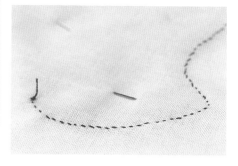

8. Once all pieces have been appliquéd, press the foundation from the wrong side and trim it to the desired size, including the seam allowances.

NEEDLE-TURN APPLIQUÉ

This technique involves turning under the appliqué seam allowance as you stitch. For best results, use a straw or milliners needle. The extra length of these needles aids in tucking fabric under before taking stitches.

1. Prepare the appliqué pieces following Freezer-Paper Method 4, which begins on *page 8–7,* or by completing steps 1 and 2 of the Basting Method on *page 8–2.* Pin, baste, or glue an appliqué piece in place on the appliqué foundation.

2. Working with a length of thread no longer than 18", insert the needle into the wrong side of the appliqué foundation directly beneath the edge of the appliqué piece. Bring your needle up between the appliqué and the foundation. Use the point of the needle to sweep the seam allowance under about 1" or so ahead of your stitching and secure the fabric with your thumb. The edge of the freezer-paper template or the drawn line serves as your guide for how much to turn under.

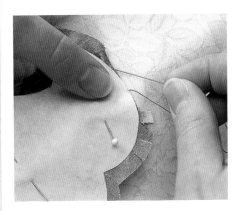

3. Hold the needle parallel to the edge of the appliqué with the needle's point at the spot where the thread just exited. Slide the point of the needle under a thread or two along the appliqué's rolled edge. Give the thread a gentle tug to bury the stitch in the fabric and allow the appliqué shape to rise up off the foundation.

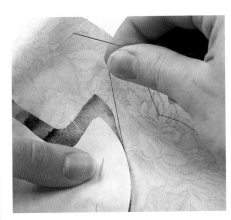

4. Then place the tip of the needle into the appliqué foundation and rock it forward, bringing the tip up into the rolled appliqué edge about 1/8" to 3/16" away from the previous stitch. Pull the needle through and gently tug the thread to bury the stitch as before.

5. Continue in the same manner around the entire appliqué, taking tinier stitches around inside corners and curves where the seam allowances are more scant. Use the needle point to manipulate the seam allowance to lie flat in outside curves.

6. End the thread by knotting it on the wrong side of the foundation, beneath the appliqué piece.

7. Once all pieces have been appliquéd, press the foundation from the wrong side and trim it to the desired size, including the seam allowances.

TACK STITCH

This technique uses appliqué pieces that have had the seam allowances turned. (For more information, see Preparing Appliqué Pieces, which begins on *page 8–2.*)

For best results, use a sharp, between, straw, or milliners needle.

1. Prepare the appliqué pieces by turning the seam allowances under. Pin, baste, or glue an appliqué piece in place on the appliqué foundation.

2. Working with a length of thread no longer than 18", insert the needle into the wrong side of the appliqué foundation directly beneath the edge of the appliqué piece. Bring the needle up through the rolled edge of the appliqué piece.

3. Insert the needle down into the foundation right next to the appliqué edge where it came up.

4. Bring the needle back up through the edge of the appliqué piece about ¹⁄₁₆" from the first stitch. Continue in the same manner to stitch the appliqué piece to the foundation.

5. Once all pieces have been appliquéd, press the foundation from the wrong side and trim it to the desired size, including the seam allowances.

RUNNING STITCH

This method results in a more primitive or folk art look. It uses appliqué pieces that have had the seam allowances turned under. (For more information, see Preparing Appliqué Pieces, which begins on *page 8–2.*)

For best results, use a sharp, between, straw, or milliners needle.

1. Prepare the appliqué pieces by turning the seam allowances under. Pin, baste, or glue an appliqué piece in place on the appliqué foundation.

2. Working with a length of thread no longer than 18", insert the needle into the wrong side of the appliqué foundation directly beneath the edge of the appliqué piece. Bring the needle up through the appliqué piece about ¹⁄₁₆" from the rolled edge.

3. Weave the needle in and out through both the edge of the appliqué piece and the foundation, staying about ¹⁄₁₆" from the outside edge of the appliqué. Rock the needle in and out, taking small, evenly spaced stitches. Continue in this manner to secure the appliqué piece to the background.

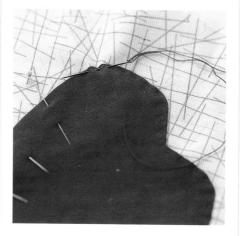

4. Working with perle cotton and a larger needle, you can produce a larger running stitch (see *below right*), sometimes called a utility stitch or big stitch. The standard running stitch done in matching thread is shown *below left*.

5. Once all pieces have been appliquéd, press the foundation from the wrong side and trim it to the desired size, including the seam allowances.

REVERSE APPLIQUÉ

With this method, the foundation fabric is sewn on top of the appliqué fabric. The foundation is then cut away to reveal the appliqué fabric underneath.

For best results, use a straw or milliners needle.

1. Make a template for each appliqué piece. (See Making Appliqué Templates on *page 8–1.*) Make an overlay for the complete appliqué pattern. (See Overlay Method on *page 8–16.*) *Note:* If you're making templates and overlays for letters and/or numbers, keep them on a straight baseline and mark the center point of each word or series of numbers.

2. Mark the center of the foundation fabric. Position the overlay on the foundation fabric, aligning the marked centers. Pin the overlay in place. Slide a template under the overlay into position.

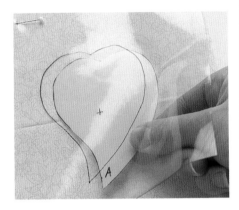

3. Flip back the overlay and, using an erasable marking tool, carefully trace around the template on the foundation fabric.

4. Place the appliqué fabric right side up, directly beneath the traced motif on the foundation fabric. Baste around the outer edges of the motif, 5/16" away from the traced lines.

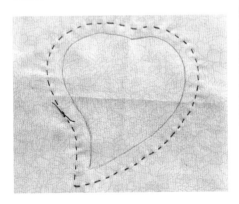

5. Starting in the middle of the motif, cut away a small portion of the foundation fabric, cutting 3/16" inside the traced line to create an edge for turning under.

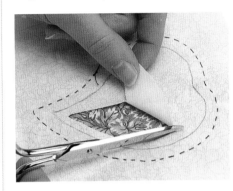

6. Turn the raw edge under and slip-stitch the folded edge to the appliqué fabric beneath. Clip curves as necessary to make the edge lie flat.

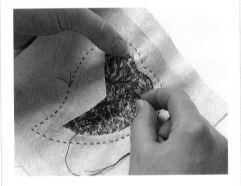

7. Continue cutting away the foundation fabric a little at a time, turning under the raw edge and stitching the folded edge to the fabric below until you have revealed the entire motif.

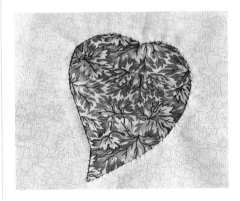

TIPS FOR HAND APPLIQUÉ

- Work in a clockwise or counterclockwise direction, whichever is more comfortable for you.

- At inside points, make your stitches close together to prevent thread from raveling where you have clipped into the seam allowance. Secure an inside point with a single stitch.

- At an outside point, stitch right up to the point, then rotate the appliqué foundation and continue stitching down the next side.

- If the foundation fabric shows through the appliqué fabric, cut away the foundation beneath the appliqué after the stitching is complete. Carefully trim the underlying fabric to within 1/4" of the stitching (see photo *below*). Be careful not to cut into the appliqué fabric.

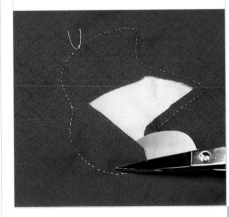

8. Once you've completed the appliqué, turn it over and trim the appliqué fabric to within ¼" of the seam allowance.

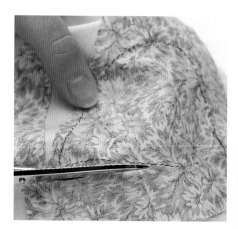

9. Press the foundation from the wrong side and trim to the desired size, including the seam allowances.

MACHINE APPLIQUÉ

BEGINNING AND ENDING STITCHING

1. To begin stitching, bring the bobbin and needle threads to the top; this helps prevent thread tangles and snarls on the wrong side of your work. To begin this way, put

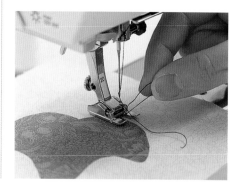

the presser foot down and take one stitch. Stop and pull the bobbin thread to the top.

2. Set your machine for a narrow zigzag or satin stitch. Holding the bobbin and needle threads to one side, take a few stitches on a curve or straight edge; do not start at an inner or outer point. (If your machine has a variable stitch length, you may wish to set your stitch length at 0 and take a few stitches, one on top of the next, to lock threads in place at the start.) Reset your machine to the desired stitch setting; stitch about 1" and trim off the thread tails. Or, when the appliqué work is completed, use a needle to draw the thread tails to

ABOUT STABILIZERS

Stabilizers are used beneath appliqué foundations to add support and eliminate puckers and pulling on the fabric as you machine-appliqué. Some stabilizers are temporary and are removed once stitching is complete (as in the photo *below,* where the stabilizer is removed by holding it firmly on one side of the stitching and gently pulling it away from the other side). Others are permanent and remain in the quilt or are only partially cut away after stitching. Many brands are available. Two of the most common types are tear-away and water-soluble stabilizers. Freezer paper also may be used as a stabilizer. Experiment with a variety of types to determine which works best for you.

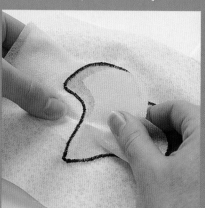

TIP: For machine appliqué, use a 60/8, 70/10, 75/11, or 80/12 sharp needle. For best results, use a smaller number needle for lighter weight, finer fabrics, and monofilament threads; use a larger number needle for medium-weight fabrics and cotton threads. Sewing on flannel or working with decorative threads requires larger or specialty needles (see Chapter 1—Tools, Notions, & Supplies).

the wrong side of the work and bury them in the stitching.

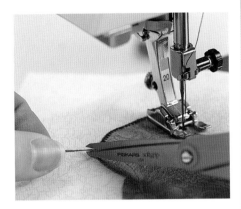

3. To end, stitch one or two threads past the point where the stitching began and take one or two backstitches to secure the thread. (If your machine has a variable stitch length, you may wish to set your stitch length at 0 and take a few stitches, one on top of the next, to lock the threads in place.)

SATIN OR ZIGZAG STITCH APPLIQUÉ

Variable-width satin or zigzag stitch makes a smooth, professional-looking finish on appliqué edges. Choose a thread color that complements or matches your appliqué fabric. Select a stitch width that corresponds to the size of the piece being appliquéd. Larger pieces can accommodate a wider, denser

appliqué stitch than smaller appliqué shapes can.

With a machine satin stitch, it is not necessary to turn under the appliqué piece's edges because the entire outer edge is held in place by the zigzag or satin stitch. The outer edge of the stitch just grazes the appliqué foundation. Depending

---

SEWING MACHINE SETUP FOR MACHINE APPLIQUÉ

- Make certain your machine is clean and in good working order.

- Install a new size 60/8, 70/10, 75/11 or 80/12 sharp embroidery needle in your machine.

- Wind a bobbin with cotton 60-weight embroidery thread or bobbin-fill thread.

- Thread the needle with matching- or complementary-color cotton 60-weight embroidery thread.

- Set your machine for a zigzag stitch with a width between 1 and 1.5mm or about ⅛" wide. Set the stitch length just above (not at) the satin-stitch setting, or between .5 and 1mm.

- If possible, set your machine in the "needle down" position, and set the motor at half speed.

---

upon the stability of your fabric, the appliqué design, and your personal preference, you can use fusible web, pins, or fabric glue to hold the appliqué pieces in place for machine stitching. Use a stabilizer behind the appliqué foundation (see About Stabilizers *opposite*).

1. Position the presser foot so that the left swing of the needle is on the appliqué and the right swing of the needle is just on the outer edge of the appliqué, grazing the appliqué foundation.

2. Begin stitching on a curve or straight edge, not at an inner or outer point.

TIP: To produce uniform stitches when doing machine appliqué, work slowly and sew at an even pace.

PIVOTING AT CORNERS, CURVES, AND POINTS

The position of your needle is critical when pivoting fabric to round a curve or turn a point or corner. Use the following illustrations to guide you in knowing when to pivot. In each case, you will need to place your needle down in the fabric before pivoting. In each illustration the arrows indicate stitching direction, and the dots mark where the needle should be down for pivoting.

Turning Corners–Method 1

With this method the stitches cross over one another in the corners.

1. Stop with the needle down in the fabric on the right-hand swing of the needle.

TIP: Mark edges of circular or oval appliqué pieces with the hours of a clock. Pivot the fabric at each hour.

2. Raise the presser foot and pivot the fabric. Lower the presser foot and begin stitching to the next edge.

Turning Corners–Method 2

With this method the stitching lines abut, but they do not cross over one another.

1. Stop with the needle down in the fabric on the left-hand swing of the needle.

2. Raise the presser foot and pivot the fabric. Lower the presser foot and turn the handwheel until the right-hand swing of the needle is just about to go into the foundation fabric. Lift the presser foot and reposition the foundation fabric so the tip of the needle is above the point where the needle thread is coming out of the appliqué. Lower the presser foot and begin stitching to the next edge.

Pivoting Inside Curves

Stop at the first pivot point with the needle down in the fabric on the left-hand swing of the needle. Raise the presser foot, pivot the fabric slightly, and begin stitching to the next pivot point. Repeat as needed to round the entire inner curve.

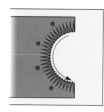

Pivoting Outside Curves

Stop at the first pivot point with the needle down in the fabric on the right-hand swing of the needle. Raise the presser foot, pivot the fabric slightly, and begin stitching to the next pivot point. Repeat as needed to round the entire outer curve.

TIP: Pivoting evenly around curves takes practice. Keep an eye on the space between your stitches as you work around the appliqué. To maintain evenness between your stitches, pivot more often on a gentle curve than a sharp one.

Pivoting Inside Points

1. With a marking tool, mark a line extending from the upcoming edge of the appliqué into the center. On the line, measure from the point a distance equal to your stitch width; mark the location with a dot.

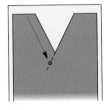

2. Stitch to the bottom of the inside point, stopping with the needle down in the fabric on the left-hand swing of the needle. The needle should be at the dot on your drawn marked line.

3. Raise the presser foot and pivot the fabric. Lower the presser foot and turn the handwheel until the right-hand swing of the needle is just about to go into the foundation fabric. Lift the presser foot and reposition the foundation fabric so the tip of the needle is above the point where the needle thread is coming out of the appliqué. Lower the presser foot and begin stitching to the next edge.

MACHINE APPLIQUÉ TROUBLESHOOTING TIPS

THIS MACHINE-APPLIQUÉ STITCHING IS CORRECTLY PLACED. The outside edge of the stitch is just grazing the appliqué foundation.

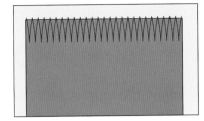

THIS STITCHING IS TOO FAR INSIDE the edge of the appliqué piece, so fabric threads from the appliqué will fray and poke out around the edges.

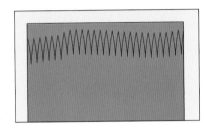

HERE THE STITCHES ARE TOO FAR OUTSIDE the edge of the appliqué piece, so it may pull loose from the foundation.

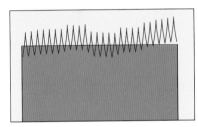

GAPS WILL OCCUR in the stitching if your needle is down in the fabric on the wrong side of the needle swing when you pivot.

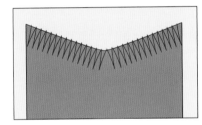

YOUR STITCHES WILL SLANT if you try to pull or push the fabric through curves, rather than lifting the presser foot and pivoting the fabric.

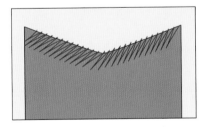

PIVOTING TOO SOON on an inside point will leave an incomplete line of stitches at the point.

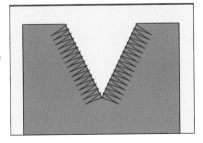

Pivoting Outside Points

Shapes with outside points are among the more difficult to appliqué. This method requires you to taper your stitch width at the point. If your project requires you to appliqué around this shape, practice first on scraps to perfect your technique.

1. Stitch along the first edge of the appliqué, keeping the stitch width consistent until the left-hand swing of the needle begins to touch the opposite outside edge of the point. Stop with the needle down in the fabric on the left-hand swing of the needle.

2. Gradually reduce your stitch width and continue sewing toward the point. Keep the right- and left-hand swings of the needle just grazing the outer edges and taper your stitch width until it's 0 at the point. Stop with the needle down in the fabric.

3. Raise the presser foot and pivot the fabric. Lower the presser foot and begin stitching away from the point, increasing the stitch width at the same rate that you decreased it until you have returned to the original stitch width. Pivot the fabric slightly as needed to keep the right-

hand swing of the needle grazing the foundation at the right-hand edge of the appliqué piece.

This method uses monofilament thread in the needle and the blind hem stitch to make virtually invisible stitches. *Note:* Contrasting thread was used in the photos that follow for illustration purposes only.

SEWING MACHINE SETUP FOR MOCK HAND APPLIQUÉ

- Make certain your machine is clean and in good working order.

- Install a new size 60/8, 70/10, or 75/11 embroidery needle in your machine.

- Wind a bobbin with cotton 60-weight embroidery thread.

- Thread the needle with lightweight, invisible, nylon (monofilament) thread. Use clear thread for light-color fabrics; use smoke-color invisible thread for medium- and dark-color fabrics.

- Set your machine for a blind hem stitch with the stitch width and length each set at 1mm. This stitch takes 2 to 5 straight stitches, then a zigzag, then 2 to 5 more straight stitches before zigzagging again.

Stitch a test sample using the same threads and fabrics as in your project. The distance between each zigzag should be ⅛" maximum, and the width of the zigzag should be the width of two threads. When you are finished, you should be able to see the needle holes, but no thread. If you gently pull on the edge of the appliqué, the stitching should be strong and without gaps.

Check the stitch tension on the test sample. There should be no bobbin thread showing on the top and no loops of nylon thread on the bottom. If the bobbin thread is showing on the top, loosen the top tension gradually until the bobbin thread no longer shows. Turn the sample over. If there are loops of nylon thread on the bottom, you've loosened the top tension too much.

1. Prepare the appliqué pieces following Freezer-Paper Method 3 on *page 8–6*.

2. Position an appliqué piece so that the needle goes into the appliqué foundation right next to it. The needle should be so near the fold of the appliqué piece that it touches the fold but does not stitch through it.

When the needle jumps to the left, the stitch should be totally on the appliqué piece.

When the needle jumps to the right to complete a zigzag stitch, the needle should again be against the edge of the appliqué piece but go through the foundation only.

3. When you come to inside and outside points, make sure to secure them with with several stitches. Make certain the needle always touches the fold of the appliqué so no edges are missed.

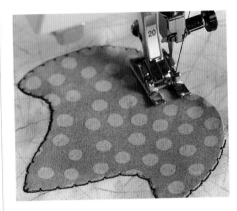

4. Continue stitching around the appliqué. When you reach the location where the stitching began, stitch over the beginning stitches to

MOCK HAND APPLIQUÉ TROUBLESHOOTING TIPS:

- If your stitching shows, you may be stitching too far from the edge of the appliqué. If you miss stitching into the appliqué with the zigzag, the stitches will be visible.

- If there are gaps in your stitching, the stitch length may be too long.

- If you see too much of the zigzag stitch, its width is too big.

secure the threads. To lock your stitches, backstitch only two or three stitches.

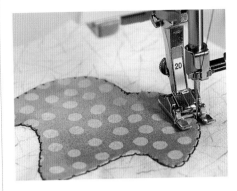

5. When the stitching is complete, check all the edges of the appliqué to make sure no areas were left unstitched. On the wrong side, carefully trim away the foundation fabric from within each stitched shape, leaving a ¼" seam allowance.

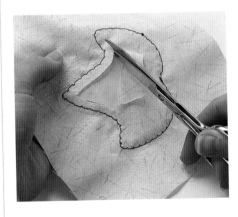

6. Using a spritzer bottle, spray water on the inside of the appliqué's seam allowances, making sure to wet the areas that were glued over the freezer paper.

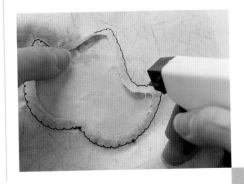

7. Remove the paper. You'll find that once the water dissolves the glue, the freezer paper will slip right out.

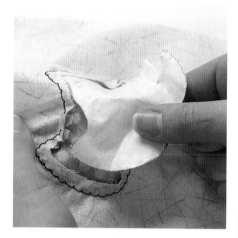

8. When the freezer paper has been removed from all appliqués, place a thick bath towel atop your pressing surface and lay the appliqué facedown on the towel. Cover the back of appliqué with a pressing cloth; press with a warm iron. (The towel prevents edges of the appliqués from being flattened by the iron.)

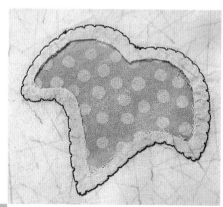

Note: Contrasting thread is used here for illustration purposes only. If monofilament thread had been used, no stitching line would be visible on the right side of the fabric.

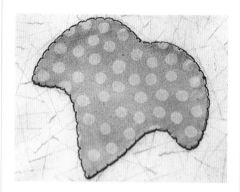

STRAIGHT STITCH APPLIQUÉ

1. Prepare the appliqué pieces following the desired method. (For more information, see Preparing Appliqué Pieces beginning on *page 8–2.*) Pin, baste, or glue the appliqués in place.

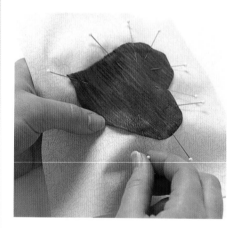

2. Set the stitch length at 0. Beginning on a straight edge or a curve, take two or three stitches about ⅛" from the outer edge of the appliqué to anchor the thread. Hold the thread tails out of the way to prevent thread snarls on the underside. *Note:* Remove pins before the needle reaches them.

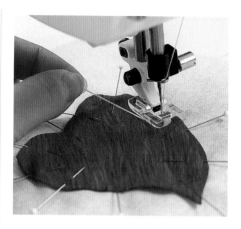

SEWING MACHINE SETUP FOR STRAIGHT STITCH APPLIQUÉ

- Make certain your machine is clean and in good working order.

- Install a new size 60/8, 70/10, 75/11, or 80/12 sharp embroidery needle in your machine.

- Wind a bobbin with cotton 60-weight embroidery thread.

- Thread the needle with thread in a color that matches the appliqué or a lightweight, invisible nylon (monofilament) thread.

- Set your machine for a straight stitch with the stitch length at 12 to 15 stitches per inch.

Stitch a test sample using the same thread and fabrics as your project. If your tension is properly adjusted, no bobbin thread will show on the top of your appliqué.

3. Adjust the stitch length to the desired number of stitches per inch (12 to 15) and continue sewing around the appliqué edge, staying ⅛" from the outer edge.

4. To stitch inner and outer curves, stop with the needle down, lift the presser foot, pivot the appliqué foundation, lower the presser foot, and continue sewing.

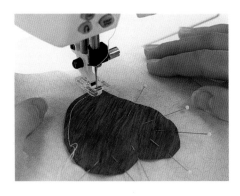

5. To end your stitching, gradually reduce the stitch length to 0 as you meet the point where the stitching began. Make the last two or three stitches next to the stitches where you started. Do not backstitch or overlap stitches.

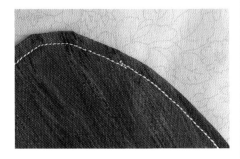

Note: Contrasting thread was used in the photographs for illustration purposes only. In the photograph, monofilament thread was used on the sample *below right,* so the stitching line does not appear as visible on the right side of the appliqué.

DECORATIVE STITCH APPLIQUÉ

This technique is often done on a sewing machine using the blanket or buttonhole stitch. Other decorative stitches also may be used, such as the featherstitch. (For information on decorative stitches done by hand, see Chapter 13—Specialty Techniques.)

1. Prepare the appliqué pieces following the desired method. (For more information, see Preparing Appliqué Pieces beginning on *page 8–2.)* Pin, baste, or glue the appliqués in place.

2. Use a tear-away stabilizer beneath the appliqué foundation. (See About Stabilizers on *page 8–22.)*

3. Beginning on a straight edge or a curve, take a few stitches; hold the thread tails out of the way to prevent

SEWING MACHINE SETUP FOR DECORATIVE STITCH APPLIQUÉ

- Make certain your machine is clean and in good working order.

- Install a new size 80/14 embroidery needle in your machine.

- Wind a bobbin with cotton 60-weight embroidery thread in a neutral color.

- Thread the needle with matching- or contrasting-color, cotton, 60-weight embroidery thread. Use black, cotton, 40-weight embroidery thread in the needle for a folk art look.

- Set your machine for the desired stitch length and width.

Stitch a test sample using the same thread and fabrics as your project. If your tension is properly adjusted, no bobbin thread will show on the top of your appliqué.

thread snarls on the wrong side of your project. The right swing of the needle should graze the appliqué foundation. The left swing of the needle should be completely on the appliqué piece.

4. For inside curves, stop with the needle down in the fabric on the left needle swing, lift the presser foot, pivot the appliqué foundation, lower the presser foot, and continue sewing.

5. For outside curves, stop with the needle down in the fabric on the right needle swing, lift the presser foot, pivot the appliqué foundation, and continue sewing.

6. Adjust the stitch length as necessary at corners and where the stitching meets at the end.

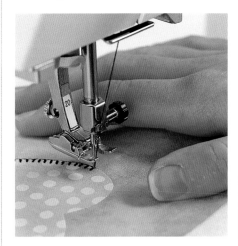

FUSIBLE-WEB APPLIQUÉ

To finish the edges of appliqué pieces that have been fused to the appliqué foundation, follow the instructions for Satin or Zigzag Stitch Appliqué, which begin on *page 8–23*, Decorative Stitch Appliqué on *page 8–29*, or Hand Embroidery Stitches in Chapter 13—Specialty Techniques. Be sure you have prepared your appliqués with a sew-through fusible web. (See Preparing Appliqué Pieces—Fusible Web Method beginning on *page 8–10.*)

WOOL APPLIQUÉ

Felted wool—wool that has been napped and shrunk—is easy to work with because the edges will not ravel so there is no need to turn them under. Use templates to cut felted wool into appliqué pieces. Do not include seam allowances. (See Making Appliqué Templates, which begins on page 8–1.)

Use a basic running stitch or decorative hand- or machine-embroidery stitches to attach wool appliqués to an appliqué foundation. Or, for added dimension, tack wool appliqué pieces at their centers only.

To felt wool for use in appliqué, machine-wash it in a hot-water/cool-rinse cycle with a small amount of detergent, machine-dry, and steam-press. It is the disparity in temperatures, along with the agitation, that causes the wool to felt. If you wish to use wool from a piece of clothing, cut it apart and remove the seams so it can shrink freely.

Assembling the Quilt Top

9

ASSEMBLING THE QUILT TOP

ONCE YOU'VE PLANNED YOUR QUILT and have cut and pieced or appliquéd the blocks, it's time to sew them together and perhaps add a border or two. Knowing the fundamentals of setting blocks together and adding borders will help you assemble a quilt top accurately.

SQUARING UP THE BLOCKS

Often the quilt you are assembling is one you've worked on from start to finish. Sometimes, you may have set the blocks aside for a while before you begin the quilt top assembly. Still other times, you may receive a set of finished quilt blocks from another source, and your first experience working with them is when you're ready to sew them together. However you've acquired the blocks, it is essential that all blocks be squared up before they're assembled into a quilt top. If you piece together your quilt top with some blocks that are too large and ease in the excess fabric, you'll end up with a quilt that has waves. If you piece your quilt with some blocks that are too small and try stretching the fabric to fit, you'll have a quilt that isn't square at the corners and pulls in, creating drag lines across the surface.

Measure each block to be certain they are all the same size. Check to be sure they have ¼" seam allowances on all edges and that the corners are square. Use a large, acrylic square ruler atop the block to check your work.

If you have cut accurately and used ¼" seams throughout the piecing process, the blocks will be the correct size.

If you are squaring up a block to a dimension that is not easily visible on the ruler, use pieces of narrow masking tape on the underside of the ruler to create a guide. Place the inside edge of the tape on your measurement line, so you can see at a glance if a block is too small.

SETTING THE QUILT BLOCKS

The word *set* refers to how the blocks are arranged in the quilt top. Blocks can be put together in a variety of ways, including block to block, or with sashing and/or setting squares. (See Chapter 4—Planning the Quilt Top for information on choosing a setting for your quilt blocks.) As a review, here are several assembly options for straight and diagonal (on point) block settings.

TROUBLESHOOTING TIPS:

What can you do if some blocks are too small?

- Discard blocks that don't measure up and make replacements using accurate ¼" seam allowances.

- Restitch blocks, making sure to use accurate ¼" seam allowances.

- Add borders to blocks to bring them to a uniform size. Borders may be added around the entire block or just to one or two sides.

What can you do if some blocks are too large?

- Discard blocks that don't measure up and make replacements using accurate ¼" seam allowances.

- Restitch blocks, making sure to use accurate ¼" seam allowances.

- If the margin the block is off is minimal (⅛" to ¹⁄₁₆"), you may trim it. Recognize that you may be trimming into the seam allowance, thus cutting off points of angled pieces or visually altering the finished look of a block relative to the other blocks in the quilt.

Straight Set, Block-to-Block

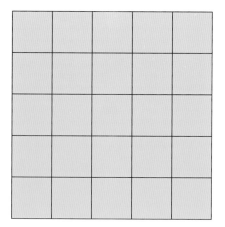

Straight Set with Continuous Sashing

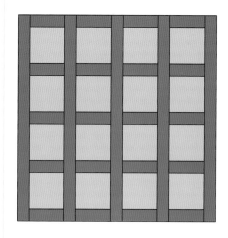

Diagonal Set with Floating Blocks

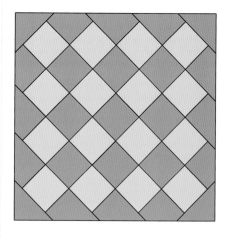

Straight Set with Alternate Squares

Straight Set with Sashing Strips and Squares (Cornerstones)

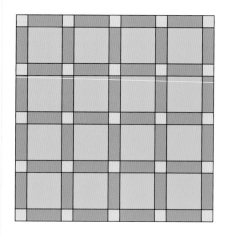

Diagonal Set with Continuous Sashing

Straight Set with Alternate Blocks

Diagonal Set

Diagonal Set with Sashing Strips and Squares

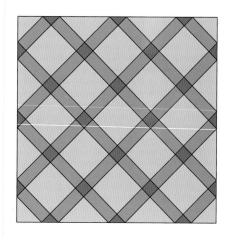

Vertical or Zigzag Set

ASSEMBLING STRAIGHT-SET BLOCKS AND ROWS

(See Chapter 4—Planning the Quilt Top for information on choosing a straight setting for your quilt blocks.)

1. After selecting the desired straight-set block arrangement, lay out the blocks in horizontal rows. *Note:* Fabric squares were substituted for pieced blocks in the photographs that follow. If you are including sashing between blocks, layout the sashing pieces now, too.

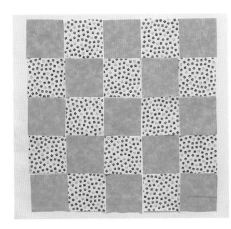

2. With right sides together and raw edges aligned, join together the blocks (or blocks and sashing pieces) in each row.

3. Press the seam allowances to one side, pressing each row in alternate directions. For example, press the seam allowances in row 1 and all odd-numbered rows to the right, and press the seam allowances in row 2 and all even-numbered rows to the left. Then when you assemble the rows, the alternated seam allowances will lock together, ensuring matching seams.

4. Pin together rows 1 and 2, taking care to match the seam intersections. You may need to ease the blocks a slight bit to ensure that the raw edges align. If one row is significantly shorter or longer, check your seam allowances to see if one is too narrow or too deep. If so, remove the seam and restitch it before joining the rows. Sew the rows together, backstitching at the beginning and end to secure the seam line and stabilize the quilt edge. Trim any threads and/or dog-ears.

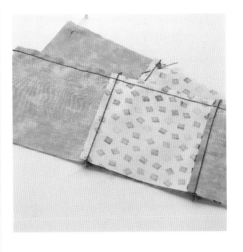

5. Continue joining rows in pairs (for example, join row 3 to row 4, row 5 to row 6, and so forth).

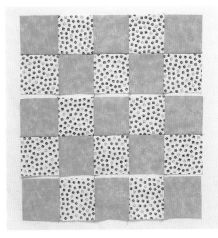

6. Then sew together the joined rows to complete the quilt center. Press all seam allowances in the same direction.

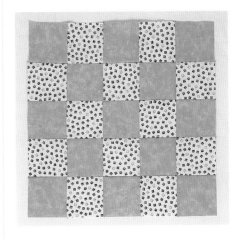

ASSEMBLING DIAGONALLY SET BLOCKS AND ROWS

(See Chapter 4—Planning the Quilt Top for information on choosing a diagonal setting for your quilt blocks.)

Quilt tops with blocks set diagonally, or on point, can be a bit more challenging to piece than straight-set blocks. Because you are sewing in diagonal rows, you may have a greater tendency to stretch or distort the quilt blocks as you piece them together.

It is essential to cut side setting triangles and corner setting triangles so the straight grain edge will be along the outer edges of the quilt. This will help prevent your quilt from becoming distorted or sagging. (See Chapter 5—Cutting for complete information on cutting setting triangles and setting squares. *Note:* Some quilters prefer to cut their side and corner setting triangles ½" to 1" larger than required and trim away the excess fabric after piecing the top. The measurements given in the Quick Reference Chart for Setting Triangles and Setting Squares in Chapter 5 are mathematically correct and do not allow for any excess fabric.)

Seams don't match? Did you square up your blocks? If so and the blocks still don't line up in rows the way you'd like, take the time to remove stitching and rejoin blocks until the seams do match.

1. After selecting the desired diagonally set block arrangement, lay out blocks and setting squares in diagonal rows. If you are including sashing between blocks, lay out the sashing pieces now, too.

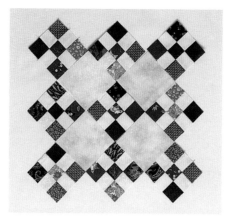

2. Add the side setting triangles and corner setting triangles to the layout.

3. With right sides together and raw edges aligned, join together the blocks (or blocks and sashing

pieces) in each row. Sew the setting triangles to the ends of each row. Do not add the corner triangles.

4. Press the seam allowances to one side, pressing each row in alternate directions. For example, press the seam allowances in row 1 and all odd-numbered rows to the right, and press the seam allowances in row 2 and all even-numbered rows to the left. Then when you assemble the rows, the alternated seam allowances will lock together, ensuring matching seams.

TIP: Reverse Sewing Direction by Row
Some quilters like to alternate the sewing direction of their rows when assembling a quilt center. If you tend to pull on your rows of blocks as you stitch them together and notice any distortion in the finished quilt top, try stitching one row left to right, the next right to left.

5. Pin together rows 1 and 2, taking care to match seam intersections. You may need to ease the blocks a slight bit to ensure that the raw edges align. If one row is significantly shorter or longer, check your seam allowances to see if one is too narrow or too deep. If so, remove the seam and restitch it before joining the rows. Sew the rows together, backstitching at the beginning and end to secure the seam line and stabilize the quilt edge. Trim any threads and/or dog-ears.

TIP: If you're having difficulty aligning seams when sewing rows together, try sewing with the seam allowances on top facing away from you as you guide the rows under the presser foot. This forces the top seam to butt up to the lower seam so the two automatically lock together.

6. Continue joining rows in pairs (for example, join row 3 to row 4, row 5 to row 6, and so forth). Then sew together the joined rows.

7. Sew the setting corner triangles to the pieced rows to complete the quilt center. (The ¼" seam allowances of the corner triangles will extend beyond the edge of the quilt center.) Press all seams allowances in the same direction. Trim any threads and dog-ears.

Note: If you chose to cut your side and corner triangles larger than specified, you will need to trim them now, leaving a ¼" seam allowance outside the corners of the pieced blocks.

BORDERS

Just as a mat and frame enhance a picture, borders can make a big difference in the finished appearance of your quilt. There are myriad possibilities for adding a single or multiple rows of borders to a quilt (see Chapter 4—Planning the Quilt Top for information on choosing a border design for your quilt).

ADDING STRAIGHT BORDERS

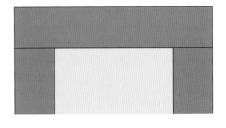

1. Place the assembled quilt center on a flat surface. *Note:* You may wish to use the chart on *page 9–6* along with steps 1 through 4 that follow. To determine the border strip width to cut, add ½" for seam allowances to the desired finished border strip width.

For border strips, measure the quilt center in both directions through the center to ensure straight sides and square corners. Measuring along the edges is less accurate because they may have stretched during assembly.

DETERMINING YARDAGE FOR STRAIGHT BORDERS

The border strip width will be cut the desired finished width plus ½" for seam allowances.

SIDE BORDER STRIPS:

Measure vertically (top to bottom) through the center of the quilt center (including seam allowances).

For side edges, you will need 2 strips, each = _____" long (A)

For example, if the measurement is 40", including seam allowances, (A) = 40".

TOP AND BOTTOM BORDER STRIPS:

Measure horizontally (side to side) through the center of the quilt center (including seam allowances). _____"

Multiply width of side border strips (including seam allowances) by 2.

Add to first measurement +_____"

Subtract 1" for seam allowances -1"

For top and bottom edges, you will need 2 strips, each =_____" long (B)

For example, if the measurement is 30", including seam allowances, and the width of the side border strips is 3", including seam allowances, then 30" + (3" × 2) - 1" = 35" (B).

YARDAGE REQUIRED TO CUT BORDER STRIPS LENGTHWISE:

FOR BORDER WIDTH UP TO 10½":

Divide larger of (A) or (B) by 36" = _____ yards

For example, if (A) measures 40" and (B) is 35", (A) is larger than (B), so 40" (A) divided by 36" = 1.11 yards, which rounded up would be 1⅛ yards. Note: With a border up to 10½"-wide, you can cut at least four border strips the length (parallel to the selvage) of the 42"-wide fabric. In some cases, if your border strips are narrower, you may be able to cut more strips from the length.

FOR BORDER WIDTH 10¾" TO 20":

Divide (A + B) by 36" = _____ yards

For example, if the quilt center measures 60×40" and you want to add a 15"-wide border, 60"(A) + 40"(B) = 100" of border length needed divided by 36" = 2.77 yards, which rounded up would be 2⅞ yards. Note: With a border up to 20"-wide, you can cut at least two border strips the length (parallel to the selvage) of the 42"-wide fabric. In some cases, if your border strips are narrower, you may be able to cut three strips from the length.

YARDAGE REQUIRED TO CUT BORDER STRIPS CROSSWISE:

Take measurements for (A) and (B) as described above.

(A + B) × 2 = ____ (C), or total inches of border needed.

Divide (C) by 42" (round up to next whole number) = _____ (D)
or number of strips that will need to be cut.

Add 1 strip to allow for diagonal seaming of border strips + 1 = _____ (E)

Multiply (E) × width of border, then divide by 36" = _____ yards

For example, if 40" (A) + 35" (B) × 2 = 150" (C) of border needed. 150" (C) divided by 42" = 3.57 rounded up would be 4 (D) strips to cut. 4 (D) + 1= 5 (E) strips. 5 (E) strips × 3"-wide border, divided by 36"= .42 or ½ yard. Note: For information on piecing crosswise border strips, see page 9-8.

2. To determine the length of the border strips for the side edges, measure through the center of the quilt center from top to bottom.

3. To determine the length of the top and bottom borders, measure through the center of the assembled quilt center from side to side. Add twice the width of the side border strip (including seam allowances), then subtract 1" (for the seam allowances). For example, if the quilt center measures 18" from side to side and the side border strips are 2½" wide, add 18" + 5" - 1" = 22". In this case, you would cut your top and bottom border strips 2½×22" long.

Cut border strips on the lengthwise grain of fabric whenever possible. The lengthwise grain has less stretch than crosswise grain and is more stable. Cut borders on crosswise grain only when the amount of fabric is limited.

4. Cut the border strips on the lengthwise grain of fabric for less stretch and more stability. Cut on the crosswise grain only if the quantity of yardage on hand is limited. Rotary-cut straight borders whenever possible (see Chapter 5—Cutting for more information on cutting border strips).

5. Fold each side border strip in half crosswise and press lightly to mark the center.

6. Fold the pieced quilt center in half and press lightly to mark the center of the side edges.

7. With right sides together and raw edges aligned, pin and sew the border strips to the side edges of the pieced quilt center with ¼" seam allowances, matching the center fold lines. If you need to ease in a slight amount of fullness, sew with the

longer fabric piece next to the feed dogs.

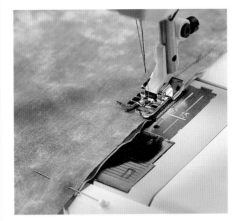

8. Press the seam allowances toward the border.

9. Repeat steps 5 and 6 to mark the centers of the top and bottom border strips and the pieced quilt center.

If you need to press a dark seam allowance toward a light piece, trim the sewn darker seam allowance slightly to prevent it from showing through.

10. Pin and sew the top and bottom border strips to the top and bottom edges of the quilt center as before.

11. Press the seam allowances toward the border.

12. Repeat the steps as necessary to add additional borders.

TIP: Aligning Fold Marks
When you fold and press to mark the center edges of the assembled quilt center and border strips, fold so the layers will nest. Fold the quilt center with the right side inside; press. Fold the border strips with the wrong sides inside; press. The two folds will snuggle together to make a perfect match.

PIECING CROSSWISE BORDER STRIPS

Cutting borders lengthwise is preferable to cutting them crosswise. But if you have a limited amount of the "perfect" fabric available for your quilt project, cutting crosswise strips may be your only option. Follow these steps to join crosswise border strips with diagonal seams.

1. Cut crosswise fabric strips the desired width of the border plus ½" for seam allowances. Cut enough strips to equal the total length needed for each side of the quilt, plus one extra strip. The extra strip will provide you with enough additional length to allow for the fabric that is lost as a result of diagonal seams.

2. Position the strips perpendicular to one another with the raw edges aligned and right sides together.

3. Mark, then join the strips with diagonal seams to make a border strip. *Note:* In most cases, diagonal seams are

preferable to straight seams because they are visually less distracting in the finished quilt.

4. Press the seam allowance open.

5. Trim the seam allowance to ¼". Trim the border strip to the desired length, including seam allowances.

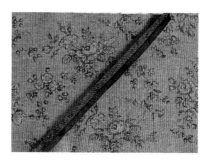

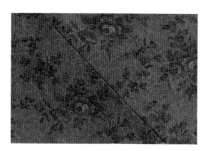

ADDING STRAIGHT BORDERS WITH CORNER SQUARES OR BLOCKS

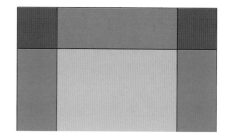

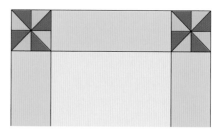

1. Lay the quilt top on a flat surface. *Note:* You may wish to use the chart opposite along with steps 1 through 5 that follow. To determine the border strip width to cut, add ½" for seam allowances to the desired finished border strip width.

2. To determine the length of side border strips, measure through the center of the assembled quilt center from top to bottom (including seam allowances).

3. To determine the length of top and bottom border strips, measure through the center of the quilt center from side to side (including seam allowances).

4. To determine the dimensions of corner squares or blocks, measure the width of the side border strip including seam allowances.

5. Cut the border strips on the lengthwise grain of the fabric, if possible. It has less stretch and more stability than the crosswise grain.

6. Fold each side border strip in half crosswise and press lightly to mark the center.

7. Fold the quilt center in half and press lightly to mark the center of the side edges.

8. With right sides together and raw edges aligned, pin and sew the side border strips to the side edges of the quilt center with ¼" seams, matching the center fold lines. Press the seam allowances toward the border.

9. Sew a corner square or block to each end of the top and bottom border strips. Press the seam allowances toward the border strip.

DETERMINING YARDAGE FOR STRAIGHT BORDERS WITH CORNER SQUARES OR BLOCKS

The border strip width will be cut the desired finished width plus ½" for seam allowances.

SIDE BORDER STRIPS:

Measure vertically (top to bottom) through the center of the quilt center (including seam allowances).

For side edges, you'll need 2 strips, each ⟶ = _____" long **(A)**

For example, if the measurement is 40", including seam allowances, (A) = 40".

TOP AND BOTTOM BORDER STRIPS:

Measure horizontally (side to side) through the center of the quilt center (including seam allowances).

For top and bottom edges, you'll need 2 strips, each ⟶ = _____" long **(B)**

For example, if the measurement is 35", including seam allowances, (B) = 35".

CORNER SQUARES (PIECED BLOCKS MAY BE SUBSTITUTED):

Measure the width of the side border (including seam allowances) _____

Multiply sum by 4 _____"

For corner squares or blocks, you'll need 4 squares from a __"-long strip **(C)**

For example, if finished width of the side border is 3", (3" + ½") x 4 = 3½ × 14" long strip needed. You will subcut the strip into four 3½" squares.

YARDAGE REQUIRED TO CUT BORDER STRIPS LENGTHWISE:

FOR BORDER WIDTH UP TO 10½":

Divide larger of (A) or (B) by 36" = _____ **yards**

For example, if (A) measures 40" and (B) is 35", (A) is larger than (B), so 40" (A) divided by 36" = 1.11 yards, which rounded up would be 1⅛ yards. Note: With a border up to 10½"-wide, you can cut at least four border strips the length (parallel to the selvage) of the 42"-wide fabric. In some cases, if your border strips are narrower, you may be able to cut more strips from the length.

FOR BORDER WIDTH 10¾" TO 20":

Divide (A + B) by 36" = _____ **yards**

For example, if the quilt center measures 60×40" and you want to add a 15"-wide border, 60"(A) + 40"(B) = 100" of border length needed divided by 36" = 2.77 yards, which rounded up would be 2⅞ yards. Note: With a border up to 20"-wide, you can cut at least two border strips the length (parallel to the selvage) of the 42"-wide fabric. In some cases, if your border strips are narrower, you may be able to cut three strips from the length.

YARDAGE REQUIRED TO CUT BORDER STRIPS CROSSWISE:

Take measurements for (A) and (B) as described above.

(A + B) × 2 = _____ **(D)**, or total inches of border needed.

Divide (D) by 42" (round up to next whole number) = ____ **(E)** or number of strips that will need to be cut.

Add 1 strip to allow for diagonal seaming of border strips + 1 = _____ **(F)**

Multiply (F) × width of border, then divide by 36" = _____ **yards**

For example, if 40" (A) + 35" (B) × 2 = 150" (D) of border needed. 150" (D) divided by 42" = 3.57 rounded up would be 4 (E) strips to cut. 4 (E) + 1= 5 (F) strips. 5 (F) strips × 3"-wide border, divided by 36"= .42 or ½ yard. Note: For information on piecing crosswise border strips, see page 9-8.

10. Pin and sew the borders to top and bottom edges of the quilt center, matching center fold lines, ends, and seams. Press the seam allowances toward the border.

TROUBLESHOOTING TIP:

Having trouble getting the border strip to fit?
Compare the measurements of your assembled quilt top with the mathematical dimensions of the finished quilt top given in the pattern. Do this by taking your finished block width (or length) times the number of blocks and finished sashing width (or length) times the number of pieces. Are your measured dimensions the same as the pattern's dimensions? If the two figures are similar, use the pattern measurements for the border sizes. If the figures are quite different, use your actual quilt center measurements to figure border strips measurements and make any adjustments to border embellishments as you proceed.

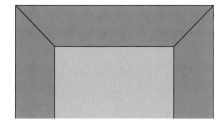

1. Lay the assembled quilt center on a flat surface. *Note:* You may wish to use the chart opposite along with steps 1 through 4 that follow. To determine the border strip width to cut, add ½" for seam allowances to the desired finished border strip width.

2. To determine the length of the side border strips, measure through the center of the quilt center from top to bottom, then add twice the finished width of the border to allow for mitering, plus 1" for seam allowances.

3. To determine the length of the top and bottom border strips, measure through the center of the quilt center from side to side, then add twice the finished width of the border to allow for mitering, plus 1" for seam allowances.

4. Cut the border strips on the lengthwise grain of the fabric, if possible. It has less stretch and more stability than the crosswise grain.

5. Fold each border strip in half crosswise and press lightly to mark the center. (See the tip for Aligning Fold Marks on *page 9–7.*) Fold the assembled quilt center in half and press lightly to mark the center of the side edges.

6. To ensure accuracy when pinning border strips to the quilt top, measure and mark the length of the quilt center on each side. Divide the quilt center's length by 2, and measure this amount in both directions from the center crease on the border strip. Make a mark at each measured point, which should correspond to the quilt center corner.

7. With right sides together and centers and corner marks aligned, pin a side border strip to one side edge of the quilt center, allowing the excess border strip to extend beyond the corner edges. Sew together, beginning and ending ¼" from the quilt center's corners. Repeat with the opposite side border strip.

8. Repeat steps 6 and 7 with top and bottom border strips. Press the seam allowances toward the border strips.

9. With the wrong side up, overlap the border strips at one corner.

10. Align the edge of a 90° right triangle with the raw edge of a top border strip so the long edge of the triangle intersects the seam in the corner. With a pencil, draw along the edge of the triangle between the border seam and the raw edge.

11. Place the bottom border strip on top and repeat the marking process.

DETERMINING YARDAGE FOR MITERED BORDERS

The border strip width will be cut the desired finished width plus ½" for seam allowances.

SIDE BORDER STRIPS:

Measure vertically (top to bottom) through the center of the quilt center
(including seam allowances). _____"

Determine finished width of border _____

Add twice the finished width of the border to allow for mitering + _____"

Add 1" for seam allowances + _____"

For side borders you will need 2 strips, each = _____" **long (A)**

For example, if the side edge measurement is 40", including seam allowances, and the finished width of a border strip is 3", then 40"+ 6" + 1" = 47" (A).

TOP AND BOTTOM BORDER STRIPS:

Measure horizontally (side to side) through the center of the quilt center
(including seam allowances) _____"

Determine finished width of border _____

Add twice the finished width of the border to allow for mitering + _____"

Add 1" for seam allowances + _____"

For top and bottom borders you will need 2 strips, each = _____" **long (B)**

For example, if the measurement is 35", including seam allowances, and the finished width of the border is 3", then 35" + 6" + 1" = 42" (B).

YARDAGE REQUIRED TO CUT BORDER STRIPS LENGTHWISE:

FOR BORDER WIDTH UP TO 10½":

Larger of (A) or (B) divided by 36" = _____ **yards**

Using the example above, (A) is larger than (B), so 47" (A) divided by 36" = 1.30 yards, which rounded up would be 1⅓ yards Note: With a border up to 10½"-wide, you can cut at least four border strips the length (parallel to the selvage) of the 42"-wide fabric. In some cases, if your border strips are narrower, you may be able to cut more strips from the length.

FOR BORDER WIDTH 10¾" TO 20":

Divide (A + B) by 36" = _____ **yards**

For example, if the quilt center measures 60×40" and you want to add an 11"-wide border, 60" + 22" + 1"= 83"(A) and 40" + 22" +1"= 63"(B). 83" + 63" divided by 36" = 4.05 yards, which rounded up would be 4⅛ yards. Note: With a border up to 20"-wide, you can cut at least two border strips the length (parallel to the selvage) of the 42"-wide fabric. In some cases, if your border strips are narrower, you may be able to cut three strips from the length.

YARDAGE REQUIRED TO CUT BORDER STRIPS CROSSWISE:

Take measurements for (A) and (B) as described above.

(A + B) × 2 = ____ (C), or total inches of border needed.

Divide (C) by 42" (round up to next whole number) = _____ **(D)**
or the number of strips that will need to be cut.

Add 1 strip to allow for diagonal seaming of border strips + 1 = _____ **(E)**

Multiply (E) × width of border, then divide by 36" = _____ **yards**

For example, if 47" (A) + 42" (B) × 2 = 178" (C) of border needed. 178" (C) divided by 42" = 4.24, which rounded up would be 5 (D) strips. 5 (D) +1=6 (E) strips. 6 (E) strips × 3"-wide border, divided by 36" = .5 or ½ yard. Note: For information on piecing crosswise border strips, see page 9-8.

12. With the right sides of adjacent border strips together, match the marked seam lines and pin.

13. Beginning with a backstitch at the inside corner, stitch exactly on the marked lines to the outside edges of the border strips. Check the right side of the corner to see that it lies flat.

14. Trim the excess fabric, leaving a ¼" seam allowance.

15. Press the seam open.

16. Repeat steps 9 through 15 to mark and sew the remaining border corners in the same manner.

MULTIPLE BORDERS WITH MITERED CORNERS

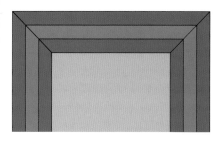

If you are making more than one mitered border, join strips for each edge together lengthwise (matching the center lines) and sew the joined border strips to the assembled quilt center edges as a unit. Press the seam allowances in alternate directions on adjoining border edges and the seam allowances will match more easily at the miter line.

APPLIQUÉ BORDERS

Appliquéing borders may be done before or after the border strips are joined to the quilt center, depending on your personal preference.

APPLIQUÉING BORDER STRIPS BEFORE JOINING THEM TO THE QUILT CENTER

If you wish to appliqué your border strips before joining them to the quilt center, follow these steps.

1. Some patterns that call for the appliqué to be done before the borders are added will have the border strips cut larger than necessary to assure that fabric "taken up" in appliqué stitching will not affect the overall desired size of the finished border. You may wish to cut your border strips longer and wider than specified if the pattern does not allow for this.

2. Appliqué the pieces using your desired method (see Chapter 8—Appliqué for more information on appliqué methods). If you do add excess width and length, do not place appliqué pieces too near the outside edge, as they could be cut off in trimming the outer edge, or covered by the binding. Do not add any appliqués at the border strip ends that will cover or come within 1" of a straight or mitered seam.

3. After appliquéing is completed, trim the border strips to the specified size if excess allowance was added. Join the border strips to the assembled quilt center following the instructions for your desired method (see Adding Straight Borders on *page 9–5* or Adding Mitered Borders on *page 9–10)*.

4. Complete the unfinished appliqué where it crosses or comes near the seams.

APPLIQUÉING BORDER STRIPS AFTER JOINING THEM TO THE QUILT CENTER

If you wish to appliqué your border strips after joining them to the quilt center, follow these steps.

1. Some patterns call for the outer edge of the border strips to be trimmed after the appliqué is added to allow for the fabric that might be "taken up" in appliqué stitching. You may wish to cut your border strips larger than specified if the pattern does not allow for this.

2. Join the border strips to the assembled quilt center following the instructions for the desired method (see Adding Straight Borders on *page 9–5* or Adding Mitered Borders on *page 9–10)*.

3. Appliqué the pieces using your desired method (see Chapter 8— Appliqué). If you added excess width and length to your strips, do not appliqué pieces too near the outside edge, as they could be cut off in trimming, or covered by the binding.

4. After appliquéing is completed, trim the border strips to the specified size if excess allowance was added.

PIECED BORDERS

Borders made up of blocks or pieced units are sewn to quilt edges in the same way as straight borders are. Follow the instructions for Adding Straight Borders on *page 9–5* or Adding Straight Borders with Corner Squares or Blocks on *page 9–8* to create the desired length border strips from blocks or pieced units. (See Chapter 4—Planning the Quilt Top for information on how to design a pieced border.) Pay special attention to the layout of the pieced blocks and, if the units are directional, how they turn the

corners. It is best to have all four corners of a quilt top match.

If this isn't possible, use corner blocks rather than pieced units to avoid taking the focus off the center of your quilt.

Make sure that the finished size of your border block divides evenly into the finished size of your assembled quilt center. This will prevent you from having to use partial blocks in the border.

PIECED BORDERS WITH DIAGONALLY SET BLOCKS

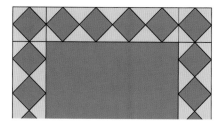

Borders that contain blocks or units set diagonally, or on point, are easiest to use on a plain quilt center or a quilt center with blocks set on point. Refer to the Quick Reference Chart for Diagonal Measurements of Standard Blocks in Chapter 5— Cutting for mathematical help in planning a diagonally set border. Make sure that the finished size of your border block divides evenly into the finished size of your pieced quilt center. This will prevent you from having to use partial blocks in the border. (For information on designing a diagonally set border, see Chapter 4—Planning the Quilt Top.)

SCALLOPED BORDERS

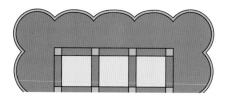

Scallops on borders are marked after the border strips are sewn to the assembled quilt center. They are cut after the hand or machine quilting is complete. To plan a scalloped border, follow these steps.

1. Once the border strips have been added, measure the width and length of the assembled quilt top.

2. Decide on the approximate width of each scallop. In choosing a width, select a number that is divisible into both the width and length of your quilt top. Use the approximate width to determine how many scallops per edge. For example, if your quilt top measures 50×70" and you'd like each scallop to be 10" wide, the top and bottom borders would have five scallops each and the side borders would have seven scallops each.

3. Draw the desired scallop on a strip of paper as long as a border. (Rolls of adding machine paper work well for marking shallow scallops.) In this example, you would place two dots 10" apart on the top edge of the paper to mark the top of the scallop. Draw a line between these dots. Make another set of dots between 1" and 2" directly below the first marks. The depth between the first and second marks will determine how deep the indentations or Vs are in the scallops (the sharper the V, the more difficult it is to bind).

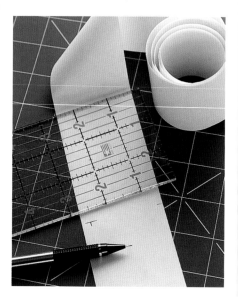

4. Using a compass, jar lid, plate, or other rounded edge as a guide, join the second set of marks with a gentle curve that just touches the line drawn between the first set of marks.

5. Once you've created a scallop you like, draw it along the complete length of the paper strip to make a template. Repeat to make as many different-size templates as needed.

6. Position the paper templates on the quilt top and check the corners. You will need to blend the curves of the scallops to round the corners. Once you've blended the edges of one corner, make a paper template of it and trace three more identical paper templates for the remaining corners. Use your paper templates to mark the pattern on your quilt top (see Chapter 5—Cutting for information on marking your quilt top).

Directional borders are those which have designs running in a particular sequence or order. For instance, sawtooth borders are made up of a series of triangle-squares. Since borders need to appear the same on all four sides, careful planning is required to turn corners smoothly and keep the design moving in the right direction. Sketch your border on paper before proceeding with assembly. Occasionally, directional borders require a special corner unit or block to make the transition from side to side (see Chapter 4— Planning the Quilt Top for more information).

SPACER BORDERS

Spacer borders are plain borders that are sewn between the quilt center and outer pieced borders. Think of a spacer border as an inside mat or one part of a double mat on a framed picture. Spacer borders are a good solution when the dimensions of the pieced border and the pieced quilt center are not compatible, or whenever you'd like to have some visual breathing room between the quilt center and the outer border.

Spacer borders can be the same width on all sides of a quilt, or they can be one width on the sides and another on the top and bottom.

When the same fabric used for the assembled quilt center is used for a spacer border, it can make the center blocks appear to float within the confines of the spacer border.

A spacer border of contrasting fabric calls attention to the separation between the quilt center and the outer border.

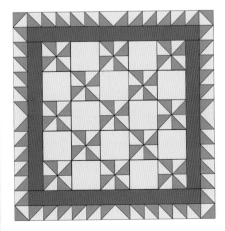

USING BORDER PRINTS FOR MITERED BORDERS

Mitered borders made of a print or striped fabric add complexity to the look of a quilt with little extra work. You may need to purchase extra fabric so all the corners will match.

MITERED BORDER-PRINT BORDERS ON A SQUARE QUILT

If you are making a square quilt with a border print border, place like motifs at the center of each side edge so the mitered corners and edges will match.

1. Determine the yardage and measurements for your border strips following Determining Yardage for Mitered Borders on *page 9–11*. The yardage needed depends on the pattern repeat of the border print across the width of the fabric. For example, if you're making a 4"-wide finished border and the motif is repeated every 6" across the width of the fabric, all borders can be cut from one length of fabric. If you are making a 4"-wide finished border and the motif you wish to use is printed only once across the width of the fabric, only one border can be cut from one length of fabric. You will need a total of four lengths to make the border.

2. Cut the four border strips from the same lengthwise repeat of the border print.

3. Join the border strips to the assembled quilt center following the instructions for Adding Mitered Borders on *page 9–10*, beginning with Step 5.

MITERED BORDER-PRINT BORDERS ON A RECTANGULAR QUILT

1. Determine the yardage and measurement for your border strips following Determining Yardage for Mitered Borders on *page 9–11*. The yardage needed depends on the pattern repeat of the border print across the width of the fabric, the pattern repeat of the border print along the length of the fabric, and where the border strips will join. Cut the two side border strips first from the same lengthwise repeat of the border print, selecting a motif to be at their centers.

2. Join each side border strip to the side edges of the quilt center, following directions given in Adding Mitered Borders on *page 9–10,* steps 5 through 7.

3. Fold the border strip corners back at 45° angles as if to miter.

4. Cut the top and bottom border strips from the same lengthwise repeat of the border print, selecting the same motif used at the center of the side border strips for the centers of the top and bottom border strips.

5. Lay the quilt center with its attached side border strips right side up on a work surface. Align the centers of the top border strip and upper edge of the quilt center, allowing the excess top border strip to extend under the side border strips.

6. Make a pleat at the center of the top border strip and pull the border strip fabric into the pleat until the desired motif appears at a corner. Pleat an equal amount of fabric from each side of center on the top border strip.

7. Fold the pleat to the wrong side of the top border strip and pin. The pleat should align with the marked midpoint on the top edge of the quilt center.

8. Pin the border strips with right sides together at the corners.

9. Sew the pleat along the fold lines. Trim the seam allowance to ¼" and press open. Then sew the border strip to the quilt center, joining the corners following Adding Mitered Borders on *page 9–11*, beginning with Step 9.

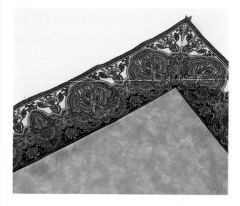

10. Repeat steps 5 through 9 to add the bottom border strip.

My Notes for Assembling the Quilt Top

Batting & Backing

10

TABLE OF CONTENTS
CHAPTER 10—Batting & Backing

QUILTER TESTED FOR ACCURACY

YOUR BEAUTIFUL QUILT TOP DESERVES A BATTING AND BACKING that will enhance the finished project and be suited to its use. Historically, quiltmakers used whatever natural fibers were on hand for the quilt's middle layer or batting, but today's quilters can choose from natural and synthetic products that have a variety of characteristics.

BATTING

Batting is the soft layer between the quilt top and backing that gives a quilt dimension and definition and offers warmth.

Because it comes in various thicknesses and fibers, it can make a quilt flat or puffy, stiff or drapable. It is available by the yard or packaged to fit standard bed sizes.

The batting you use should complement the nature and use of your finished quilt. Check package labels, talk to other quilters, and test samples to find the batting with the qualities that are important for your project.

MANUFACTURING PROCESS

All battings start out as individual fibers that are carded and processed into a sheet or web. Without further treatment, these battings would be difficult to use as the unbonded fibers would come apart or clump together inside a quilt. An untreated batting also would be susceptible to bearding or fiber migration (when

batting fibers come through the quilt top).

To make a sheet or web of batting more stable, and hence more useable, it's either bonded or needle-punched, treatment processes that result in battings with different characteristics.

BONDING

Manufacturers chemically bond batting fibers by adding a resin or using heat. Resin bonding helps wool or polyester battings resist bearding.

Bonded batts usually have a higher loft and airier appearance than needle-punched batts. A bonded batting holds up well with use and does not require extensive quilting. If a batting is not bonded, it can be difficult to work with and have an uneven appearance.

NEEDLE-PUNCHED

This treatment process involves running a barbed needle through the batting fibers to "tangle" them and provide some stability to the web. For additional stability, a scrim—a loosely woven piece of fabric that resembles a net—can be added to a batting sheet or web before it's needle-punched.

The loft of needle-punched batting varies according to the number of layers used in the manufacturing process. The fewer the layers, the lower the loft; the lower the loft, the better fine-quilting details can be seen.

BLEACHING

Natural batting fibers are ecru in color. They can be bleached to create bright white battings for use with white or very light-color fabrics.

Carefully read the manufacturer's label to learn the specific qualities of a particular batting.

BEARDING

Some battings beard, or have fibers migrate through the quilt top, more than others, but any bearding is a problem when light battings are used with dark fabrics, or the reverse. Test battings with your quilt's fabrics to see if bearding will be a problem. (See Testing on *page 10-5* for more information about selecting the best batting for your project.) Make sure you're not using an untreated batting. Though bearding can be attributed to a problem with your batting choice, it also could be caused by a very loosely woven fabric. Knowing what qualities to watch for can make a significant difference in your satisfaction with the finished quilt.

TIP: Try black batting. It is difficult to avoid bearding when quilting large areas of black fabric. If you're working on a dark-color quilt, you may wish to consider a black batting.

DRAPABILITY

The density or sparseness of the quilting and the loft of the batting will affect the drape, or relative stiffness or softness, of the finished quilt. In general, a thinner batting and more dense quilting will result in a quilt with a softer drape. A thicker batting in a quilt that has been tied, rather than heavily quilted, will have less drape.

GRAIN LINE

Battings can have a grain line just as fabric does. The lengthwise grain is stable and doesn't have much give, while the crosswise grain will be stretchy. In order to prevent unwanted distortion, match the batting's lengthwise grain with the backing fabric's lengthwise grain. Quilt the lengthwise grain first to limit distortion.

LOFT

The thickness of a batting is referred to as its loft. Differing loft levels result in differing appearances in a finished quilt. Refer to the chart at *right* to choose a loft compatible with your finishing method.

Keep in mind that the higher the loft, the less drapability in the finished quilt.

RESILIENCY

Resiliency refers to the batting's ability to regain its original shape. A resilient batting, such as one made from polyester, will spring back when unfolded and resist creasing. This may be a desirable feature if you want a finished quilt with a puffy appearance. Cotton battings are less resilient and more prone to creasing, but some of their other qualities may compensate and make their use desirable. A cotton/polyester blend batting is somewhere in between in terms of resilience.

WARMTH

Cotton battings have the ability to absorb moisture, thus offering cooling comfort in the summer and a natural warmth in the winter. Wool battings provide warmth with little weight. Synthetic fibers, such as polyester, lack the breathability of natural fibers.

WASHABILITY AND SHRINKAGE

Although polyester and wool battings resist shrinkage, cotton battings can shrink from 3 to 5 percent. Check the package label, then decide whether or not to preshrink a batting. Some quilters prefer the puckered, antique look that comes from a batting that shrinks after it's been quilted.

Choose a batting for your project based on the finished quilt's intended use and desired appearance.

QUILTING DISTANCE

The distance between quilting stitches is largely determined by batting qualities. The manufacturer's label will specify the maximum distance between stitching rows. If you exceed the recommended maximum distance, your batting will shift and bunch up later.

If you know you want to tie your finished quilt project, it is essential that you select a quilt batting that allows a wide distance between stitches. A heavily quilted design will require a different choice of batting. Always refer to the package label to see if the batting you're considering is compatible with the amount of quilting you plan to do on your project.

QUICK REFERENCE CHART
BATTING LOFT AND CORRESPONDING FINISHING METHODS

Consider how you'll be quilting your project and use the chart below to select an appropriate batting loft.

LOW LOFT	MEDIUM LOFT	HIGH LOFT
Hand and machine quilting	Hand and machine quilting	Tied quilts, comforters

QUICK REFERENCE CHART
GENERAL BATTING CHARACTERISTICS

BATTING TYPE	ADVANTAGES	DISADVANTAGES	CHARACTERISTICS
100% Cotton	Natural fiber so batting breathes. Resists fiber migration. Readily available.	May have seeds and plant residue that can release oils and stain the quilt. Often cannot be prewashed. Shrinks 3 to 5% when washed. May be too dense for beginning hand quilters to needle.	Can give a puckered appearance if washed after quilted. Soft, drapable. Good for experienced quilters' fine, hand-quilting stitches or machine quilting.
Cotton/Polyester Blends: 80/20, 50/50	Some natural fibers so batting breathes. Resists fiber migration. Easy for beginning hand quilters to needle. Readily available.	Some shrinkage, which can be avoided in many cases, if desired, by prewashing.	Low to medium loft. Drapable. Good for hand quilting and machine quilting.
Wool and Wool Blends	Natural insulator. Preshrunk. Available in black.	May have inconsistent loft. May need to be encased in cheesecloth or scrim if not bonded.	Blend of fibers from different animal breeds. Resiliency enhances quilting stitches. Soft, drapable. Good for hand and machine quilting.
Silk	Good choice for quilted garments. Does not shrink. Can be washed.	Expensive. Not widely available. Damaged by exposure to direct sunlight.	Has excellent body and drape. Lightweight. Good for hand quilting and machine quilting.
Flannel	Lightweight alternative to traditional batting. Readily available.	Extreme low loft limits quilting pattern development.	100% cotton. Lightweight, thin. Good for machine quilting.
Polyester	Resilient, lightweight. Cannot be harmed by moths or mildew. Readily available. Available in black.	Synthetic fibers lack breathability.	Available in many lofts. Suitable for hand quilting and machine quilting. High loft is good for tied quilts, comforters.
Fusible	No need to prewash. Eliminates need for basting. Good choice for small projects.	Limited batting options and sizes. Adds adhesive to quilt. Difficult for hand quilters to needle.	Good for machine quilting. Eliminates need for basting.

QUICK REFERENCE CHART
BATTING OPTIONS AT A GLANCE

Find the finishing method you'll be using, then follow the appropriate column based on a few quick decisions. These options are very general recommendations meant to illustrate the process you'll go through to select a batting for your next project. Before making a final decision, carefully weigh all your options based on the complete information provided in this chapter.

WILL YOU BE HAND QUILTING?

Will your stitching be high density?	Will your stitching be medium density?	Will your stitching be low density?
Choose a low-loft batting.	Choose a medium-loft batting.	Choose a high-loft batting.
Batting options could include 100% cotton, cotton/polyester blend, or wool.	Batting options could include a cotton/polyester blend or wool.	This combination is not recommended as stitching will be lost in the batting's loft.

WILL YOU BE MACHINE QUILTING?

WILL YOU BE TYING THE QUILT?

Will your stitching be high density?	Will your stitching be low density?	Will you have few ties?
Choose a low-loft batting.	Choose a medium-loft batting.	Choose a medium- to high-loft batting.
Batting options could include cotton, cotton/polyester blend, or wool.	Batting options could include wool or a cotton/polyester blend.	Batting options could include polyester.

TIP: Is it possible to join two pieces of batting?
If your batting is too small, you can join two batting pieces to make the necessary size. Follow this process to prevent a seam line ridge where the pieces join. Overlap the batting pieces by several inches. Rotary-cut a rolling curve through the overlapped area. Remove the excess and butt the curved edges together. Use a herringbone stitch (diagram at *right*) to join the two pieces. (See Chapter 13— Specialty Techniques for complete instructions on the herringbone stitch.)

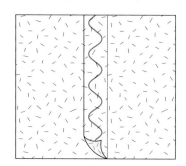
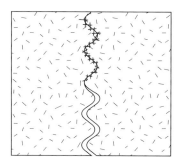

INTENDED USE

Consider the intended use of your quilt. Is it a baby quilt that will be washed and dried extensively? Will it be placed on a child's bed and get pulled and tugged? Are you making a wall hanging that needs to maintain sharp, crisp corners? Or are you making a quilt that you want to drape loosely over a bed and tuck beneath the pillows? Is it an heirloom project that will be used sparingly and only laundered once every few years? Or is it a decorative item that will never be washed? Is it a table runner that needs to lie extremely flat? Questions such as these will help you evaluate which batting is best for your project.

DESIRED APPEARANCE

Consider the fabrics in the quilt top and the backing. Are they light or dark colors? If you select a dark batting, will it show through the fabric? Would a white batting beard through the top?

Did you wash and dry your fabrics before making your quilt top, or do you want the layers to shrink as one after you've finished the project to result in an antique appearance?

What loft do you want your quilt to have? Do you want it to be big and puffy or flat and drapable?

QUILTING METHOD

Do you plan to quilt your project by hand or machine, or are you tying it? Do you want to use perle cotton and a utility stitch to create a folk art look?

The batting type dictates the spacing between rows of quilting, so determine whether you want dense or sparse stitching before selecting a batting. The manufacturer's label will specify the maximum distance. If you exceed this distance when quilting, your batting will shift and bunch up, causing your finished project to look uneven. If you want to tie a project, select a batting that specifies a wide distance between stitches.

FIBERS

Consider whether you want natural, synthetic, or a blend of fibers. Each has different qualities. (For more information, see the Quick Reference Chart General Batting Characteristics on *page 10–3*.)

SIZE

The quilt batting needs to be larger than the quilt top to allow for take-up during quilting and for stabilization when using a quilting frame. Add 6" to both the length and width measurements to allow an extra 3" of batting around the entire quilt.

TESTING

To be sure that you'll be satisfied with your choice of batting, test it with similar fabrics, thread, quilting technique, and washing process (if desired) used in the quilt top.

Use the note pages at the end of this chapter to record your results for future reference. Since same-type battings from different manufacturers can vary in qualities and results, keeping records of the battings you use and your personal preferences will help you make future selections.

In addition, when looking at other quilters' finished projects, ask the makers what battings they used. The answers can help you determine the finished appearance you prefer.

BACKING

Most quilters use a single fabric for the quilt back, thus keeping the focus on the quilt top. Some, however, enjoy adding a design to the quilt back, almost making the quilt reversible.

There are many options if you want to use multiple fabrics in your backing. You can piece leftover fabrics from the quilt top or from an entirely different quilt project.

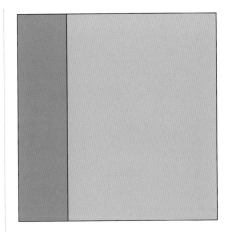

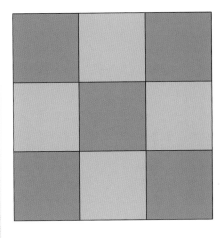

If you have unused blocks from the quilt top, join them to create a pieced quilt back.

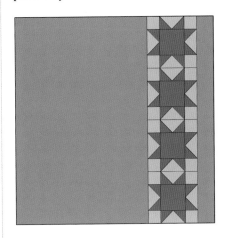

Another option is to enlarge a block used on the quilt top and use it as a focal point on the quilt back.

You could include a novelty print or a piece of treasured fabric "too good" to cut into pieces.

A quilt back is also a wonderful place to showcase an embroidered verse, a photo-transfer collage, or a sampling of coordinating test blocks remaining from previous projects.

If you're concerned about the quality of your hand or machine quilting, choose a backing fabric that will camouflage your stitches, such as a particularly busy one or one that matches the thread color used on the quilt top.

Although muslin is an inexpensive option for a quilt back, keep in mind that it shows every quilting detail and does little to enhance the beauty of your finished quilt.

Consider that a pieced back with many seams can make hand quilting difficult, since the needle must pierce several layers of fabric. A pieced back is of less concern when you're machine-quilting.

Backing fabrics should have the same care requirements as the quilt top and should be preshrunk if the quilt top fabrics were.

PREPARE THE BACKING FABRIC

Like batting, the quilt back needs to be larger than the quilt top to allow for fabric that is taken up during quilting and for stabilization when using a quilting frame. Always add 6" to both the length and width measurements so you have an extra 3" of fabric all around.

Trim off the selvage of all backing fabrics. The selvage edge is tighter than the rest of the yardage and can cause puckering or inward curving in your finished quilt if it is used as a part of the backing.

PLANNING THE QUILT BACK

If your quilt top is wider or longer than your backing fabric width, you will need to piece the backing. If seams are necessary, you need to decide whether you want the seams on the back to be horizontal or vertical.

If your quilt is 40 to 60" wide, horizontal seams save on yardage.

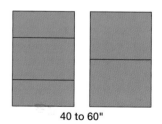

40 to 60"

If your quilt is wider than 60", you may use one or two vertical seams.

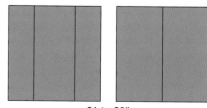

61 to 80"

QUICK REFERENCE CHART
BACKING YARDAGE GUIDE

QUILT TOP WIDTH	SEAM ORIENTATION	YARDAGE TO PURCHASE
40–60"	Horizontal	2 × width +12" ÷ 36"=
61–80"	Vertical	2 × length +12" ÷ 36"=
81–120"	Vertical	3 × length +18" ÷ 36"=

EXAMPLES

Width × Length	Seam Orientation	Figures	Add 6" per piece	Divide by 36"	Purchase
47×74"	Horizontal	47"× 2 widths	94"+12"=	106"÷36"=	3 yds.
70×84"	Vertical	84"× 2 lengths	168"+12"=	180"÷36"=	5 yds.
95×110"	Vertical	110"× 3 lengths	330"+18"=	348"÷36"=	9⅔ yds.

A quilt 81 to 120" wide requires a backing that is pieced with two vertical seams.

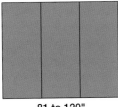

81 to 120"

The quilt top's measurement determines how many pieces are in the backing. For example, if one dimension of your quilt top is less than 36", you can use a single piece of 45"-wide fabric for the backing. This width will cover the 36" dimension plus the additional 6". In this case, add 6" to the remaining quilt top dimension and divide by 36" to determine the yardage necessary. *Note:* The calculations assume 42" of usable fabric can be cut from a 44/45"-wide fabric.

Manufacturers offer fabrics in widths of 60", 90", and 108", but they are available in a limited color and design assortment.

TIP: Bedsheets for backing—don't do it!
Although it's tempting to use a bedsheet because of its size, sheets don't make good quilt backs. The thread count is much higher in sheeting than in common quilting fabrics. The tighter weave causes the needle to break the sheet's threads when it pierces through, rather than pushing between the threads as it does with quilting fabric, thus leaving holes and diminishing the stability of the sheet.

BACKING FOR A QUILT TOP 40–60" WIDE

Horizontal seams are most economical for quilts that are 40 to 60" wide.

Determine the width of the quilt top. Multiply this measurement by 2. Add 12", then divide by 36" to find the yardage you need to purchase for backing.

For example, if your finished quilt top is 50" square, you'll need a backing piece that measures 56" square. To figure backing yardage, multiply $50" \times 2 = 100"$; $100" + 12" = 112"$; 112" divided by $36" = 3.11$ yards. In this case you should purchase a minimum of $3\frac{1}{8}$ yards of 44/45"-wide backing fabric. *Note:* The calculations and diagrams assume 42" of usable fabric can be cut from a 44/45"-wide fabric.

Piecing Method 1

To piece your quilt back with two horizontal seams, first cut off a length of 56" (42×56"). Then cut two 8×56" pieces from the remaining 56" length. For added stability, use $\frac{1}{2}$" seam allowances when piecing the quilt backing. Sew an 8"-wide piece to each long side of the first piece to make a pieced back that measures 56" square. Press the seam allowances open.

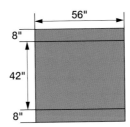

Piecing Method 2

To piece your quilt back with a single seam, first cut off a length of 56" (42×56"). Then cut a 15×56" piece from the remaining fabric. For added stability, use $\frac{1}{2}$" seam allowances when piecing the quilt backing. Sew together the two pieces along a pair of long edges to make a pieced back that measures 56" square. Press the seam allowances open.

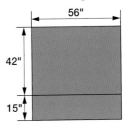

Piecing Method 3

To piece your quilt back and have the horizontal seam centered, cut the fabric length in half. For added stability, use $\frac{1}{2}$" seam allowances when piecing the quilt backing. Sew together the two pieces along a pair of long edges to make a pieced back that measures 56×83". Press the seam allowances open. When layering the backing, batting, and quilt top, position the batting and quilt top so that the backing seam is centered. Then trim off the excess backing fabric.

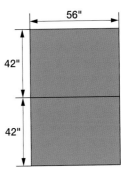

BACKING FOR A QUILT TOP 61–80" WIDE

Vertical seams are most economical for quilts that are 61 to 80" wide.

Determine the length of the quilt top. Multiply this measurement by 2. Add 12", then divide by 36" to find the yardage you need to purchase for backing.

For example, if your quilt top is 65×80", you'll need a backing piece that measures 71×86". To figure backing yardage, multiply 80" × 2 = 160"; 160" + 12" = 172"; 172" divided by 36" = 4.77 yards. In this case you should purchase a minimum of 4⅞ yards of 44/45"-wide backing fabric. *Note:* The calculations and diagrams assume 42" of usable fabric can be cut from a 44/45"-wide fabric.

Piecing Method 1

To piece your quilt back with one vertical seam, cut the fabric length in half crosswise. For added stability, use ½" seam allowances when piecing the quilt backing. Sew the two pieces together along a pair of long edges to make a pieced back that measures 83×86". Press the seam allowances open.

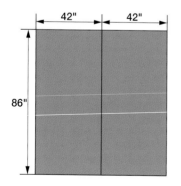

Piecing Method 2

To piece your quilt back with two vertical seams, cut the yardage in half crosswise (42×86"). Cut one of the pieces in half lengthwise to get two 21×86" pieces. For added stability, use ½" seam allowances when piecing the quilt backing. Sew one narrow piece on either side of the first piece to make a pieced back that measures 82×86". Press the seam allowances open.

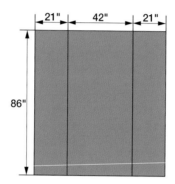

BACKING FOR A QUILT TOP 81–110" WIDE

Vertical seams are most economical for quilts that are 81 to 110" wide.

Determine the length of the quilt top. Multiply this measurement by 3. Add 18", then divide by 36" to find the yardage you need to purchase for backing.

For example, if your quilt top is 85×100", you'll need a backing piece that measures 91×106". To figure backing yardage, multiply 100" × 3 = 300"; 300" + 18" = 318"; 318" divided by 36" = 8.83 yards. In this case you should purchase a minimum of 8⅞ yards of backing fabric.

Piecing Method

The only efficient way to piece a backing this large is with two vertical seams. Cut the total yardage into three equal lengths of 106". For added stability, use ½" seam allowances when piecing the quilt backing. Sew together the three lengths along long edges to make a pieced back that measures 124×106". Press the seam allowances open.

When layering the backing, batting, and quilt top, you'll have excess fabric on the side edges. You can choose to evenly space the seams or have them offset. Once the backing is positioned, trim off the excess backing fabric, leaving an extra 3" of fabric on all edges.

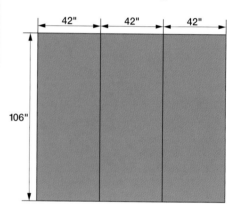

Hand & Machine Quilting

11

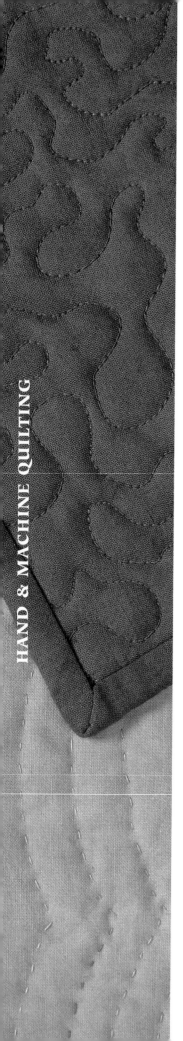

TABLE OF CONTENTS
Chapter 11—Hand & Machine Quilting

QUILTER TESTED FOR ACCURACY

ONCE YOU'VE COMPLETED YOUR QUILT TOP, it's time to layer it with the batting and backing. Once the layers are in place, the process of quilting can begin. Whether you choose to quilt by hand or machine, the quilting designs you choose for your project can enhance the beauty, intricacy, or simplicity of your quilt. Knowing the hows and whys of this important part of quiltmaking will assist you in making the right choices for your particular quilt.

MARKING THE QUILT TOP

Quilting designs generally are marked on a quilt top before it's layered with batting and a backing. First select a marking method according to your project; several options follow. Then select the appropriate marking tool, keeping in mind that some marking tools are more permanent than others (see Chapter 1—Tools, Notions, & Supplies for more information).

> **TIP:** To better see how a precut stencil's design will look when it's stitched, use a pencil to lightly trace through the stencil's cutout design onto tracing paper.

Secure your quilt top to a large, flat work surface with tape or clips to prevent shifting. Position your quilting design in the center of your quilt top to begin. Reposition your design and quilt top as needed to mark the entire quilt center or quilt top. Before marking your borders, see Adjusting Border Designs to Fit on *page 11–15* for more information.

USING A TRACING METHOD

There are several tracing methods to choose from when you wish to transfer a quilting design to a quilt top. Because these methods involve placing a light source behind the layered quilting design and quilt top, tracing works best on small-to medium-size projects.

Light Bulb and Glass-Top Table

1. Place a bright light beneath a glass-top table. Or, pull apart a table that accommodates leaves and place a piece of glass or clear acrylic over the opening.

2. Tape the quilting design to the top of the glass. Secure the quilt top over the design and trace the design onto the fabric.

Light Box

1. Tape the quilting design to a light box. Turn on the light source.

2. Secure the quilt top over the design, and trace the design onto the fabric.

Sunny Window

1. Tape the quilting design to a clean, dry window on a sunny day.

2. Tape the quilt top over the design and trace the design onto the fabric.

USING STENCILS AND TEMPLATES

1. To transfer a quilting design using a stencil or template, place the pattern on the quilt top and secure it in place with tape or weights.

2. Mark the pattern on the fabric.

USING TEAR-AWAY PATTERNS

1. Mark the quilting design on tracing paper, tissue paper, or tear-away stabilizer. You will need to make one pattern for each time the design will be used on the quilt top.

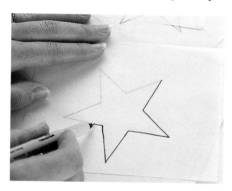

2. Baste or pin the pattern to the quilt top. Quilt along the design lines through both the paper and the quilt.

3. Gently tear the paper patterns away from the quilt top.

USING PERFORATED PATTERNS

1. Mark the quilting design on sturdy paper. Sew over the paper's design lines with a sewing machine and an unthreaded needle (or trace the lines with a needle-pointed tracing wheel).

2. Secure the quilt top to a firm surface, then secure the perforated pattern to the quilt top. Go over the perforations with chalk, pounce, or stamping powder.

TIP: What's a quilt sandwich? Quilters use this term to describe the quilt top, batting, and backing once they've been layered together.

USING TAPE

Use quilter's tape, painter's tape, or masking tape to mark straight-line quilting designs. (See Chapter 1—Tools, Notions, & Supplies for more information on tapes.) The tape can be put in place before or after the quilt layers are sandwiched together. Reposition the tape as needed until the quilting is complete, then remove it.

To avoid a sticky residue on fabric, do not leave tape in place for extended periods of time.

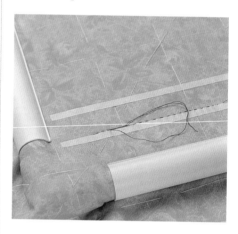

TIP: What's the difference between a stencil and a template? Both are patterns. A template is a pattern created by marking around a shape. A stencil is a pattern through which a design is transferred. Stencils have slits in the surface for you to mark through them, while a template's outer edge is in the shape of its design.

You can make your own stencils and templates or purchase them ready-made at a quilt shop.

PREPARE THE BATTING

Once your quilt top is marked, it's time to prepare the batting. (For complete information on selecting a batting, see Chapter 10— Batting & Backing.)

1. Remove the batting from its packaging and spread it out on a large flat surface to allow the folds to relax overnight. Or, fluff the batting in a clothes dryer for a few minutes on an air-dry setting to remove wrinkles.

2. Trim the batting so that it's at least 3" larger on all sides than the quilt top.

ASSEMBLE THE LAYERS

Take your time layering the quilt top, batting, and backing. Being careful at this point will save frustration when quilting. It is best to assemble the layers on a large, flat surface where the entire quilt top can be spread out.

1. If the quilt backing is pieced, press all the seam allowances open. This will prevent added bulk when you are quilting.

2. Place the quilt backing wrong side up on a large, flat surface.

Tape, clip, or otherwise secure the quilt backing to the work surface.

3. Center and smooth the batting in place atop the quilt backing. If desired, baste the batting and backing together with a single large cross-stitch in the center to prevent the layers from shifting. (This is especially important if you are working on a surface that is smaller than your quilt top.)

4. Center the quilt top right side up on top of the batting. To be sure that it is centered, fold it in half with right side inside. Align the center fold of the quilt with the center of the batting, then unfold the quilt top and smooth out any wrinkles.

5. Square up the quilt top (for more information, see Chapter 9— Assembling the Quilt Top). To check that you have not stretched or pulled the quilt top out of alignment during the layering process, place a large, square ruler in one corner. The edges of the ruler should be flush with the quilt top's edges. If the quilt is squared up, pin the border in that corner to hold it in place. Repeat in the remaining three corners. If the quilt top is not square, repeat Step 4, taking care not to stretch the quilt top out of shape.

6. Pin or baste all the layers together, beginning at the center. Be careful not to shift the layers, and work toward the edges, smoothing fabrics as you go. (Refer to the basting instructions that follow for additional information.)

THREAD BASTING

This method is most common for hand quilters because it works better in a hoop than pins.

1. With stitches about 2" long, baste the three layers together by stitching a horizontal line and a vertical line through the center of the quilt sandwich to form quadrants on the quilt top. Then baste diagonally in both directions.

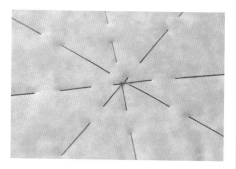

2. Add basting stitches 3 to 4" apart over the entire surface of the quilt top (or follow the batting manufacturer's directions for spacing). *Note:* If you'll be quilting in a hoop, use 1 to 2" long basting stitches spaced 1 to 2" apart. Because the hoop will be repeatedly

> **TIP:** Having trouble basting a large quilt without the layers shifting? Often the problem is not having a large enough work space to lay the entire quilt flat. Working on the floor is less than desirable and hard on your back.
>
> If work space is at a premium in your home, see if there's basting space at your local quilt shop, community center, or church. The large tables often found in these places can be pushed together to make a surface that's easy to work around without having to adjust the quilt.

moved and repositioned, the shorter stitch length and closer stitches will help prevent shifting.

PIN BASTING

Machine quilters generally pin baste because it is easier to remove pins rather than basting threads from underneath stitching.

1. Pin the three layers together with rust-proof safety pins, making a horizontal line and a vertical line through the center of the quilt sandwich to form quadrants on the quilt top. *Note:* Rust-proof pins won't stain fabrics if left in place for an extended period of time.

2. Add pins over the surface of the quilt top at 3 to 4" intervals.

SPRAY BASTING

Basting sprays are best for small quilt projects, such as wall hangings. Follow the manufacturer's directions to adhere the layers to one another. Take care not to overspray, which can lead to a

> **TIP:** If you're assembling a quilt on a table that is smaller than the quilt backing, center the fabric on the table top so equal lengths hang down on each side like a tablecloth.

gummy buildup on your quilting needle. (See Chapter 1—Tools, Notions, & Supplies for more information on basting sprays.)

Hand quilting results in broken lines of stitches and a quilt with a soft look. Methods of hand quilting vary as much as quilters do. Adapt the techniques that follow to suit your style.

Practice pays when it comes to hand quilting. If you're new to the process, start with straight lines, then try to echo patterns. As you gain proficiency, you'll be motivated to do more, which will lead to even better results.

Small, evenly spaced stitches are the hallmark of hand quilting. A beginner should aim for evenly spaced, uniform-size stitches. Your quilting stitches will generally decrease in size as you gain experience.

HAND-QUILTING SETUP
(See Chapter 1—Tools, Notions, & Supplies for more information on hand-quilting tools, supplies, and work space setup.)

> **TIP:** If you're basting a quilt on a small table or in limited space, consider thread-basting the batting and backing together before basting the quilt top into the quilt sandwich. This extra step will give you better control and help prevent shifting as you baste all three layers.

Some hand quilters like to hold their quilts loosely in their laps as they stitch, a method referred to as "lap quilting."

Wooden hoops or frames are often used to hold quilt layers together for quilting, keeping them smooth and evenly taut. The layers of a quilt should be basted together before inserting them into a hoop or frame.

Some quilters prefer hoops to frames because they are smaller and lighter, take up less storage space, are portable, and can be retightened as needed.

The size and style you choose—whether it's a hoop you can hold in your lap, a hoop attached to a floor stand, or a large quilting frame—depends upon your personal preference and the mobility you

desire. You may wish to try several types before deciding which works best for you. (See Chapter 1—Tools, Notions, & Supplies for more information.)

Hand quilters most often use a size 10 or 12 between needle and 100% cotton hand-quilting thread. (Hand-quilting thread differs from machine-quilting thread in that it is heavier and is usually coated to help it glide more easily through the fabric.)

Be sure that you're comfortably seated, with the hoop or frame at an angle you can easily see and reach without straining your shoulders, arms, and hands. The quilt layers should be securely basted so they won't shift.

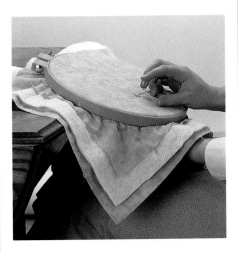

STARTING AND STOPPING HAND-QUILTING STITCHES

Stitch with an 18" length of hand-quilting thread in your needle. You'll begin and end your stitching by burying the thread tail between the layers of the quilt; this prevents knots from showing on the front or back of the quilt.

Securing Thread to Begin

1. With your needle threaded, hold the thread tail over the needle, extending it about ½" above.

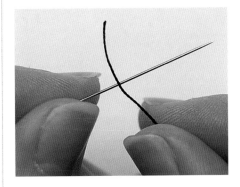

2. Holding the thread tail against the needle with one hand, use your other hand to wrap the thread around the needle clockwise two or three times.

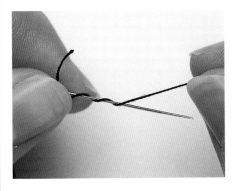

3. Pinching the thread tail and wraps with your thumb and forefinger, grasp the needle near the point and gently pull it through the thread wraps.

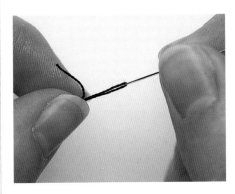

4. Continue pinching the thread wraps until the thread is pulled completely through and forms a small, firm knot near the end of the thread tail. This is called a quilter's knot.

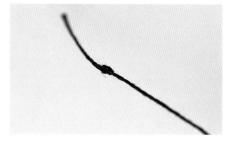

5. Insert the needle into the quilt through the quilt top and batting, but not into the backing, a few inches from where you want to quilt.

Bring the needle back to the surface in position to make the first stitch.

TIP: To decide if your quilting thread contrasts or blends the way you wish, practice your quilting designs on quilt sandwiches made from the same fabrics used in your quilt. If the color is not right, experiment with thread a shade lighter or darker.

6. Tug gently on the thread to pop the knot through the quilt top and embed it in the batting.

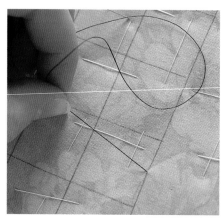

Securing Thread to End

1. Wind the thread twice around the needle close to the quilt top, as if making a French knot.

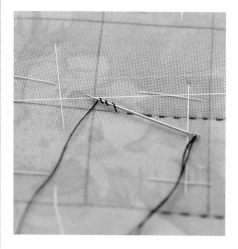

2. Holding the thread wraps next to the quilt top, run the needle tip through the quilt top and batting layers only.

3. Rock the needle tip back up, bringing the needle out ½ to 1" away from the stitching.

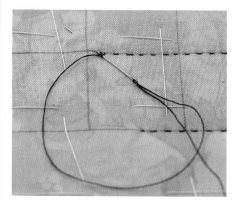

4. Tug gently on the thread to pop the knot through the quilt top and embed it in the batting.

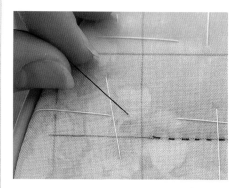

5. Holding the thread tail taut, clip the thread close to the quilt top, releasing the end to snap below the surface of the quilt top.

HAND-QUILTING RUNNING STITCH

For this classic hand-quilting stitch, wear a thimble on the middle finger of your stitching hand.

1. Hold the needle between your thumb and index finger. Place your other hand under the quilt, with the tip of your index finger on the spot where the needle will come through the quilt back. With the needle angled slightly away from you, push the needle through layers until you feel the tip of the needle beneath the quilt.

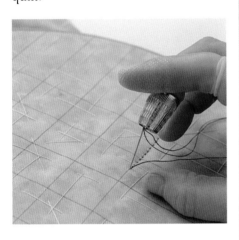

2. When you feel the needle tip, slide your finger underneath the quilt toward you, pushing up against the side of the needle to help return it to the top. At the same time, with your top hand roll the needle away from you. Gently push the needle forward and up through the quilt

layers until the amount of the needle showing is the length you want the next stitch to be.

3. Lift the eye of the needle with your thimble finger, positioning your thumb just ahead of the stitching. Rock the eye of the needle upward until the needle is almost perpendicular to the quilt top and the tip is in the fabric. Push down on the needle until you feel the tip beneath the quilt again.

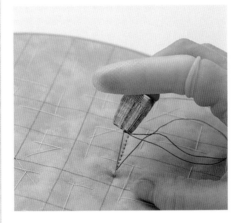

4. As in Step 2, push the needle tip with your underneath finger and roll the eye of the needle down and forward with your thimble finger to return the needle tip to the top.

5. Repeat this rock-and-roll motion until the needle is full.

6. Pull the needle away from the quilt top until the stitches are snug.

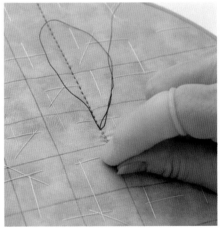

Remember that uniformity in stitch length is more important than the actual length of individual stitches.

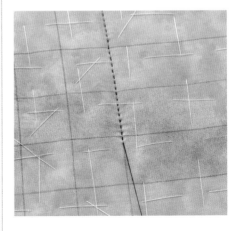

HAND-QUILTING STAB STITCH

Although it's less commonly used than the running stitch, some hand quilters prefer the stab stitch. Wear a thimble on the middle finger of both your hands.

1. Hold the needle between your thumb and index finger. Place your other hand under the quilt. Put the needle tip in the fabric with the needle straight up and down. Push the needle through layers and pull it completely through with your underneath hand.

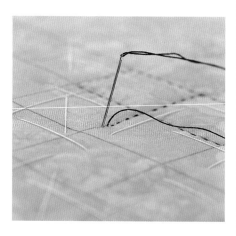

2. With the underneath hand, push the needle back through all the quilt layers to the top a stitch distance from where it went down; pull the needle and thread completely through all the layers with the upper hand to complete a quilting stitch.

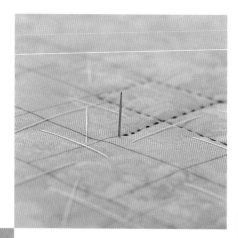

3. Repeat this stab-and-pull-through motion, making one quilting stitch at a time. Remember that uniformity in stitch length is more important than the actual length of individual stitches.

TRAVELING WITH THE NEEDLE

If you finish a line of hand-quilting with plenty of thread still in your needle, you may want to move to another area without knotting your thread and starting again. The technique for doing so is referred to as "traveling," which is often used for continuous quilting designs such as feathers. If the distance you need to travel is more than 1 to 2", however, it is best to knot the thread and begin again.

1. When you finish a line of stitching, run the needle point through the quilt top and batting only, moving it towards the next quilting area. If you are using a contrasting thread color that is darker than the quilt top, be sure to slide the needle deep into the batting. Bring the needle tip out about half a needle length away. Do not pull the needle all the way through unless you have reached the point where the next stitching line is to begin.

2. If you have not reached the starting point of the next stitching line, grasp the tip of the needle only. Leaving the eye of the needle between the quilt layers, pivot the needle eye toward the point where the next stitching line will begin.

3. With a thimble on your middle finger, push the tip of the needle, eye first, toward the next starting point. Bring the eye of the needle out at the starting point, pulling out the entire needle, eye first. Begin stitching where desired.

HAND-QUILTING DESIGNS

The designs that can be created with hand quilting are almost limitless. You can create straight lines of quilting stitches or intricate curves. For inspiration, see Quilt as Desired on *page 11–13*.

MACHINE QUILTING

Though some believe machine quilting to be a modern method, there are examples that date back to the early days of sewing machines. With the versatility of today's sewing machines, as well as the expanded availability of long-arm quilting machines outside the commercial market, machine quilting continues to grow in popularity. With practice and perseverance you can create keepsake-quality quilts with your sewing machine.

Machine-quilting stitches are continuous and even, giving a quilt a precise look. Just as in hand-quilting, practice pays when it comes to machine quilting. If you're new to the process, start with straight lines that are stitched from edge to edge to avoid lots of stopping and starting. Then try grid patterns and more intricate designs. As you gain proficiency and become more comfortable working with your sewing machine in this way, you'll be motivated to do more, which will lead to even better results.

> **TIP:** To avoid having the entire quilt beneath the sewing-machine arm at one time, begin working at the center of a quilt and work toward one edge. Complete half of the quilt top, then turn it around and quilt the other half, keeping in mind any directional motifs you may be stitching.

MACHINE-QUILTING SETUP

(See Chapter 1—Tools, Notions, & Supplies for more information on machine-quilting tools, supplies, and work space setup.)

Make sure your machine is clean and in good working order. Arrange a large, flat working surface that's even with the bed (throat plate) of the machine. It is important that the work surface support the weight of the quilt to prevent pulling and shifting of layers. Make certain the quilt layers are securely basted.

Be sure that you're comfortably seated, with the machine in a position that allows you to see and reach without straining your shoulders, arms, and hands.

For straight-line machine quilting, set up your machine with a walking (even-feed) foot and a straight-stitch throat plate. (Free-motion machine quilting requires a different presser foot. See Free-Motion Quilting on *page 11-11* for information on this technique.) Set the stitch length for 8 to 12 stitches per inch.

The style of needle most often

> **TIP: What's a long-arm quilting machine?**
> A long-arm quilting machine holds a quilt taut on a frame, which allows the quilter to see and work on a larger portion of the quilt at one time than would be possible with a standard sewing machine. The machine head moves freely, allowing the operator to quilt in all directions. These machines are most often used by professional machine quilters.

used is a sharp 80/12. You can experiment with smaller needles (75/11 or 70/10) if you feel the holes left in the fabric by the needle are too large.

The most common thread choice is 50-weight, three-ply, 100% cotton machine-quilting thread. If you want the finished stitches to be invisible, use very fine, transparent, nylon, monofilament thread (.004 mm) in the needle and lightweight cotton or bobbin-fill thread in the bobbin.

STARTING AND STOPPING MACHINE-QUILTING STITCHES

1. At the beginning of a line of stitching, pull the bobbin thread to the quilt top. Lock the stitches by setting the machine's stitch length to the shortest setting and sewing forward about ¼".

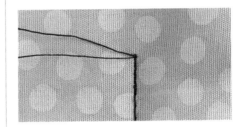

> **TIP:** Some machine quilters wear special gloves with grippers on the palms for better control as they shift the quilt on the machine bed when quilting.

2. Stop sewing, reset the stitch length to the preferred setting, and continue sewing.

3. To finish a line of stitching, return the machine's stitch length to the shortest setting, and sew forward about ¼".

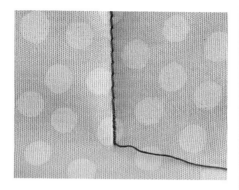

4. Raise the presser foot, remove the quilt, and clip the threads.

IN-THE-DITCH MACHINE QUILTING

Quilting "in the ditch" means stitching just inside a seam line.

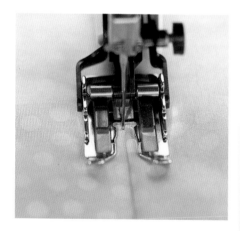

The stitches disappear into the seam, which makes a patch, block, or motif stand out from its background. It is one of the easiest methods to do by machine.

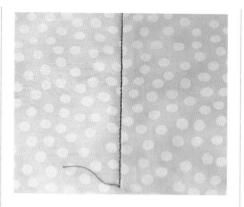

1. Attach a walking (even-feed) foot. Find the lengthwise center seam line of the basted quilt sandwich. With the needle just to one side of that seam line, sew along it from border to border.

2. Turn the quilt crosswise; adjust all the layers so they are smooth. Stitch the crosswise center seam in the same manner.

TIP: Don't Force-Feed the Quilt into the Machine
Feed the fabric up to the walking foot gently, but don't push the fabric ahead. Pushing it causes tucks at the crossing of each seam. Try not to stretch the quilt top or force it under the needle as that will cause the batting to pull, which will distort the finished quilt.

3. Return the quilt sandwich to the lengthwise direction and stitch in the ditch along the seam lines in a quadrant to the right of the center seam, working from the center outward toward the border.

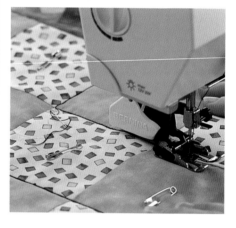

4. Turn the quilt and stitch in the ditch on the seam lines in a quadrant on the opposite side of the center line, again working from the center outward toward the border.

5. Repeat in the remaining two quadrants of the quilt.

CHANNEL OR GRID MACHINE QUILTING

When you want straight lines that do not necessarily follow the seam lines, you can do channel or grid quilting.

Channel Quilting

Channel quilting consists of parallel rows of straight lines going in one direction across a quilt top. Some sewing machines come with a quilting bar that attaches to the machine to serve as a guide for evenly spaced rows. Use the bar when your quilting rows are farther apart than a presser foot width or when the guides on your machine bed are covered. The bar is particularly useful when you're quilting straight rows across a large project.

When channel quilting, you need to mark at least the center line on your quilt top before you begin stitching. Follow the steps described in In-the-Ditch Machine Quilting, *opposite,* anchoring the center line first, then stitching each half of the quilt. Work from the center outward

> **TIP:** Let the large work surface around your sewing machine support the weight of the quilt as you machine-quilt. Avoid letting the quilt drop to the floor and create drag. If you have limited work surface, adjust an ironing board to the height of your sewing machine bed to help support the quilt's weight.

toward the border until an area is completely quilted.

Grid Quilting

Grid quilting involves stitching parallel rows of straight lines in two directions across a quilt top. When quilting in a grid, you need to mark at least the horizontal and vertical center lines on your quilt top before you begin stitching. The same quilting bar used for channel quilting can help keep rows straight for grid quilting. Follow the steps described in In-the-Ditch Machine Quilting, *opposite,* anchoring the center lines first, then stitching quadrant by quadrant until finished.

FREE-MOTION QUILTING

Free-motion machine quilting is used to stitch curved lines and designs. You sew with the machine's feed dogs in the down position in order to control the stitch length and direction.

It takes practice to achieve the steadiness and speed control necessary for creating small, uniform-size stitches. Start with a small project and simple quilting designs and work up to a larger quilt with more complicated designs.

1. Attach a darning foot to your sewing machine and drop or cover the feed dogs.

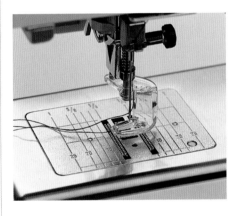

2. Position the basted quilt sandwich beneath the darning foot. Bring the bobbin thread to the surface of the quilt top.

3. Lower the presser foot. *Note:* Even though the darning foot does not touch the quilt top when the

> **TIP:** If your sewing machine does not allow you to drop the feed dogs, tape a business card over them to prevent them from grabbing the fabric beneath the presser foot.

presser foot is lowered, lowering it before stitching will help prevent the quilt from "jumping" up and down as the needle goes in and out; it also engages the tension discs which will make your stitches more even and taut.

Hold both the needle and the bobbin threads in one hand. Take three to six stitches in the same area to lock the stitches. Move the quilt sandwich in the direction you wish to go. (With the feed dogs down, the fabric layers will not move unless you move them.)

4. Clip the thread ends.

5. Begin stitching, moving the quilt sandwich slowly with the machine stitching at a medium-fast, constant speed. Glide the fabric layers in the direction they need to go. Do not turn the quilt. Because the feed dogs are lowered, you will be able to move the quilt sandwich freely from side to side and front to back. Use as little hand pressure as possible to move and control the quilt.

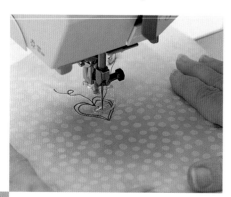

6. End your stitching by taking three to six stitches in the same area to lock the stitches. Remove the quilt top from the machine and clip the thread ends.

FOLDING A LARGE PROJECT FOR MACHINE QUILTING

When you're working on a large quilt, it can be difficult to control the bulk of many fabric layers, especially between the needle and the inside of the machine arm. Many machine quilters find it is easier to roll the project and work on small areas at a time.

1. Evenly roll or fold up opposite sides of the quilt sandwich. Secure the sides as desired. *Note:* Quilt shops often carry clips specially designed for this purpose.

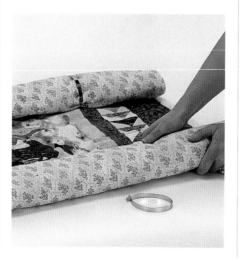

2. Evenly roll or fold up a remaining quilt side, again securing as desired.

3. Place the project beneath the needle and presser foot and begin quilting.

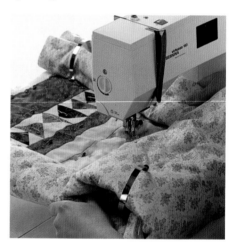

4. Reroll or refold the layered quilt sandwich to stitch new areas.

MACHINE-QUILTING DESIGNS

Machine quilting can produce almost a limitless number of designs. Besides the straight lines and intricate curves described on previous pages, there are quilting designs created specifically for sewing machines. The advantage of these designs is that they involve minimal starting and stopping. Arrows on the stitching patterns indicate the direction you should sew. For inspiration, see Quilt as Desired, *opposite.*

TYING A QUILT

Tying, or tufting, is a quick alternative to hand or machine quilting. A tie is a stitch taken through all three layers of the quilt and knotted on the quilt top surface or, occasionally, on the back of the quilt. Tied quilts have a puffier look than those that are quilted. For extra puffiness, use a thicker than customary batting or multiple layers of batting. Make certain the batting you select is appropriate for tying, because there will be large unquilted areas between ties. (See Chapter 10—Batting & Backing for more information on selecting a batting.)

1. Use perle cotton, sport-weight yarn, or narrow ribbon for the ties and a darner or chenille needle (see Chapter 1—Tools, Notions, & Supplies for more information on needles). Make a single running stitch through all quilt layers, beginning and ending on the quilt top and leaving a 3" tail.

2. Make a single backstitch through the same holes and all three layers, ending on the quilt top.

3. Clip the thread, yarn, or ribbon, leaving a second 3" tail.

4. Tie the tails in a square knot (right over left, then left over right) close to the surface of the quilt. Avoid pulling too tight and puckering the fabric.

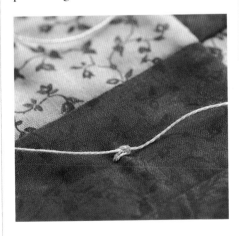

5. Clip the thread tails as desired.

QUILT AS DESIRED

Instructions for making a quilt generally come with detailed steps, numerous patterns, and helpful diagrams. How you should quilt the project often goes unsaid. Many quiltmakers simply quilt in the ditch or in an allover meandering pattern because they don't know what else to do.

If "quilt as desired" is your only instruction, those three words needn't leave you wondering how to proceed. Instead, look at them as an invitation to begin the next phase of completing a fabulous quilt project.

QUESTIONS TO ASK

Take some time and ask yourself the following questions. They'll help you make decisions on how to quilt your project.

Is this a quilt I hope will remain in my family for several generations?
When creating an heirloom quilt, consider quilting the project with elaborate designs and intricate details. For other projects, simple quilting designs that are easy to complete may be more appropriate.

Is this quilt going to be laundered often?
Select machine quilting for quilts that will receive lots of use.

How much time do I have to complete this quilt?
Save hand quilting for projects where you can afford to invest the time. If time is limited but you want to hand-quilt a project, select easy-to-do designs and motifs.

What's my preferred quilting method, by hand or by machine?
Just as when selecting a project, if you're excited about the process you've chosen, you'll be more likely to finish it successfully. Whether you want to hand- or machine-quilt may also affect your choice of a quilting design, as some lend themselves better to one technique than the other. For example, if you're going to machine-quilt, a continuous line design is often the best option since there will be less starting and stopping.

Do I want my quilting stitches to be visible in the quilt top?
Whether quilting by hand or machine, save intricate, close quilting for projects that will showcase the stitching and more basic designs for those with busier fabrics and more pieces where it's likely the quilting stitches won't show.

Does this quilt have a traditional, folk art, or contemporary mood?
Sometimes the feel of a quilt will drive the quilting design. For example, a traditional quilt may call for a feathered wreath design, but a folk art quilt may look best with big stitches quilted in perle cotton.

FINDING INSPIRATION

Ideas for quilting motifs and designs don't have to be limited to the precut stencils, templates, and books of quilting designs available at your local quilt shop. Look around you for inspiration.

One way to generate designs is to think about your project's theme. For example, if you're making a Christmas quilt, consider holiday-related items, such as ornaments,

strings of lights, trees, holly, garland, mittens, snowflakes, reindeer, and stockings, as potential quilting motifs. Evaluate the possibilities based on difficulty and where they might work best on your quilt.

A round ornament could be stitched as a simple circle, for instance, while a reindeer would probably require a stencil. A wavy line with occasional loops could represent garland on a narrow inner border.

Another place to find a quilting design is within the quilt's fabrics. Are there motifs in one of the prints, such as oak leaves or flowers, that could work as a the quilting design?

The architecture of buildings can provide numerous concepts. The exteriors of old brick buildings often provide interesting grid arrangements that can be translated into quilting patterns, for instance. Wrought-iron fences and gates might suggest beautiful scrollwork, perfect for border designs. Door arches, moldings, or pressed-tin ceilings may offer ideas for your next medallion-style quilt.

Even household items, such as picture frames, jewelry, and kitchen tiles, can produce quilting design ideas. The bubbles in an aquarium, for example, may suggest the perfect pattern for a goldfish quilt.

Examine both new and old quilts that you like. Ask yourself: Why do I like this quilt? What about it appeals to me? Is it the pieced or appliquéd pattern? Is it the colors? Or is it the quilting design that brings it all together?

QUILTING TERMINOLOGY

Understanding some general quilting terms will help you select a design for your next project.

Allover designs, particularly geometrics, can be stitched over an entire quilt without regard to shapes or fabrics (see photos 9 and 10 on on *page 11–18*). Allover designs can be quilted from either the top side or the backing.

Backgrounds and fillers fill in open interior spaces, such as setting squares, circles, or hearts with stitching. You can stitch squares, diamonds, clamshells, or other small regular shapes (see Photo 6 on *page 11–17* and Photo 7 on *page 11–18*). You also can stitch these shapes in the background outside an appliqué or quilted motif. The closely spaced lines of a filler tend to flatten the area, creating a low-relief, textured appearance.

Big, or utility, stitches require a heavier thread, such as perle cotton, and a large hand stitch. They result in a folk art appearance (see Photo 11 on *page 11–18*).

Echo quilting involves stitching multiple lines that follow the outline of an appliqué or other design element, repeating its shape (see photos 4 and 5 on *page 11–17*). The evenly spaced quilting lines should be ¼ to ½" apart. You can use echo quilting to completely fill a background.

In the ditch means stitching just inside a seam line (see Photo 3 on *page 11–17*). The stitches disappear into the seam, which makes a patch, block, or motif stand out from its background. It's an easy method to do by machine.

Outline quilting is done ¼" from a seam line or edge of an appliqué shape, just past the extra thickness of the pressed seam allowance (see photos 1 and 2 on *page 11–17*). If you want to quilt closer to a seam line, choose the side opposite the pressed seam allowance.

Stippling, also called allover meandering or puzzle quilting, can be stitched by hand or machine. It involves random curves (see Photo 8 on *page 11–18*), straight rows of regularly placed stitches (lined up or staggered), or random zigzags. For the best effect, stippling should be closely spaced.

BORDER DESIGNS AND BALANCE

Borders and quilt centers are usually quilted separately. While one option is to leave the border unquilted, that tends to make the final project look unbalanced. That's also the result if the border quilting doesn't fit the rest of the project. Don't skimp on quilting in the borders; try to keep the amount of quilting equal to the rest of the quilt.

To balance your quilting designs, include the borders when you begin thinking about quilting designs for your blocks. Think about what will coordinate with or complement the quilting designs you've selected for the rest of the quilt top.

If you've selected a particular motif or design for the quilt center, is there a way to continue that same motif or a variation of the motif in the border? For example, if the blocks are quilted with a simple flower, can it be repeated in the border, maybe adding a connecting vine-and-leaf pattern? If you are crosshatching the blocks, can you crosshatch through the border as well?

As you select your quilting designs, evaluate the fabric used in the border. Is it a solid or a subtle print that will really show off a quilting design? Or is the fabric so busy it will hide any type of quilting?

If you have a solid inner border and a print outer border, you may want to quilt a recognizable pattern in the solid border, where it will show up better, then crosshatch or stipple the busier fabric.

For more inspiration, examine photos 29 to 39, which begin on *page 11–21*. They show border quilting designs that complement their quilts.

AUDITIONING DESIGNS

Once you have an idea for a border quilting design, it's best to create a paper template or tracing paper overlay to see how the design will fit in the length of your borders and how it will turn the corners. Use a temporary quilting pencil or marker to draw it on your quilt top. Always test the pencil or marker on scraps of the fabrics used in the quilt top before marking on the actual top. (See Marking the Quilt Top, which begins on *page 11-1,* for more information.)

ADJUSTING BORDER DESIGNS TO FIT

There is no single formula for success in adjusting border designs to fit a quilt. Because of the variety of factors involved—border width and length, quilting design width and repeat—the ways to adjust a border design are numerous.

An important consideration as you adjust the design is that it is best for all sides and corners to match. The most challenging method is to adjust the length of a continuous design. However, there are options other than adjusting a border design's width and length.

Extending the Quilt Center Design

If an overall design, such as crosshatching or stippling was used on the quilt center, consider extending it onto the borders as well.

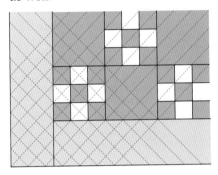

Meandering Vine Design

Meander a vine design along each border. When you reach the corners, be sure to turn the design in an identical manner, creating mirror images in opposite corners of the quilt.

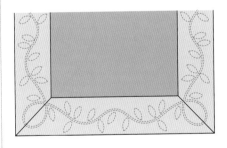

TIP: Choose a border design that fills the border's width well, keeping in mind you don't want the quilting to go too near the seam allowance or you'll risk covering it with the binding.

Repeated Block Design

Repeat a block design used in the quilt center in the border (or choose a different design), evenly spacing the design along the length. Pay particular attention to the direction of the motifs. You may wish to point them all in one direction if the motif has a definite top and bottom. Or you can point all the designs toward or away from the quilt center.

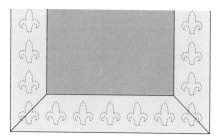

Combining Elements

If you choose a rhythmic or wavy design, such as swags or feathers, but the motifs don't fit your border length, consider combining them with a block design at the midpoint of each border.

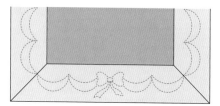

Adjusting the Length of the Design

Adjusting a continuous line design takes the most time and effort of any adjustment, but when completed results in a design which appears to seamlessly circle the entire quilt. The instructions that follow are for modifying a stencil design. Drawing the design first on paper (shelf liner or freezer paper) will prevent you from incorrectly marking your quilt top.

Though the steps of adjusting border designs are generally the same, how you choose to add or take out extra length so that the design fits is unique to each project.

As a rule, it's best not to modify a design at the corners. Instead, adjust the design somewhere near, but not at, the midpoint.

1. Cut two lengths of paper, one equal in width and length to the quilt's finished side borders and one equal in width and length to the top/bottom borders. Do not include the seam allowances. (If your quilt is square, one strip will do.) Label the strips and mark the center of each.

2. Trace the stencil's corner design on the ends of each strip. Use the registration marks on the stencil to make sure your design is properly aligned on the paper border.

3. Align the center registration mark on the stencil with the midpoint marked on the border. Beginning from this point, slide the stencil between the midpoint and corner to figure how many repetitions of the design will fit. The alterations will likely be different for the side and top/bottom borders.

If the amount of design adjustment is small, you may be able to adjust a bit of length in one motif without noticeably altering the design. *Note:* If the amount to be added or reduced is too great, the design will be distorted, calling attention to the motif that was squeezed or stretched to fit.

If the amount is significant, you will need to add or delete a part of several motifs to make the adjustment. When doing so, keep in mind the overall shape of the design and use the stencil as much as possible to trace the design on the paper.

4. Once you're pleased with the paper patterns, transfer the modified design to the quilt top. (See Marking the Quilt Top on *page 11–1*.)

Refer to the quilting designs and ideas that follow for inspiration
when planning the hand or machine quilting design for your own quilt.

Photo 1

This example of outline quilting was done with perle cotton ¼" inside the center shape, then 1" inside that.

Photo 2

The outline quilting of Job's Tears, a traditional pattern done here in classic 1930s reproduction prints, was stitched ¼" inside each pattern piece, as well as ¼" from the edge of each four-pointed star.

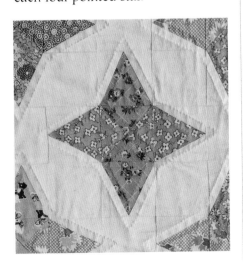

Photo 3

The metallic thread used here to stitch in the ditch makes the quilting a design element. Often, however, in-the-ditch quilting is nearly invisible as the thread disappears into the seams.

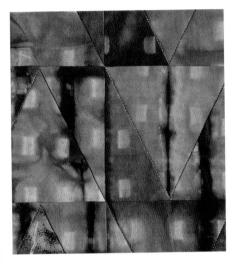

Photo 4

These needle-turn appliquéd flowers are surrounded by widely spaced echo quilting, which gives the quilt a casual look.

Photo 5

Echo quilting can be done with closely spaced concentric lines that simply follow the contours of the appliqué pieces, as was done in this fusible-appliqué project.

Photo 6

Clamshells, simply partial circles stacked in rows, fill a portion of this quilt's background. This pattern can be stitched by hand or by machine.

Hand & Machine Quilting

Photo 7
Diagonal lines—here stitched in pairs at 45° angles to the seam allowances for a trellis design—also can fill backgrounds.

Photo 8
Stippling provides texture and interest behind a pattern, such as this appliqué shape. This project was stippled by machine.

Photo 9
The traditional Baptist fan quilting design, the result of concentric arcs stitched over an entire quilt top, lends an antique feel to this project.

Photo 10
Viewed from the back, this allover machine-quilted design reveals free-form loops and feathers. On the front, this type of allover quilting blends sampler blocks of many hues.

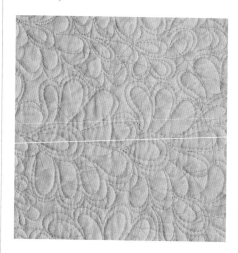

Photo 11
The aptly named "big stitch," a quick, simple, hand-quilting technique, results in this primitive, folk-art look.

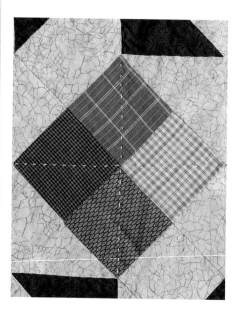

Photo 12
The layers of this Nine-Patch quilt are tied together with perle cotton for a simple, unfussy feel.

Photo 13

Kaleidoscope, a traditional block, naturally gives the illusion of movement. To accentuate the spin in the design, the maker machine-quilted circles in each block.

Photo 14

Maple Leaf blocks in autumn colors made the designer think of a rainy fall day, so she quilted overlapping circles to create the illusion of leaves floating on the water.

Photo 15

Carefully placed concentric circles add interest to these simple star blocks.

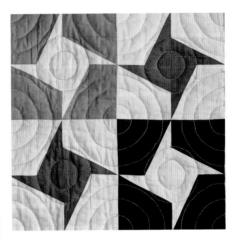

Photo 16

The designer of this colorful quilt chose a swirling spiral pattern for each setting square to offset the angular piecing.

Photo 17

A puffy wool batting made machine-quilting this project an excellent choice. This serpentine stitch is easy enough for beginners.

Photo 18

This quilting design, inspired by Mother Nature, is fittingly called a spider web pattern.

Photo 19

Bright, playful colors called for a fun, free-motion design of loops and scallops.

Photo 20

Nautical quilting designs abound in this sailboat quilt. Hand-stitched waves fill the white border, and a swirling pattern adds motion to the water and sky.

Photo 21

The quiltmaker stitched simple leaf shapes into and around this Tree block.

Photo 22

Quilted logs and quilted smoke curling from the chimney were natural choices for this Log Cabin block.

Photo 23

A patchwork dinosaur marches across a background of quilted pebbles.

Photos 24 and 25

The floral print backing (first photo) offered the quilter a chance to outline-quilt the flower and leaf motifs, which resulted in an easy overall design on the quilt top (second photo).

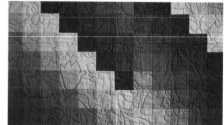

Photo 26

Several different designs fill the background of this wall hanging, and the quilting stitches in the borders follow the motifs in the fabric.

Photo 27

This closer look at one of the wonderful geometric patterns quilted in the previously shown wall hanging illustrates how a plain background can be made special.

Photo 28

The details stitched into these pumpkins, including vine tendrils, bring the orange shapes to life.

Photo 29

This quiltmaker went outside the box when she quilted family members' handprints in this wide border.

Photo 30

An elongated orange peel design in the border simply stops before the corner, then resumes in the adjacent border. The corner is quilted with a totally different design.

Photo 31

Diagonal lines radiating from the center of the quilt fill a wide inner border. The dark, outer border provides space to add a wispy cable design with a related, but not connected, corner.

Photo 32

To complement this quilt's starry-night theme, the quiltmaker machine-stitched fireworks, or chrysanthemum, shapes in the inner border.

Photo 34

The center section of this quilt is stitched with an interlocking orange peel design. The leaves in the border, joined with deeply arched vines, are half the orange peel design.

Photo 36

Arches connect simple teardrop shapes in this border. Using contrasting perle cotton on the dark flannel produced a country look.

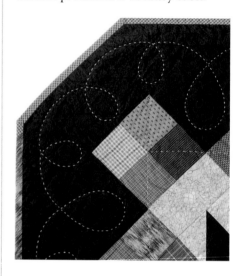

Photo 33

The machine-quilted leaf border adds to the mood of a delicately colored floral quilt.

Photo 35

Diagonal lines that mimic the quilting lines of the quilt center and pieced border are used on the wide outer border.

Photo 37

The border's lovely curved quilting, done with a heavier specialty thread, complements the quilt center's elaborate embroidery.

Photo 38

A pleasant scalloped edge frames a classic looped border in this vintage quilt. The traditional crosshatching creates a wonderful backdrop for the appliquéd blocks.

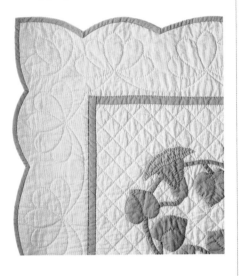

Photo 39

Cookie cutters were used as patterns for the stars casually scattered around the plaid border of this homespun quilt.

Photo 40

Machine-embroidered blanket stitching gives these appliquéd sunflowers delightful spiral centers.

Photo 41

Random big stitches using contrasting perle cotton on a cream-color background adds specks of color for a creative filler.

Photo 42

Machine-embroidered stars in the flower centers anchor these three-dimensional blooms and offer attention-grabbing details.

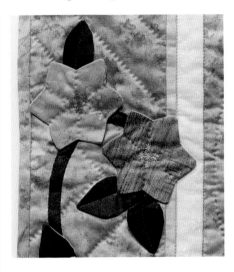

Photo 43

The lines outlining this angel's wings are faux stitches. They were drawn on with a permanent-ink pen.

Photo 44

Variegated thread stitched in concentric teardrop shapes fills the black diamond shape with vibrant color that complements the quilt's brilliant fabrics.

Photo 45

Machine stitching with a double needle easily creates perfectly parallel diagonal lines, which here crisscross the star and continue into the setting squares and borders.

Photo 46

Use machine embroidery to add artistic details to an otherwise plain border.

Photo 47

Tie satin ribbons into bows and tack them to a simply pieced quilt top to create a soft, feminine-looking bed cover.

My Notes for Hand & Machine Quilting

My Notes for Hand & Machine Quilting

Binding & Finishing

12

TABLE OF CONTENTS
Chapter 12—Binding & Finishing

BINDING YOUR QUILT, ADDING A LABEL, AND PERHAPS STITCHING ON A HANGING SLEEVE bring you the satisfaction of a completed project. Here, as with the rest of the quiltmaking process, creativity is enhanced when you're able to make informed decisions about techniques. When you're adding these finishing touches it's the perfect time to be thinking ahead to your next quilt.

PREPARING THE QUILT FOR BINDING

Taking the time to properly prepare the quilt for binding will result in a better finished appearance. *Note:* If you plan to use the backing fabric as binding, see Self-Binding beginning on *page 12–8* for information on preparing the quilt.

> **TIP:** If your quilting is more than 1" from the outer edges, baste the layers together around the entire quilt ⅜" from the edges. This will prevent the outside of your quilt from ruffling and stretching as the binding is added.

1. Lay the quilted project faceup on a rotary-cutting mat on a flat surface.

2. Position a large acrylic square ruler in one corner of the quilt, aligning adjacent edges of the ruler with adjacent edges of the quilt top. Place a long acrylic ruler above the square ruler, aligning the long edge with the quilt top edge. Using a rotary cutter, cut away the batting and backing that extend beyond the quilt top edge.

Reposition the rulers and cutting mat as needed to trim around the entire quilt. *Note:* Aligning the square ruler on two edges before positioning the second ruler enables you to square up the quilt corner, keeping your quilt straight. A slight bit of the quilt top edge is sometimes trimmed away. If one corner is significantly off when you align the ruler, refer to Chapter 9—Assembling the Quilt Top for information on squaring up quilt blocks.

If you do not wish to rotary-cut the excess batting and backing, mark the cutting line along the ruler edge, then use scissors to trim on the line.

BINDING LENGTH

Determine how much binding you will need to go around all sides of your quilt. Many patterns list the number of binding strips or the total length needed to complete a project.

If you need to determine the binding length yourself, lay the quilt flat and measure through the center of each border strip (do not measure along the outer edge of the quilt); add the lengths of each side together. Add approximately 15" to allow for diagonally seaming strips and finishing the ends of continuous binding (binding in one long strip with no breaks except where it begins and ends).

DETERMINING BINDING TYPE AND WIDTH

Before cutting your binding strips, you need to decide whether you want single-fold or double-fold (French-fold) binding. Also determine whether you want to cut the binding on the straight grain or bias grain. If you are working on a project that has curved or scalloped edges, you will need to cut your strips on the bias grain.

SINGLE-FOLD BINDING

Single-fold binding, as its name implies, is a single thickness of fabric. It requires less fabric than double-fold binding, but also provides less protection for a quilt's edges. Because of this, single-fold binding is generally used in quilts that will not be handled frequently, such as wall hangings, miniature quilts, and quilts with curved or scalloped edges where less bulk in the binding is desired.

Single-fold binding is cut twice the desired finished binding width plus ½" for seam allowances. For example, for ¼"-wide finished single-fold binding, cut 1"-wide binding strips. The binding strips for single-fold binding can be cut on the straight or bias grain. If you are binding a quilt with curved edges, cut your strips on the bias grain.

QUICK REFERENCE CHART
BIAS STRIP WIDTH

Use this chart to determine how wide to cut fabric strips for the type of binding you choose.

	SINGLE-FOLD	DOUBLE-FOLD (French-fold)
Desired Finished Width	Width To Cut Strip	Width To Cut Strip
¼"	1"	1½"
⅜"	1¼"	2"
½"	1½"	2½"
⅝"	1¾"	3"
¾"	2"	3½"
⅞"	2¼"	4"
1"	2½"	4½"

DOUBLE-FOLD BINDING

Double-fold, or French-fold, binding is the most common binding type. It provides the most durable finish on a quilt's edges. It is cut wider than single-fold binding because it is pressed in half (doubled) before it is attached to the quilt top. Double-fold binding is cut four times the desired finished binding width plus ½" for seam allowances. For example, for ½"-wide finished double-fold binding, cut 2½"-wide binding strips. The binding strips for double-fold binding can be cut on the straight or bias grain. If you are binding a quilt with curved edges, cut your strips on the bias grain.

SELF-BINDING

This method of binding uses the quilt backing, rather than separate strips, as binding. (See Self-Binding beginning on *page 12–8* for more information.)

STRAIGHT-GRAIN BINDING

For most quilts, binding strips may be cut on the straight grain. Use a fabric's crosswise straight grain rather than its lengthwise grain for more give and elasticity. If your quilt has curved edges, cut the strips on the bias (see *opposite* for details).

1. Cut crosswise strips the desired width (see Determining Binding Type and Width beginning on *page 12–1*), cutting enough strips to equal the total length needed.

TIP: SQUARING UP THE QUILT

After quilting, the sides of your quilt may be slightly different in length. You can equalize the difference by measuring through the middle of the quilt both horizontally and vertically, and using these measurements (plus seam allowances) when figuring the binding length of each side.

You may wish to trim the quilt until the sides are equal, but if the amount you're trimming is significant, keep in mind that you may alter the proportion and balance of the borders. You may also alter the distance between quilting motifs and the quilt edge from one border to the next.

2. Position and pin the strips perpendicular to one another with the raw edges aligned and right sides together. Mark, then join the strips with diagonal seams to make one continuous binding strip.

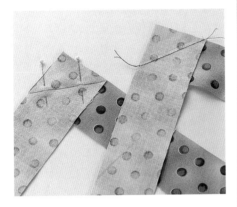

3. Trim the excess fabric, leaving ¼" seam allowances. Press the seam allowances open. Trim the dog-ears.

BIAS BINDING

When binding a quilt that has curved edges, cutting your strips on the bias grain will help the binding lie flat.

CUTTING BIAS STRIPS

1. Begin with a fabric square or rectangle. Use a large acrylic ruler to square up the edge of the fabric and find the 45° angle.

2. Cut enough strips to total the length needed, handling the edges carefully to avoid stretching and distorting the strips.

3. Position and pin the strips perpendicular to one another with

the raw edges aligned and right sides together. Mark, then join the strips with diagonal seams to make one continuous binding strip.

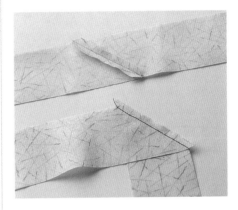

4. Trim the excess fabric, leaving ¼" seam allowances. Press the seam allowances open. Trim the dog-ears.

MAKING CONTINUOUS BIAS FROM A SQUARE

Rather than cutting individual bias strips, you can cut and seam a square to make a continuous bias strip.

1. Cut a square from your binding fabric on the straight grain. Use the chart *below* to determine the size of square you need.

QUICK REFERENCE CHART
AMOUNT OF CONTINUOUS BIAS THAT CAN BE CUT FROM A SQUARE

To calculate the length of a continuous bias strip that can be cut from a square, find the square's area (multiply the square's measurement by itself) and divide by the desired width of the bias strip.
For example, to figure the total inches of 2½"-wide bias a 12" square yields, multiply 12×12 and divide by 2.5 = 57".

Bias width	1"	1¼"	1½"	1¾"	2"	2¼"	2½"
12" square	144"	115"	96"	82"	72"	64"	57"
18" square	324"	259"	216"	185"	162"	144"	129"
27" square	729"	583"	486"	416"	364"	324"	291"
36" square	1,296"	1,036"	864"	740"	648"	576"	518"

2. Cut the square in half diagonally to form two triangles.

3. With right sides together, align two short triangle edges. Sew the triangles together with a ¼" seam allowance to make a parallelogram. Press the seam allowances open.

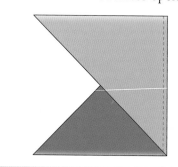

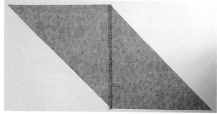

4. Use a quilt marker or pencil and a ruler to draw lines parallel to the long bias edges, spacing the lines the desired width of the binding strip. For example, space the lines 1½" apart for a 1½"-wide binding strip.

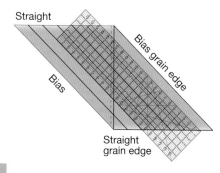

5. With right sides together, bring the straight-grain edges together and align the raw edges. Shift one straight-grain edge so the top corner is offset by the width of one drawn line.

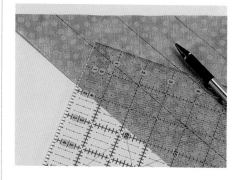

6. Sew the offset edges together using a ¼" seam allowance. Press the seam allowances open.

7. At the extended edge, begin cutting on the drawn lines to make one continuous bias strip.

Trim the strip's ends so they are square.

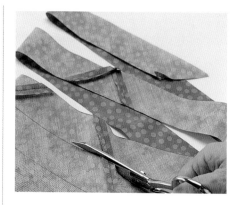

PREPARING BINDING

SINGLE-FOLD BINDING

Single-fold binding requires little preparation before being sewn to the quilt.

1. With the wrong side inside, fold under 1" at one end of the binding strip; press.

2. You may wish to turn under and press a ¼" seam allowance on one long edge of the strip before joining the other long edge to the quilt. This pressed edge will be hand-stitched to the back of the quilt after the binding strip is sewn to the quilt top.

DOUBLE-FOLD (FRENCH-FOLD) BINDING

1. With the wrong side inside, fold under 1" at one end of the binding strip; press.

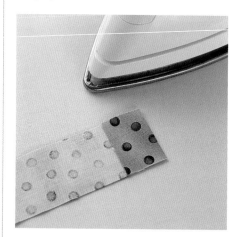

Binding & Finishing

2. With wrong side inside, fold the strip in half lengthwise and press.

SEWING ON BINDING

The instructions that follow can be used to attach single-fold or double-fold binding.

Binding is generally attached to a quilt with a ¼" seam allowance. This leaves ¼" of binding showing on the

> **TIP:** When pressing a long continuous binding strip in half, place two straight pins in your ironing surface with each shaft inserted to make an opening equal to half the width of the strip. Slide the end of the folded strip end beneath the pins, then steadily pull the strip beneath the soleplate of a warm iron. The pins will fold the strip in half as it is pulled along. *Note:* Periodically lift the iron to prevent scorching the ironing board.

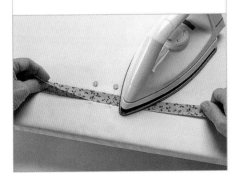

quilt front and the balance of the binding turned to the quilt back.

If you prefer a narrower or wider binding to show on the quilt front, adjust the width of your seam allowance to equal the binding width that you want to show on the quilt front. (To determine how wide to cut your binding, see Determining Binding Type and Width beginning on *page 12–1.)*

Cut and sew a sample binding strip on a layered quilt sandwich to be sure your strips are wide enough to cover the stitching line on the quilt back.

CONTINUOUS BINDING WITH MITERED CORNERS

The photographs that follow show double-fold binding. If you use single-fold binding, the raw binding edge (the edge not turned under) is the one to align with the edge of the quilt. (See Preparing Binding—Single-Fold Binding *opposite.)*

1. Beginning in the center of the bottom edge, place the binding strip against the right side of the quilt top, starting with the folded end and aligning the binding strip's raw edges with the quilt top's raw edge.

2. Starting 2" from the folded end, sew through all the layers. End your stitching line before you reach the

corner at a distance equal to the width of the seam allowance. For example, if you are sewing with a ¼" seam allowance, you would stop sewing ¼" from the corner. Backstitch, then clip the threads. Remove the quilt from beneath the sewing-machine presser foot.

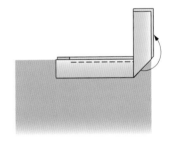

3. Fold the binding strip upward, creating a diagonal fold, and finger-press.

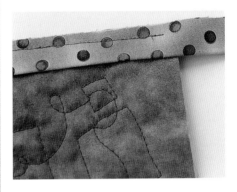

4. Holding the diagonal fold in place with your index finger, bring the binding strip down in line with the next edge, making a horizontal fold that aligns with the first raw edge of the quilt.

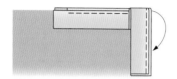

5. Begin sewing again at the top of the horizontal fold, stitching through all layers.

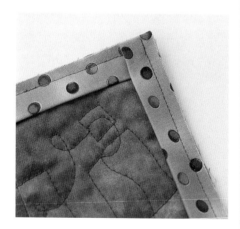

6. Sew around the quilt, turning each corner in the same manner. When you return to the starting point, lap the raw end of the binding strip inside the folded end.

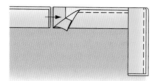

7. Finish sewing to the starting point. Backstitch to secure.

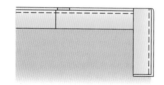

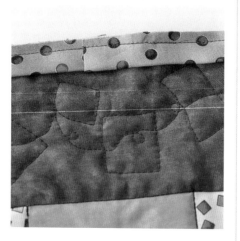

8. Turn the binding over the edge of the quilt to the back. Hand-stitch the binding to the backing fabric, making sure to cover the binding stitching line. Hand-stitch the folded edge of the binding down where the binding strips meet.

9. Fold a miter in each corner as you reach it. Take a stitch or two in each fold to secure it.

JOINING BINDING ENDS WITH NO OVERLAP

Some quilters prefer to seam the ends of a binding strip together, rather than overlapping them as described in Continuous Binding with Mitered Corners, steps 6 and 7, *left*. Seaming the ends means less bulk.

1. Prepare the binding strips as for double-fold (French-fold) binding, but do not fold under an end. (See Preparing Binding—Double-Fold Binding, which begins on *page 12–4*.)

2. Beginning in the center of the bottom edge, place the binding strip against the right side of the quilt top; align the binding strip's raw edges with the quilt top's raw edge and leave a 6 to 10" tail (the larger the project, the longer the tail).

3. Starting 6 to 10" from the end (depending on the length of your binding strip tail), sew the binding to the quilt following steps 2 through 5 under Continuous Binding with Mitered Corners, which begins on *page 12–5*. Stop sewing when you are within 10 to 20" from where you began stitching.

4. Remove the quilt from under the presser foot and place it on a flat surface.

5. Lay the first binding tail in place on the quilt top, aligning the raw edges. Repeat with the second binding tail. Crease the second binding tail where it meets the first tail's straight cut end. From the crease, measure the distance of the binding strip's cut width.

For example, these binding strips were cut 2" wide, so we measured 2" from the crease and cut the second tail straight across at that mark.

6. Open the tails; with right sides together, place one on top of the other at a right angle.

7. Join the strips with a diagonal seam. Before stitching, check to be sure the strips are not twisted. Trim the seam allowance to ¼" and finger-press open.

8. Fold the binding strip in half lengthwise as it was previously. It should lie perfectly flat.

9. Continue sewing the binding strip to the starting point. Backstitch to secure.

10. Turn the binding over the edge of the quilt to the back. Hand-stitch the binding to the backing fabric, making sure to cover the binding stitching line.

BINDING INSIDE CORNERS

Sometimes a project may require you to bind around an inside corner. Knowing where to stop stitching and pivot the quilt is the key to turning an inside corner smoothly. This technique may be used with single-fold or double-fold binding.

1. Sew a binding strip to the quilt with a ¼" seam allowance. As you reach an inside corner, sew ¼" past the corner so that when you pivot, the needle will be ¼" from the next edge. Backstitch once, then return to the original stopping point. With your needle down, pivot the layers to stitch the next portion in place.

2. Use the point of a seam ripper to make the binding lie flat as necessary. Continue sewing along the edges, repeating steps 1 and 2 at each inside corner, until the binding strip is sewn to the quilt.

3. Turn the binding over the edge of the quilt to the back. Work the binding's inside corners to create a small pleat on each side.

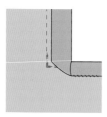

4. Hand-stitch the pleats in place, then hand-stitch the binding to the backing fabric, making sure to cover the binding stitching line.

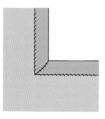

BINDING CURVED OR SCALLOPED EDGES

Use strips cut on the bias to bind a quilt that has curved edges or scallops because it has enough give to bend smoothly around the curves.

1. Prepare the bias strips as desired for single-fold or double-fold binding. (See Preparing Binding which begins on *page 12–4*.)

2. Beginning in the center of the bottom edge, place the binding strip against the right side of the quilt top, starting with the folded end and aligning the binding strip's raw edges with the quilt top's raw edge. *Note:* Do not begin at an inside point.

3. Starting 2" from the folded end, sew through all the layers, easing the binding around the curves. *Note:* Do not stretch the binding around the curves or the quilt edges will cup once the binding is turned to the quilt back.

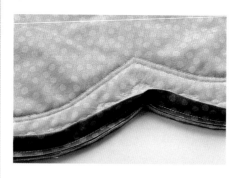

4. When you return to the starting point, lap the raw end of the binding strip inside the folded end.

5. Finish sewing to the starting point. Backstitch to secure.

6. Clip the seam allowance at each inner point.

7. Turn the binding over the edge of the quilt to the back. Hand-stitch the binding to the backing fabric, folding a small mitered tuck at each inner point. Make sure to cover the binding stitching line.

SELF-BINDING

Self-binding methods use the backing fabric to bind the quilt. This type of binding tends to be less durable than traditional binding, but can be practical when you have limited fabric on hand and want the binding to match the backing fabric.

SELF-BINDING WITH BACKING FABRIC, MITERED CORNERS

1. Mark the ¼" seam line on the quilt top. Trim the batting so it extends beyond the marked seam line the desired finished binding width. For example, if you want ½" of binding showing on the quilt front, trim the batting ½" beyond the marked seam line.

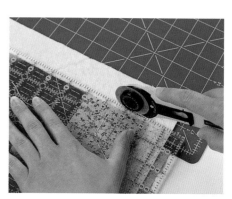

To prevent yourself from inadvertently cutting into the backing fabric, slip the edge of your rotary-cutting mat between the backing and the batting.

2. Trim the backing to leave twice the desired finished binding width plus ¼" for a seam allowance. For example, if you want a ½" finished binding, cut the backing so it extends 1¼" beyond the seam line.

3. Press one corner of the backing over the quilt top so the tip meets the corner of the marked seam line.

4. Trim the tip of the corner on the pressed line.

5. Turn up a ¼" seam allowance on the backing; press.

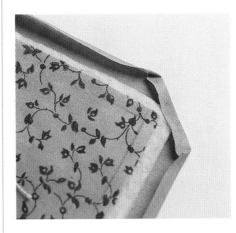

6. Fold one pressed edge of the backing over the quilt top, covering the seam line. Pin in place.

7. Fold over the adjacent edge, making a mitered corner. Hand-stitch the binding to the quilt top, making sure to cover the marked seam line.

SELF-BINDING WITH BACKING FABRIC, BUTTED CORNERS

1. If desired, mark a seam line on the quilt top ¼" from its raw edges. Trim the batting so it extends beyond the seam line to the desired finished binding width. For example, if you want ½" of binding showing on the quilt front, trim the batting ½" beyond the seam line.

To prevent yourself from inadvertently cutting into the backing fabric, slip the edge of your rotary-cutting mat between the backing and the batting.

2. Trim the backing to leave twice the desired finished binding width plus ¼" for a seam allowance. For example, if you want a ½" finished binding, cut the backing so it extends 1¼" beyond the seam line.

3. Turn up a ¼" seam allowance on opposite edges of the backing; press.

4. Fold the backing to the front again, covering the seam line; pin. In the same manner, fold, press, and pin the remaining backing edges.

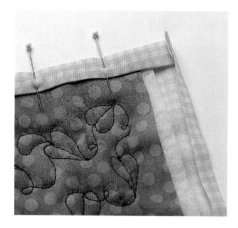

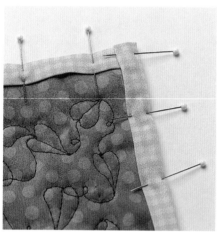

5. Hand-stitch the binding to the quilt top, making sure to cover the seam line.

KNIFE-EDGE SELF-BINDING

With knife-edge self-binding, both the quilt top and backing are turned under to meet evenly at the edges of the quilt, leaving the edges with an unbound appearance. To use this technique, quilt no closer than ½" from the quilt's edges.

1. If desired, mark a seam line on the quilt top ¼" from its raw edges. Trim the quilt top, batting, and backing to ¼" beyond the seam line.

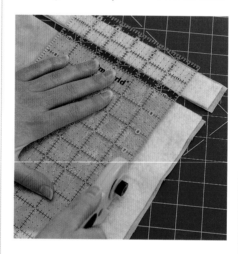

2. Fold the quilt top and backing out of the way, then trim the batting only to just beyond the seam line.

To prevent yourself from inadvertently cutting into the backing fabric, slip the edge of your rotary-cutting mat between the backing and the batting.

3. Turn opposite quilt top edges under ¼"; press. Turn corresponding backing edges under ¼"; press. Repeat with the remaining quilt top and backing edges.

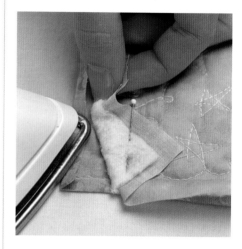

4. Align the folded edges, enclosing the batting, and pin together. Baste, if desired. Hand-stitch the folded edges together. *Note:* You may wish to finish and stabilize this area by quilting ¼ to ½" away from the folded outer edges.

These techniques for adding a special binding or finish to a quilt take a bit more time than traditional bindings, but generally add an extra element that distinguishes the quilt.

PRAIRIE POINTS

Prairie points, fabric triangles made of folded squares, add a dimensional accent to a quilt edge. To bind your quilt with prairie points, quilt no closer to the edges than ½".

1. Trim the quilt batting and backing even with the quilt top edges. If desired, mark a seam line on the quilt top ¼" from its raw edges. Then trim an additional ¼" of batting.

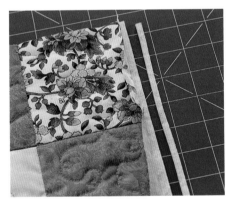

To prevent yourself from inadvertently cutting into the backing fabric, slip the edge of your rotary-cutting mat between the backing and the batting.

To make it easier to join the prairie points to the quilt top, you may wish to baste the backing out of the way.

2. Assess your project and determine a size for your prairie points. The size you choose to make your prairie points depends on the size of your quilt project. A large quilt may be able to handle large prairie points, while a small quilt could easily be overwhelmed by a border of wide prairie points.

The finished height of the prairie point will be half the size of the square minus ¼" for a seam allowance. For example, if you fold a 3" square into a prairie point, it will add 1¼" to your quilt's width on each side after being sewn to the quilt.

To figure how many prairie points are needed, first determine how much you want each prairie point to overlap. A 3" square yields a prairie point with a 3" base, but you will likely overlap your prairie points by ½ to 1", so each one will take up less than 3" of the quilt's edge. Experiment with different amounts of overlap before cutting squares to make the final prairie points. Once you've determined a size for your squares, make a few prairie points and experiment to determine the desired spacing.

3. Cut the number of squares in your desired size. Fold a square in half diagonally with the wrong side inside to form a triangle; press. Fold the triangle in half and press, making a prairie point. Repeat to make the desired number of prairie points.

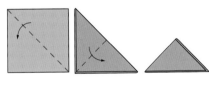

4. Pin prairie points to a side edge of the quilt top with raw edges aligned and the prairie points pointing toward the quilt center. Space them evenly and make sure all the double-folded edges face the same direction. Overlap adjacent edges or slip the single-folded edges between the double-folded edges.

5. Once you are satisfied with the placement of the prairie points, join them to the quilt top, stitching on the seam line and keeping the backing free from the stitching.

6. Repeat steps 4 and 5 along the remaining edges.

7. Turn under a ¼" seam allowance on all edges of the quilt backing; press.

8. Open up the prairie points so the points face away from the quilt center and the seam allowances turn to the inside. Pin together the backing and prairie points, enclosing the batting and seam allowances. Baste, if desired.

9. Hand-stitch the folded backing edge to the base of the prairie points, covering the machine stitching.

10. If desired, finish and stabilize the border by quilting ¼ to ½" away from the outer edges.

COVERED CORDING/PIPING

Covered cording, also called piping, is sometimes used to finish a quilt edge. To add covered cording, quilt no closer to the quilt top edges than ½".

1. Trim the quilt batting and backing even with the quilt top edges. If desired, mark a seam line on the quilt top ¼" from its raw edges. Then trim an additional ¼" of batting.

To prevent yourself from inadvertently cutting into the backing fabric, slip the edge of your rotary-cutting mat between the backing and the batting.

To make it easier to join the covered cording to the quilt top, you may wish to baste the backing out of the way.

2. Encase a length of cording in a continuous bias strip (see Cutting Bias Strips on *page 12–3* and Making Continuous Bias From a Square, which begins on *page 12–3*).

The width of your bias strip depends on the diameter of your cording. The larger the cording, the wider the bias strip will need to be. The strip needs to be wide enough to cover the cording, plus ½" for seam allowances. Regardless of the width of the bias strip, the method used to cover the cording is the same.

With the wrong side inside, fold under 1½" at one end of the bias strip, then fold the strip in half lengthwise. Insert the cording next to the folded edge, with a cording end 1" from the folded end. Using a cording or zipper foot, machine-sew through both fabric layers right next to the cording.

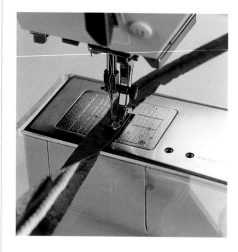

3. Beginning at the center of one edge, pin the covered cording around the quilt top with the covered cording's stitching line on the seam line.

4. Begin stitching 1½" from the folded end, stitching on the seam line and keeping the backing free from the stitching. Round the corners slightly, pivoting with the needle in the fabric at each corner and making sure the corner curves match. As you stitch each corner, gently ease the covered cording into place. Clip the seam allowance of the covered cording just next to the quilt top seam line.

5. When you get within 2 to 3" of the starting point, end the stitching. Remove 1" of stitching at each end of the cording cover and pull back the bias strip ends. Trim the cording so the ends abut and whipstitch them together.

6. Refold the bias strip so it covers the cording, lapping the folded end over the raw end. Finish stitching the covered cording to the quilt top.

7. Turn under a ¼" seam allowance on the quilt backing; press.

8. Open up the covered cording so that it sits on the quilt edge and turn the seam allowance to the inside. Pin the backing to the covered cording's seam line, enclosing the batting and seam allowances. Baste, if desired.

9. Hand-stitch the folded backing edge to the back of the covered cording, covering the machine stitching.

PIECED BIAS BINDING

You can create a scrappy border by joining straight-grain strips into sets, then cutting the sets into bias strips. Once sewn to the quilt, the pieced binding gives the appearance of diagonal stripes along the quilt's edge.

1. Cut 42"-long strips on the crosswise straight grain in the desired width or widths. (The strips may be cut in uniform or varying widths.)

2. Join the strips with ¼" seam allowances to make a striped binding set. For example, join five 1½×42" strips to make a 5½×42" binding set. Press the seam allowances open. Repeat to make the desired number of binding sets.

3. Cut bias strips from the binding sets in the desired width (see

Determining Binding Type and Width, beginning on *page 12–1* and Bias Binding, beginning on *page 12–3*).

4. Join the strips to make a continuous bias strip.

5. Prepare the continuous bias strip as for double-fold (French-fold) binding. (See Preparing Binding–Double-Fold Binding, which begins on *page 12–4*.)

6. With raw edges aligned, join the pieced binding to the quilt. (See Sewing on Binding, which begins on page *12–5*.)

7. Turn the binding over the edge of the quilt to the back. Hand-stitch the binding to the backing fabric, making sure to cover the binding stitching line.

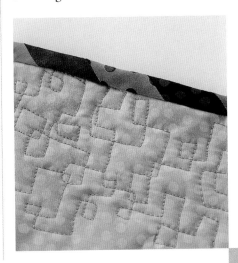

HANGING QUILTS FOR DISPLAY

If you wish to hang a quilt for display, you'll need to add tabs or a hanging sleeve. Quilts smaller than 23" square may be hung with purchased hanging clips or sewn-on tabs.

Larger quilts require a hanging sleeve attached to the back, which allows the quilt to hang straight with little distortion. The sleeve may be added before or after the binding.

ADDING A HANGING SLEEVE BEFORE BINDING

1. Assemble the quilt up to the point of attaching the binding.

2. Measure the quilt's top edge. Cut a 6 to 10"-wide strip that is 2" longer than the quilt's top edge.

3. Fold under 1½" on both short edges. Sew 1¼" from each folded edge.

4. Fold the hemmed strip in half lengthwise with the wrong side inside; pin. Join the long edges using a ¼" seam allowance to make a hanging sleeve. Do not press the seam allowance open.

5. Aligning raw edges, pin or baste the sleeve to the quilt backing.

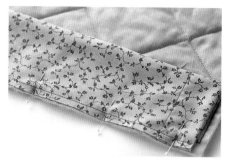

Sew the hanging sleeve and binding to the quilt at the same time, using a scant ¼" seam allowance along the edge where the sleeve is attached to accommodate the added bulk of the hanging sleeve. (See Sewing on Binding, which begins on *page 12–5* for more information on attaching binding to a quilt.)

6. Hand-stitch the binding to the hanging sleeve, covering the sleeve's stitching line.

Then hand-stitch the long folded edge of the hanging sleeve to the quilt backing. For large dowels or decorative curtain rods, allow extra ease in the side of the sleeve away from the quilt back. Before stitching down the long folded edge, fold it up about ½", then stitch in place. This will prevent the rod from creating a ridge on the front side of the quilt when it is hanging.

Stitch the short hemmed edges of the hanging sleeve to the backing where they touch.

7. Slide a wooden dowel or slender piece of wood that is 1" longer than the finished sleeve into the sleeve and hang the quilt.

ADDING A HANGING SLEEVE AFTER BINDING

1. Measure the quilt's top edge. Cut a 6 to 10"-wide strip that is 2" longer than the quilt's top edge.

2. Fold under 1½" on both short edges. Sew 1¼" from each folded edge.

3. Fold the hemmed strip in half lengthwise with the wrong side inside; pin. Join the long edges using a ¼" seam allowance to make a hanging sleeve. Press the seam allowance open and center the seam in the middle of the sleeve.

4. Center the hanging sleeve on the quilt backing about 1" below the top edge of the quilt with the seam facing the backing. Sewing through the backing and batting, hand-stitch the sleeve to the backing along both long edges and the short edges that touch the backing. For large dowels or decorative curtain rods, allow extra ease in the side of the sleeve away from the quilt back. Before stitching down the second long edge, fold it up about ½", then stitch it in place. This will prevent the rod from creating a ridge on the front side of the quilt when it is hanging.

5. Slide a wooden dowel or slender piece of wood that is 1" longer than the finished sleeve into the sleeve and hang the quilt.

ADDING HANGING LOOPS

For quilts 35" square or less, you may wish to use hanging loops instead of a full hanging sleeve.

1. Cut several 3½×5½" rectangles. Turn each rectangle's long edges under ¼"; press. Stitch ⅛" from the folded edges. Repeat with the short edges of the rectangles.

TIP: For quilts more than 60" wide, make two or three sleeves. This lets you use more nails or brackets to hold the hanging rod and more evenly distribute the quilt's weight.
    To make multiple sleeves, divide the quilt's top edge measurement by 3. Add 2" to the new measurement and cut three fabric pieces this length. Make the sleeves as previously instructed.

TIP: If you use wood dowels or rods to hang your quilts, seal the wood with polyurethane to prevent wood acids from discoloring the fabrics.

2. Evenly space the hemmed rectangles across the quilt backing 1" from the inner edge of the binding. Hand-stitch the top and bottom edges of each rectangle in place.

ADDING HOOK-AND-LOOP TAPE

This hanging method eliminates the need for a dowel but requires you to mount a lattice strip to your wall.

1. Measure the quilt's top edge. Cut a 1½"-wide strip of hook-and-loop tape 2" shorter than that measurement.

TIP: For quilts without an obvious top or side, sew sleeves along several edges. Then you can turn the quilt at least every six months and redistribute its weight, which protects your quilt from sagging and tearing.

2. Cut a 2"-wide wooden lattice strip the same length as the hook-and-loop tape strip.

3. Separate the tape halves so that you have one strip with hooks (stiffer strip) and one with loops (softer strip). Center the hook strip across the quilt backing ½" below the top edge of the quilt. Hand-stitch the entire strip to the backing, making sure the stitches don't show on the front of the quilt.

TIP: Change your wall quilts every couple of months to minimize damage from exposure to sunlight. Try to avoid hanging quilts where they'll be in direct sunlight.

4. Aligning the edges, attach the loop strip to the lattice strip using a staple gun. *Note:* A hot-glue gun may be used for this step if you're hanging a small, lightweight quilt.

5. Measure, mark, and anchor the lattice strip securely to the wall with the loop strip facing out. Place nails 1" or so in from each lattice end and in the center. Add nails, or the appropriate fastener for your wall type, between those already placed, dividing and subdividing spaces and using as many nails as needed to make sure the lattice can support the weight of the quilt.

6. Mount the quilt by aligning the hook-and-loop tape halves; press together firmly.

LABELING YOUR QUILT

Since your quilts may outlive you, it makes sense to preserve their heritage for future generations by marking them with your name, your city, and the date at a minimum. Adding other information, such as a poem, a good-will wish for the recipient, a special-occasion note, or even the fabric content and care instructions, further personalizes the quilt.

There are several ways to permanently mark a quilt. You can sign directly on the quilt using a fine-tip permanent fabric marking pen, cross-stitch, or embroidery. *Note:* Be sure to test any marking pen on a scrap of fabric identical to the quilt fabric to check for bleeding before writing on the actual quilt. (See Putting Pen to Fabric, *opposite*, for more information.)

As a guide for embroidering or cross-stitching a signature, write on tissue paper first, then stitch directly through the paper onto the fabric. After completing the stitching, gently pull away the paper.

You can also sew a separate label to the quilt backing. Purchase a premade label, or design one yourself. The fabric content of the attached label should be compatible with the quilt fabric and should be colorfast. For example, a satin or wool label on a cotton quilt might complicate the cleaning process.

To affix the label, turn under the raw edges. Using a traditional appliqué stitch (see Chapter 8—Appliqué for more information) or other decorative stitch (see Chapter 13—Specialty Techniques for more information), sew through the folded label edge, catching the quilt backing and batting in your stitches.

However you choose to label your projects, it's important to do so. It's a thoughtful act for present and future generations who may want to know: Who made this quilt?

PUTTING PEN TO FABRIC

Whether you're making one label or a whole quilt of signature blocks, use these tips to write successfully on fabric.

1. Choose a smooth, high-quality, 100%-cotton fabric. Select a fabric color that will allow the ink to show. Avoid white-on-white prints because the pattern is painted on, rather than dyed into, the fabric, which makes writing difficult and inhibits the ink penetration.

2. Prewash the fabric; cotton fabrics usually contain sizing that acts as a barrier to ink penetration.

3. Use a permanent-ink pen designed for use on fabric. A fine point (.01 diameter) writes delicately and is less likely to bleed. Lines can be made thicker by going over them more than once. For larger letters or numbers, a .05-diameter pen works well.

TIP: As an extra measure of security, affix your label to the quilt backing before you quilt the project, then quilt through the label. This way you can be certain the quilt and label won't be parted.

4. Test the pen and fabric together. Write on a fabric sample, then follow the manufacturer's directions for setting the ink. Wait 24 hours for the ink to set, then wash the sample as you would any fine quilt. The extra time it takes to run such a test will pay off in years of durability.

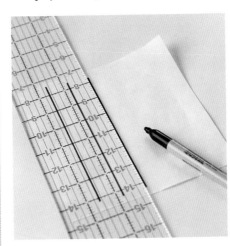

5. Stabilize the fabric and create guidelines with freezer paper. Cut a piece of freezer paper large enough to cover the fabric's writing area. Use a ruler and thick black marker to draw evenly spaced lines on the freezer paper's dull side. *Note:* This works only with light-color fabrics, which allow the lines on the freezer paper to show through.

6. Iron the freezer paper to the fabric's wrong side with a hot, dry iron. *Note:* Make several samples so you have plenty of opportunities to practice.

7. Write slowly and with a lighter touch than you normally would use for writing on paper. This allows time for the ink to flow into the fabric and lets you control the letters.

My Notes for Binding & Finishing

My Notes for Binding & Finishing

Specialty Techniques

13

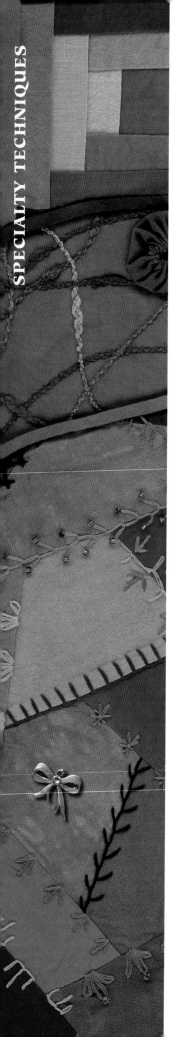

SPECIALTY TECHNIQUES

TABLE OF CONTENTS
CHAPTER 13—Specialty Techniques

AS THE ART OF QUILTING HAS EXPANDED OVER THE YEARS, SO HAVE THE DESIGN OPTIONS AND TECHNIQUES that are available to quilters. Whether you're looking for instructions on assembling a classic Log Cabin block, want to attempt trapunto for the first time, or are just ready to try something new, you'll find a host of ideas and explanations in this chapter.

LOG CABIN

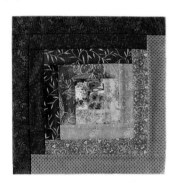

The popular Log Cabin block is simple enough for a beginner, but has so many design variations that it has held the interest of experienced quilters for generations. The success of this design depends on a strong contrast between the fabrics on either side of the diagonal that forms when the "logs" are pieced.

Traditionally, the block was made with a red center square, which represented the hearth in the log cabin home. Today's quilters use a variety of colors for the center block that may or may not match the light or dark fabrics used in the rest of the block.

Most often quilts composed of Log Cabin blocks are scrappy—

made with a multitude of fabrics. For a dramatic look, choose two high-contrasting colors, such as red and green, or light and dark variations of the same color, such as lavender and plum. (See Chapter 2—Fabric & Color for more information on contrast.)

ASSEMBLING A LOG CABIN BLOCK

A Log Cabin block is assembled in a numerical sequence, beginning at the center of the block and working in a clockwise direction around the center. Strip piecing is a quick-sew method that makes it easy to assemble multiple Log Cabin blocks without cutting individual strips for each piece of the block. To strip-piece a Log Cabin block, follow these steps.

1. Cut light and dark fabrics into 42"-long strips the desired finished width of a "log" plus ½" for seam allowances. Cut a 42"-long strip for the center square the desired finished width of the square plus ½" for seam allowances. Separate the strips into stacks of light and dark strips.

In this example, the strip for the center square was cut 2½" wide for

> **TIP: Precut Scrap Strips**
> Having strips precut makes quick work of the Log Cabin block. When cutting fabrics for other quilt projects, take leftover, odd-size pieces and cut them into 1½"-wide strips. Sort the strips into light and dark and you'll have the makings for a Log Cabin quilt in the future.

a finished 2" square, and the light and dark strips were cut 1½" wide for a 1"-wide finished "log."

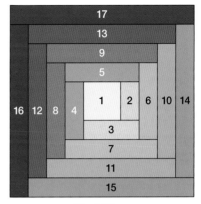

Block Diagram

2. With right sides together and long raw edges aligned, sew together the center square strip (position No. 1 in the Block Diagram, *above*) and a light strip for position No. 2. Press the seam allowance away from the center square strip.

3. Cut the pieced strips into units equal in width to the cut size of the center square strip.

In this example, the center square strip was cut 2½" wide, so the pieced strips are cut into 2½"-wide units.

4. Place a light strip for position No. 3 faceup on the sewing machine bed. Position a Step 3 unit facedown on the light strip with the center square fabric away from you.

Sew together. When you approach the end of the unit, place a second Step 3 unit next to the first with a slight space between the two and the center square fabric away from you. *Note:* For even more efficiency, continue sewing without lifting the presser foot or clipping threads.

Continue in the same manner, sewing at a slow, steady speed, until all the Step 3 units have been sewn to the position No. 3 strip.

5. Cut the pieced center units apart, trimming the edges even with the long edges of the Step 3 units. Press the seam allowances away from the center squares.

6. Repeat steps 4 and 5 to join the pieced center units to the position No. 4 strip, paying attention to the direction that the pieced center units are fed under the presser foot.

7. Continue sewing the pieced center units to strips in numerical order (see the Block Diagram on *page 13–1*) to complete a Log Cabin block. Always press the seam allowances toward the outside of the block.

SETTING OPTIONS

When joined into a quilt top, Log Cabin blocks can create many different effects. By rotating the blocks so the lights and darks are in different positions, different designs will emerge. Four setting options for Log Cabin blocks follow. (See Chapter 9—Assembling the Quilt Top for additional information on quilt settings.)

The Log Cabin block shown in these illustrations has two same-size squares for position Nos. 1 and 2. *Note:* The center square size for this block is equal to the strip width. For example, if the strips are cut 1½"-wide, each center square is 1½". This more intricate center design allows even more flexibility in creating undulating designs as you rotate the blocks.

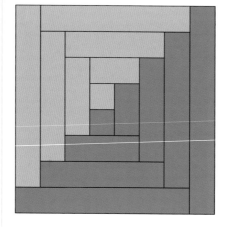

Barn Raising Set
The placement of lights and darks creates a pattern that radiates from the center of the quilt in this setting.

Streak of Lightning Set
The placement of lights and darks creates vertical rows or streaks running the length of the quilt.

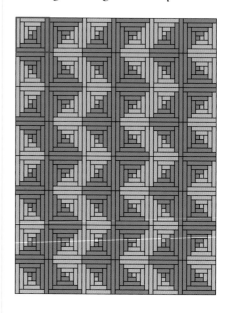

Specialty Techniques

Light and Dark Set

A pattern of blocks on point emerges as the Log Cabin blocks are rotated so lights and darks meet.

Straight Furrows Set

Diagonal bands of color move from upper right to lower left in this setting.

PREPARING THE QUILT TOP

Quilting adds texture to a quilt's surface, but if you want even more relief, trapunto, or dimensional quilting, is a technique to try. By stuffing or filling an area, then quilting it, a raised surface, or relief, is formed that gives shape to stems, leaves, or other motifs.

1. Select a quilting design with trapunto in mind. Choose a design that has definite shapes stitched around all sides, as the trapunto will bring those areas into relief. If you wish, choose one of the patterns specifically created for trapunto quilting.

2. Transfer the design onto the quilt top using a nonpermanent marking tool. (See Chapter 11—Hand & Machine Quilting for information on transferring a design onto fabric.) Cut out a muslin underlining to cover the trapunto design area. This muslin will form the backing for the area that will be stuffed. *Note:* After the trapunto is completed, the quilt top will be layered with batting and backing and finished as any other quilt.

3. Baste the muslin underlining to the wrong side of the marked design. To prevent shifting while basting, tape the corners of the muslin down, then tape the marked quilt top to a work surface.

4. Using a smaller than normal basting stitch and contrasting thread, sew just inside the marked lines of the design or motifs.

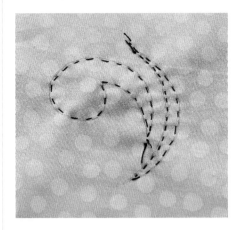

5. Turn the fabric layers with the muslin side faceup. If you will be hand-quilting the finished project, use small sharp embroidery scissors to carefully trim away the muslin underlining, except what's behind the design motifs, retaining a ¼" seam allowance. Leave small areas where you are unable to leave a ¼" seam untrimmed. *Note:* Trimming the muslin is done to reduce the bulk for hand quilting and does not have to be exact. It is not necessary to trim the muslin for machine quilting.

6. There are several ways to create the raised surface—channel, stuffed, and machine trapunto. Descriptions of each method follow. Choose one or more than one to stuff your basted shapes.

CHANNEL TRAPUNTO
To fill thin areas, such as leaf stems or veining, use channel trapunto.

1. Prepare the quilt top for trapunto. (See Preparing the Quilt Top on *page 13–3.*)

2. Thread a darning needle with 12 to 16" of cotton yarn. Working from the wrong side of the quilt top, slip the needle under the muslin underlining but not through the quilt top. Pull it through a basted channel, leaving a 1 to 2" tail of yarn at the beginning.

3. Move in and out of the muslin underlining until the channel is filled with the yarn. For wider channels, pass through the area a second time. It is best to pass through the channel twice with a single strand rather than using a doubled strand of yarn once.

4. Repeat to fill all the desired motifs, then complete the quilt as desired. (See Chapter 9—Assembling the Quilt Top for more information.)

5. Remove the basting threads.

STUFFED TRAPUNTO
To fill larger design motifs, use stuffed trapunto.

1. Prepare the quilt top for trapunto. (See Preparing the Quilt Top on *page 13–3.*)

2. Working from the wrong side of the quilt top, use small embroidery scissors to cut a small slit in the muslin underlining in the center of a motif, such as a leaf, or a section of a motif. Be careful not to cut into the quilt top fabric.

3. Working on a flat surface, insert small bits of fiberfill into the cavity with the aid of a blunt stuffing tool. Stuff only small bits at a time until the design is lightly but evenly stuffed. Avoid overfilling, which may cause the fabric surrounding the design to pucker.

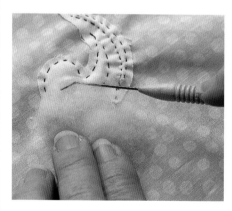

4. Turn the project over from time to time to check for distortion. If necessary, adjust the amount of fiberfill.

5. Once a motif is stuffed, use a needle and thread to whipstitch the opening in the muslin underlining closed.

6. Repeat to fill all the desired motifs, then complete the quilt as desired. (See Chapter 9—Assembling the Quilt Top for more information.)

7. Remove the basting threads.

TRAPUNTO BY MACHINE
To do trapunto completely by machine, use water-soluble thread.

1. Transfer the design onto the quilt top using a nonpermanent marking tool. (See Chapter 11—Hand & Machine Quilting for information on transferring a design onto fabric.)

2. Cut a piece of batting the size needed to cover the design area. Place the batting over the design area on the wrong side of the quilt top. Baste the batting in place.

3. Using water-soluble thread in the needle and cotton thread in a color to match the quilt top in the bobbin, stitch around a motif you want to stuff. *Note:* For illustration purposes only, contrasting thread was used in the photographs.

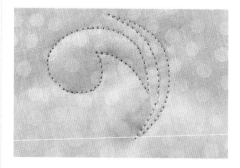

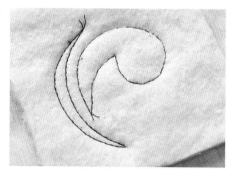

4. When stitching is complete, trim the batting away around the shape next to the stitching line, leaving the batting inside the stitching lines secured.

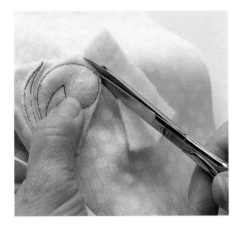

5. Repeat to fill all the desired motifs, then complete the quilt as desired. (See Chapter 9—Assembling the Quilt Top for more information.)

If you're machine-quilting, be sure to stitch over the water-soluble thread around each shape to secure the trapunto batting piece.

To make the raised areas even more prominent, quilt more heavily around each motif with closely spaced stitches, such as small stippling.

6. After the quilting and binding are complete, wash the quilt or spritz the trapunto areas with water to remove the water-soluble thread.

CRAZY QUILTING

In the late 1800s and early 1900s, quilters went a little crazy, using an array of fabrics and embellishments in their projects which came to be known as crazy quilts. Each block showcased the needlework skills of its maker. Although this quilt style was popular, the finished projects were more for decoration than for function.

One advantage of crazy quilting is that it uses foundation blocks, enabling quilters to more easily work with angled, bias-edge fabric pieces. Another attraction of this technique is that it offers the opportunity to use a variety of fabrics, such as silk, taffeta, and velvet, which aren't typically found in pieced quilts. The following steps describe crazy quilting.

1. For each block you want to make, cut a muslin square the desired size of the finished block plus ½" for seam allowances. These are your block foundations.

2. Cut a variety of fabric pieces in assorted shapes and sizes. The pieces must be cut with straight, not curved, edges.

3. Place a fabric right side up in the center of a muslin foundation square. Place a second piece right side down over the first piece, aligning straight edges along one side. Sew along the aligned edges with a ¼" seam.

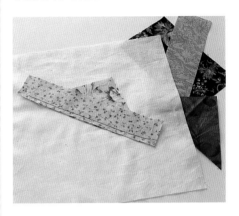

4. Press the top piece open. Trim the ends of the larger piece so that they're even with the smaller piece.

5. In the same manner, position a third fabric piece right side down on the pieced unit, aligning a pair of edges. Sew along the aligned edges with a ¼" seam. Press open and trim as before.

6. Repeat the process to fill the entire muslin foundation, trimming any fabric pieces that extend past the foundation edges.

7. Hand- or machine-embellish the finished block as desired with decorative stitches along the seam lines. (See Decorative Stitches, which begins *below,* for stitch ideas.)

8. Repeat to create the desired number of blocks. When the crazy quilt blocks are finished, lay them out as desired and sew together into a quilt top. Complete the quilt as desired. (See Chapter 9—Assembling the Quilt Top for more information.) If desired, stitch across the block seams or add ribbons, beading, buttons, or charms as embellishments (see *page 13–10* for information on surface embellishments).

(see *page 13–10* for information on surface embellishments)

DECORATIVE STITCHES BY HAND

Hand-stitching embellishment options are as limitless as the available thread types, making decorative stitches an extremely personal form of expression. Although decorative stitching has long been associated with crazy quilting, it can be found in quilts ranging from traditional to contemporary, whether embellishing seam allowances or in place of the usual straight quilting stitches.

Instructions for some more common decorative stitches follow.

BACKSTITCH

To backstitch, pull the needle up at A. Insert it back into the fabric at B, and bring it up at C. Push the needle down again at D, and bring it up at E. Continue in the same manner.

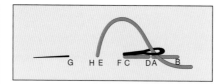

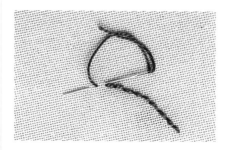

BLANKET STITCH

To blanket-stitch, pull the needle up at A, form a reverse L shape with the thread, and hold the angle of the L shape in place with your thumb. Push the needle down at B and come up at C to secure the stitch. Continue in the same manner.

You may wish to make all your stitches the same length, as shown in the illustration, or to vary the lengths, as shown in the photograph.

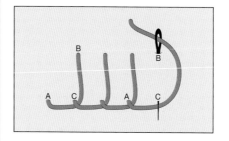

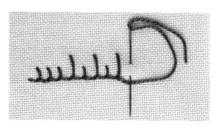

CHAIN STITCH

To chain-stitch, pull the needle up at A, form a U shape with the thread, and hold the shape in place with your thumb. Push the needle down at B, about ⅛" from A, and come up at C. Continue in the same manner.

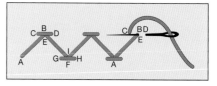

CHEVRON

To chevron-stitch, pull the needle up at A, then push it down at B. Holding the thread out of the way with your thumb, make a small stitch by bringing the needle up at C, pulling the thread taut. Then push the needle down at D and bring it up at E (same hole as B). Next push the needle down at F, pull it up at G, push it down at H, and bring it up at I (same hole as F). Pull the thread taut. Continue in the same manner.

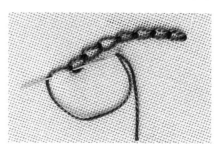

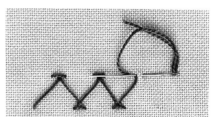

CROSS-STITCH

To cross-stitch, pull the needle up at A, then push it down at B. Bring the needle up at C, then push it down at D. Continue in the same manner. When you reach the end of a row of stitching, push the needle down at H, pull it up at I, push it down at J (same hole as F) to make an X, and pull it up at K (same hole as G). Continue in the same manner.

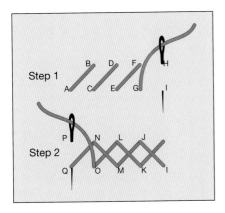

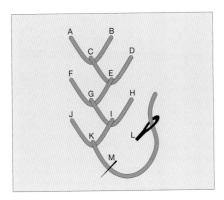

FEATHERSTITCH

To featherstitch, pull the needle up at A, form a V shape with the thread (pointing in either direction), and hold the angle in place with your thumb. Push the needle down at B, about ⅜" from A, and come up at C.

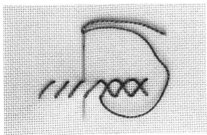

For the next stitch, form a V shape with the thread, insert the needle at D, and bring it out at E. Continue in the same manner.

There are many variations of the featherstitch. If all the V shapes fall on the same side of a seam, it looks similar to a blanket stitch. For a double or triple featherstitch, work two or three stitches on the right side of a seam, followed by two or three on the left side.

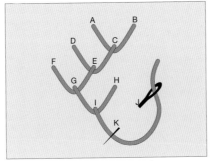

Double Featherstitch

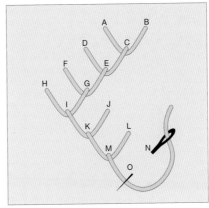

Triple Featherstitch

FRENCH KNOT

To make a French knot, pull the thread through at the point where the knot is desired (A). Wrap the thread around the needle two or three times. Insert the tip of the needle into the fabric at B, 1/16" away from A. Gently push the wraps down the needle to meet the fabric. Pull the needle and trailing thread through the fabric slowly and smoothly. Repeat for as many French knots as desired.

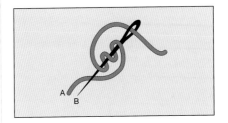

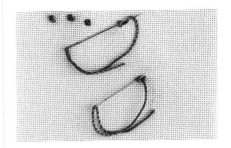

HERRINGBONE STITCH

To herringbone-stitch, pull the needle up at A, then push it down at B. Bring the needle up at C, cross the thread over the first stitch, and push the needle down at D. Pull the needle up at E, cross the thread over the second stitch, and push the needle down at F. Pull the needle up at G and continue in the same manner.

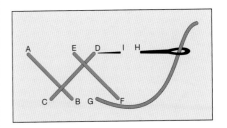

LAZY DAISY STITCH

To make a lazy daisy stitch, pull the needle up at A and form a loop of thread on the fabric surface. Holding the loop in place, insert the needle back into the fabric at B, about 1/16" away from A. Bring the needle tip out at C and cross it over the trailing thread, keeping the thread as flat as possible. Gently pull the needle and trailing thread until the loop lies flat against the fabric. Push the needle through to the back at D to secure the loop in place. Repeat for as many lazy daisy stitches as desired.

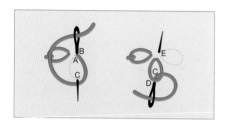

RUNNING STITCH

To make a running stitch, pull the needle up at A and insert it back

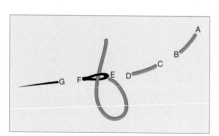

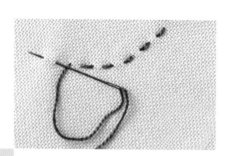

into the fabric at B, 1/8" away from A. Pull your needle up at C, 1/8" away from B, and continue in the same manner.

STAR STITCH

To star-stitch, or double cross-stitch, pull the needle up at A, then push it down at B. Bring the needle up at C, cross it over the first stitch, and push the needle down at D to make a cross. Pull the needle up at E, push it down at F, bring the needle up at G, cross it over the last stitch, and push the needle down at H to make an X. Continue in the same manner.

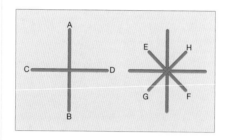

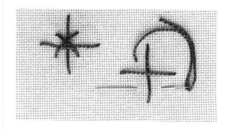

STEM STITCH

To stem-stitch, pull the needle up at A, then insert it back into the fabric at B, about 3/8" away from A. Holding the thread out of the way, bring the

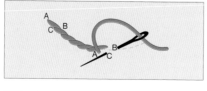

needle back up at C and pull the thread through so it lies flat against the fabric. The distances between points A, B, and C should be equal. Pull gently with equal tautness after each stitch. Continue in the same manner, holding the thread out of the way on the same side of the stitching every time.

DECORATIVE STITCHES BY MACHINE

Decorative stitches are built into many sewing machines and can be used for embellishing or quilting. Practice your machine stitches on scraps of quilted fabric so you have a sample of the stitches available. When you're finalizing your quilt design, your stitched sample will provide you with a variety of choices.

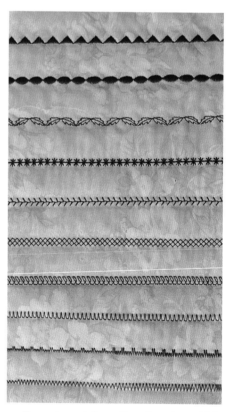

Experiment by adjusting the width and length of the decorative stitches when possible. Some stitches that

Specialty Techniques

look less desirable at their normal width and length take on a whole new look once you alter one or both factors. Be sure to mark on your stitch sample the settings that you used.

YO-YOS

A perennial favorite, the yo-yo is a circle of fabric that has been gathered to form a smaller, three-dimensional circle. Yo-yos can be sewn together to make a quilt or used as an embellishment.

Yo-yos are traditionally made by hand, and many quilters find them a good project for travel or television time. They can be made from any size fabric circle. The finished size of a yo-yo will be slightly less than half the size of the fabric circle. For example, a 3"-diameter circle will make a yo-yo approximately 1½" in diameter.

1. Cut the desired-size fabric circle using a template.

2. Begin with a sewing needle and sturdy, 100% cotton thread. Knot the end of the thread tail. While folding the raw edge of the fabric circle ¼" to the wrong side, take small, evenly spaced running stitches near the folded edge to secure it. (See the description of the running stitch *opposite.)*

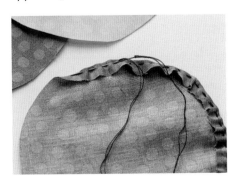

3. End your stitching just next to the starting point. Do not cut the thread. Gently pull the thread end to gather the folded edge until it forms a gathered circle. The right side of the fabric will develop soft pleats as you gather the edge. The folded-under seam allowance should roll to the inside of the yo-yo. Take a small tack stitch to hold the gathers in place, then knot your thread and cut off the thread tail.

4. To stitch yo-yos together, place the yo-yos with the gathered fronts together. Using matching thread, whipstitch them together for about ½".

Make rows of yo-yos the desired width of the finished quilt, then sew the rows together in the same manner.

Surface embellishments are finishing touches that can add texture and an element of surprise to a quilt. From buttons to beads, the options are many. Visit quilt, crafts, and art stores for items to stitch onto a quilt.

COUCHING

Fastening a thread, ribbon, or trim to a quilt's surface with small, evenly spaced stitches—couching—adds texture and dimension to a project. Couching can be done by hand or by machine and with clear monofilament or contrasting thread, depending on whether you want the anchoring stitches to show or not.

Couching by Hand

Position the decorative thread on the quilt top. Use fine thread to work small stitches ¼" to ⅜" apart over the decorative thread.

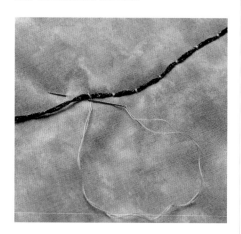

Couching by Machine

Position the decorative thread on the quilt top. Set your machine for a zigzag stitch that is slightly wider than the thread being couched. Adjust the upper tension, if necessary, or run the bobbin thread through the finger on the bobbin to increase its tension. This will pull

the needle thread to the quilt back, preventing the bobbin thread from showing on the quilt top. Zigzag-stitch over the decorative thread, making sure the swing of the needle pivots to either side of the couched thread as you stitch.

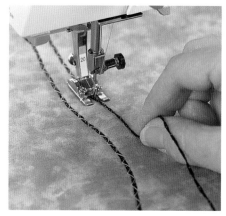

Many sewing machines have special couching feet available, which places the decorative thread or trim in a groove that stabilizes it beneath the presser foot.

Practice on scraps of quilted fabric to get the appropriate stitch width, length, and tension setting when machine-couching. Some decorative threads may flatten during couching, so it is important to stitch test samples. If the thread is being flattened too much, you may wish to try a blind hem stitch rather than a zigzag stitch.

BEADS, BUTTONS, AND CHARMS

Beads, buttons, and charms add sparkle, dimension, and texture to a quilt. Generally, it is best to add these embellishments to quilts that will not receive much handling, such as wall hangings.

Sew on the beads, buttons, or charms after quilting is complete to avoid damaging items. The method you choose for attaching them usually is driven by the desired

finished effect. *Note:* With the following methods, your stitches will show on the quilt's back. If you wish to hide your stitches, modify the techniques to run the needle through the quilt top and batting only.

Adding Round or Seed Beads Individually

Attaching single beads to a quilt surface can be tedious, but if precise placement is important, this may be the best option.

1. Thread a beading needle with matching-color cotton or monofilament thread and knot one end. Push the needle through the quilt top to the back at the point where the first bead is desired. *Note:* The knot will be covered by the first bead.

2. Take a few tiny stitches on the quilt back.

3. Push the needle from the quilt back through to the quilt top right next to the knot, and slip the first bead on the thread.

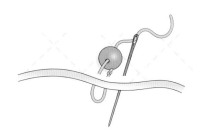

4. Place the needle into the quilt top close to the bead and pull the needle through to the back. Pull the thread taut, but do not pull too tightly or you may distort or pucker the quilt top.

5. Repeat to add additional beads. Take a backstitch after three or four beads to secure them. To backstitch, bring the needle up from the back of the quilt and thread it back through the last bead.

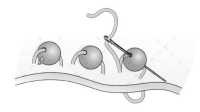

To travel short distances between beads, slide the needle between the quilt top and batting to the point of the next bead. Do not carry the thread for long distances between beads. Instead, knot your thread and begin again.

Adding Long or Bugle Beads Individually

Long, thin beads or bugle beads require a sewing technique different from round beads so they'll lie flat on the quilt.

1. Thread a beading needle with matching-color or monofilament thread and knot one end. Push the needle through the quilt top to the back at the point where the first bead is desired. *Note:* The knot will be covered by the first bead.

2. Take a few tiny stitches on the quilt back.

3. Push the needle from the quilt back through to the quilt top right next to the knot, and slip the first bead on the thread.

4. Place the needle into the quilt top close to the bead and pull the needle through to the back.

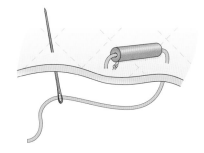

5. Push the needle to the quilt top one bead width away, as you would for a backstitch. Pull the thread taut, but do not pull too tightly or you may distort or pucker the quilt top. Make sure the bead lies flat against the quilt top.

6. Repeat to add additional beads. Take a backstitch after three or four beads to secure them. To backstitch, bring the needle up from the back of the quilt and thread it back through the last bead.

Couching a String of Beads

Attaching a string of beads by couching them to a quilt surface can be faster than adding them one at a time.

1. Thread a single strand of matching-color or monofilament thread onto a beading needle and knot one end. Bring the needle from the quilt back to the quilt top. String the desired number of beads onto the thread, leaving a few inches of thread near the needle without beads.

2. Secure the bead strand by parking the needle in the quilt. Do not remove the needle.

3. Thread a single strand of matching-color or monofilament thread onto a second beading needle and knot one end. Starting near the

knotted end of the bead strand, bring the needle up from the quilt back to the quilt front.

4. Make a couching stitch (see Couching, *opposite*) over the bead-strand thread right next to the first bead. Push the needle through to the quilt back. Pull the thread taut so that no thread shows on the quilt top near the first bead.

5. Slide the second bead next to the first and couch over the bead-strand thread right next to the second bead. Repeat to couch the remaining beads in place.

6. Once the bead strand has been couched, bring your couching thread to the quilt back and knot it off. In the same manner, bring the parked needle and bead-strand thread to the quilt back and knot the thread.

Adding Buttons and Charms

Folk art quilts often feature buttons as embellishments. In some cases, buttons are part of a quilt's ties, rather than thread alone. For added dimension, buttons can be layered one on top of another.

Charms often appear on crazy quilts. (See *page 13–5* for information on crazy quilts.) Add charms to a theme quilt to enhance the design and provide another element of interest. Quilt and crafts stores often carry packages of metal charms that work well on quilts or needlework.

Depending on the finished look you want, choose matching-color or contrasting-color thread to attach the buttons or charms to a quilt.

MACHINE EMBROIDERY

Computerized sewing machines and the expanded availability of specialty threads to noncommercial sewing enthusiasts has opened up many machine embroidery options to quilters. You may wish to use the preprogrammed designs available from sewing machine and independent software design companies. For example, sewing machines with computer programs and embroidery images make it possible to stitch designs such as the pansy bouquet *below*. You also can create your own designs using free-motion or freehand embroidery.

Most often machine embroidery is added to a quilt top before the quilt layers are assembled. Pay special attention to the stabilizer you use and the density of the designs. If the stabilizer is not removed or the designs are too dense, you may have undesirable stiffness in the embroidered areas of your finished quilt.

If your machine does not have computerized embroidery capabilities, try freehand embroidery—with a darning foot and the feed dogs dropped—which enables you to create embroidered

designs such as the iris *below,* a combination of appliqué and machine embroidery.

BOBBIN WORK

When decorative threads are too thick to thread through the sewing machine's needle, you may choose to do bobbin work. With this technique, the decorative thread is wound onto the bobbin. Trace the design on the quilt back, opposite where you want it to appear on the quilt top. *Note:* Your design on the quilt front will be a mirror-image of what is stitched on the quilt back.

Place the quilt top facedown on the machine bed. Thread matching-color or monofilament thread in the needle. Sew on the traced lines with a straight or decorative stitch, as desired. *Note:* Stitch test samples before working on a quilt.

You will not be able to see the decorative thread as you are stitching, as it will appear on the underside (quilt top). Secure the beginning and ending stitches by turning your stitch length to 0 for one or two stitches.

There are numerous specialty quilt styles. Though this book does not provide step-by-step instructions for the techniques, the information that follows can help you identify particular specialties. Many books and patterns are available that give how-to instructions for each of these types of quilting.

BARGELLO

Bargello quilts—those with a zigzag or flame pattern—look complicated but are actually quite simple. First, strips of fabric are sewn together. Then the pieced strips are cut into different widths and sewn together in a prescribed order. The peaks and valleys in the design are created by staggering the strips and varying the strip widths. Bargello variations abound.

BRODERIE PERSE

Fabrics with attractive motifs take on a second life when the motifs are cut out and appliquéd to another fabric in a technique called broderie perse. This technique was popular in the mid-1800s when the motifs generally were cut from a small piece of an expensive fabric or one that was in short supply. The motifs were then buttonhole-stitched to a less expensive fabric. Floral motifs are commonly used in broderie perse.

CELTIC (BIAS TUBE METHOD)

Celtic quilts have geometric designs and an architectural flair. Much like stained-glass quilts in technique, this type of Celtic quilt has a linear design theme. These designs often are applied to quilt tops with thin tubes of bias-cut fabric. (See Chapter 8—Appliqué for information on making bias strips and using bias bars.)

HAWAIIAN APPLIQUÉ

Intricate, symmetrical designs are the hallmark of a Hawaiian appliqué quilt. The designs result from a process similar to cutting snowflakes from paper.

To create a Hawaiian appliqué design, first make a pattern by folding a large, square piece of paper in half two times as shown *below*.

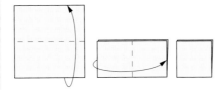

Draw an appliqué design on the paper with the design's base positioned where all the folded edges meet. Cut out the design and unfold it to see the complete motif. If you're pleased with the shape, cut the paper apart on the folds to make quarter-size patterns.

Fold the appliqué fabric in half two times. Align the cut edges of a quarter-size paper pattern with the folded edges of the folded fabric and pin in place. Cut out the appliqué shape, adding a seam allowance around the outer edges.

Unfold the fabric to reveal the appliqué shape.

Baste the appliqué shape to a foundation fabric and stitch it in place using needle-turn appliqué. (See Chapter 8—Appliqué for information on needle-turn appliqué.)

PHOTO TRANSFER

Photographic images can be transferred to fabric, resulting in a highly personalized quilt. With access to a photocopier or computer and printer, you can make your own photo transfers.

Select photo-transfer paper that is specific to or compatible with the equipment you are using. The computer or copier needs to be able to produce a mirror image of the photo or design. Otherwise, your finished photo transfer will be a reverse image of the photograph, a concern if there is lettering on a garment or a sign in the photo.

Making a photo transfer is a two-step process. First, copy the image onto the transfer paper, then press the transfer paper onto a foundation fabric using dry heat and sufficient pressure. Follow the directions that accompany your product for transferring the image and caring for the final product.

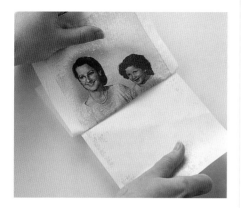

RAW EDGES

For a casual look, try leaving raw edges of a quilt exposed, as shown in the quilt at *right*. Sew the blocks with their wrong sides together so that the seams show on the quilt top. Press the seams open. Clip the seams to fringe them, or let the washer and dryer do the unraveling work.

REDWORK

Traditionally, white squares of fabric with images embroidered in red thread or floss became the basis for redwork quilts (see the photo at *right*). The quilter added stitches to preprinted squares and sewed them together in a red and white quilt.

Today, quilters use a variety of white to off-white fabrics as the foundation for redwork stitches—most often stem stitches. The embroidered designs can be combined with pieced blocks into a quilt top or joined with sashing strips. When blue thread or floss is used, the technique is aptly called bluework. (See Decorative Stitches by Hand beginning on *page 13–6* for embroidery ideas.)

SAMPLER QUILT

Rather than repeating one or two blocks throughout a quilt, a quiltmaker may use an assortment of blocks to create a sampler quilt (see the photo at *left*). This type of quilt is often used in beginning quiltmaking classes so students have the opportunity to practice different techniques. A sampler quilt works best when all the blocks are composed of the same group of coordinating fabrics and/or colors.

SASHIKO

What began as a method to mend and reinforce indigo-color work clothes in Japan—sashiko—has evolved into a quilting technique.

Sashiko is done today over one or two layers of fabric with or without a batting. It also can function as a quilting stitch. Sashiko uses thick white thread and solid-color fabrics; it involves fewer stitches per inch— five to seven stitches—than traditional quilting. The decorative patterns tend to be geometric or reflect items found in nature. Designs need to be transferred and the stitching sequence determined prior to beginning stitching.

SIGNATURE QUILT

When the settlers headed west across America, many carried a quilt signed by members of the community that they were leaving. Scores of these signature quilts can be found in antique shops, and more are being produced by quilters today (see photo at *left*). Names and notes are inscribed on the blocks in these quilts with embroidery, permanent ink, or machine stitching. (See Chapter 12—Binding & Finishing for information on putting permanent signatures with pen on fabric.)

STAINED-GLASS QUILT

The makers of stained glass and stained-glass quilts have a history of sharing patterns and designs, even though making a quilt look like a stained-glass window is a relatively new concept.

To make a stained-glass quilt, strips of ¼"-wide black bias tape are positioned over areas where different colors of fabric meet. The strips are machine-stitched down with a double needle and black thread or are stitched along each edge by hand or machine. The bias tape bends smoothly around curves and other shapes, imitating the look of leading in a stained-glass window.

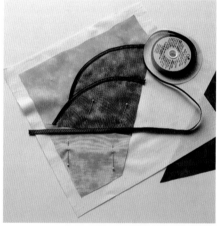

Bias tape specifically designed for stained-glass quilts is available at quilt shops. (See Chapter 8—Appliqué for information on making your own bias strips or tubes.)

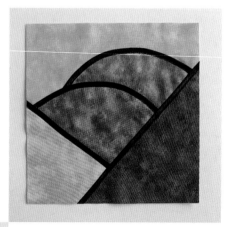

STRING PIECING

Similar to piecing a crazy quilt, string piecing involves sewing fabric strips to a foundation fabric. The strips, or "strings," can be any color combination, from scrappy to graduated color families.

The strips do not need to be a uniform width, as the foundation will prevent bias edges from distorting. This is an excellent technique for using scraps from previous quilt projects.

To begin, place two strips with right sides together atop a muslin foundation piece cut to the desired finished shape, including seam allowances. Sew along a pair of long edges, then press open the top strip. Place a third strip on the second strip with right sides together. Sew together a pair of long edges, and press open the top strip. Continue to add strips in the same manner.

Trim the strip-pieced unit even with the foundation edges, then join the trimmed units to make blocks.

WATERCOLOR OR COLOR-WASH QUILT

When an assortment of busy print fabrics is cut into small pieces and carefully positioned in a quilt top, the look of a watercolor painting emerges. Prints with multiple colors and varying values, such as florals, work well for watercolor, or color-wash, quilts.

Generally, the quilts are made from 2" squares of fabric. The key to a successful watercolor quilt is a large value range in your fabric choices. (See Chapter 2—Fabric & Color for more information about color values.) To accumulate enough prints, consider a fabric exchange with other quilters. Use a design wall to plan the design and avoid fabrics that appear solid when viewed from a distance.

Specialty Techniques

My Notes for Specialty Techniques

My Notes for Specialty Techniques

Glossary

14

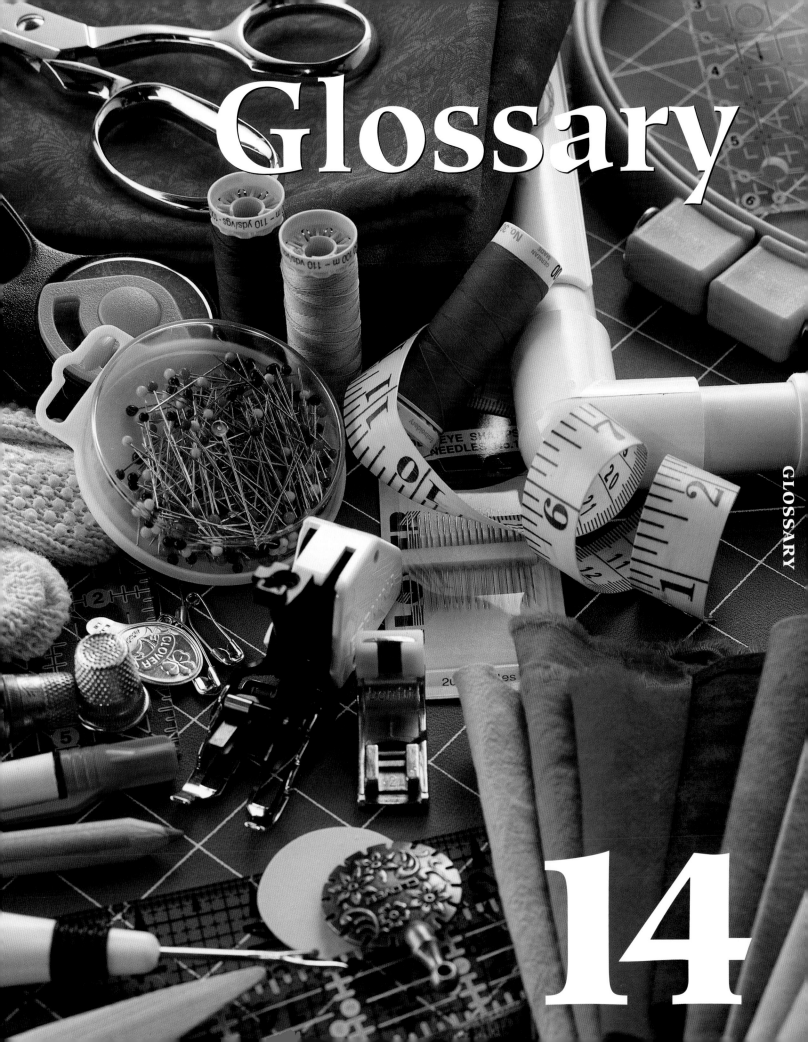

Glossary

A

Acrylic ruler: A ruler of thick, clear plastic used to make straight cuts with a rotary cutter. Available in a variety of sizes and shapes.

Acrylic template: Thick, durable plastic pattern used to trace and/or cut around. Available commercially in a variety of shapes and patterns. Can be used with a rotary cutter.

Allover quilting: Stitching that covers the entire quilt without regard for block shapes or fabric design. Can be quilted from either the top or the back side.

Alternate blocks: Plain, pieced, or appliquéd blocks used between a quilt's primary blocks. Also called alternate squares or setting squares.

Analogous color: The colors located on either side of a color on the color wheel.

Appliqué: Adding fabric motifs by hand or machine to a foundation fabric.

Appliqué sequence order: See "Stitching sequence."

Appliqué template: A pattern used to trace appliqué shapes onto fabric.

Asymmetry: When one-half of an image or block does not mirror the opposite half, the image is asymmetric.

Awl: A tool typically used in leather making to create holes. Can be used in quilting to pierce templates for marking points.

B

Background quilting: Stitching in open interior spaces, such as in setting squares. Squares, diamonds, clamshells, or other small regular shapes are commonly used as background quilting. The closely spaced lines tend to flatten the area being quilted, creating a low-relief, textured appearance.

Backing: The layer of fabric on the back of a quilt. It can be a single fabric, pieced from multiple fabrics, or created using extra blocks.

Backstitch: The process of stitching over one or two stitches to secure them. Can be done by hand or by reverse stitching on a sewing machine. Also a hand embroidery stitch.

Backstitch loop knot: Used in hand piecing to end a line of sewing. Can be made with one or two loops.

Bargello: A quilt style identified by peaks and valleys created from squares of fabric that are sewn in strips, then cut and offset before joining the strips again.

Barn Raising set: A pattern created when Log Cabin blocks are placed so the lights and darks radiate from the quilt center.

Basic sewing kit: Key components for quilting that may be requested on a class supply list. The contents include scissors, needles, and thread. Also called BSK.

Basting spray: Adhesive available in a spray can that may be used to hold the layers of a quilt together instead of thread- or pin-basting.

Basting stitch: A large, loose stitch used to hold together layers of fabric or fabric and batting. Basting stitches are usually removed after the layers are permanently joined.

Batting: The material used between the quilt top and quilt back. Commercial battings are available in a variety of fiber contents. Flannel fabric is sometimes substituted for traditional batting.

Beading: The process of adding beads to the surface of a quilt.

Bearding: The appearance of batting on the quilt surface, showing through the holes where the needle pierced the quilt top or back during the quilting process. Also called fiber migration.

Betweens: Short, fine needles used for hand piecing, hand quilting, appliqué, and sewing on binding.

Bias: Any diagonal line between the crosswise or lengthwise grain line in woven fabric. The bias grain has more stretch and is less stable than the crosswise or lengthwise grain. See also "True bias."

Bias bars: Purchased metal or heat-resistant plastic bars in varying widths that are used to make bias stems.

Bias binding: Binding strips cut on the true bias grain, resulting in a binding that can be easily positioned around curved edges. When striped fabrics are cut on the bias, the result is a "barber pole" effect.

Bias seam: When bias edges of fabric are sewn together, a bias seam results. This seam can be easily stretched and distorted and must be handled with care.

Bias stems: Fabric strips cut on the bias grain so that they are flexible enough to bend without wrinkles or puckers when making floral stems or vines for appliqué.

Bias strips: Long, thin pieces of fabric cut on the bias grain.

Big stitch: A large, evenly-spaced hand quilting stitch used to create a folk art appearance.

Binding: The finishing band of fabric that covers the raw outer edges of a quilt.

Binding foot: A specialty foot that can be attached to the machine for making and sewing binding.

Blanket stitch: A decorative machine or hand stitch used to outline appliqué pieces. Also called buttonhole stitch.

Blind hem stitch: A machine stitch used to secure appliqué pieces for mock hand appliqué. The machine takes two or three straight stitches, then a zigzag stitch.

Block: The basic unit, usually square and often repeated, from which many quilts are composed. Blocks may be pieced, appliquéd, or solid.

Block mock-up: A sample of a block made by cutting the shapes from the desired fabric and affixing them to a surface. Creating mock-up blocks allows the quilter to see how fabrics will work together when cut into smaller pieces.

Bobbin case: The portion of the sewing machine that holds the bobbin. Bobbin cases may be fixed or removable, depending on machine style and manufacturer.

Bobbin case finger: The part of the bobbin case that projects upward in some machines. It contains a hole for threading the bobbin thread through to increase the lower thread tension.

Bobbin-fill thread: A lightweight thread used in the bobbin for machine embroidery, machine appliqué, or decorative stitching. Also called lingerie thread.

Bobbin work: Winding thick decorative threads that won't fit through the machine needle onto the bobbin, then stitching from the quilt back so the bobbin thread appears on the quilt front.

Bonded batting: Batting that has been chemically processed using heat or resin to combine the fibers.

Border prints: Contained fabric designs that run lengthwise on the fabric bolt. Often these prints are cut apart and used as a quilt border.

Borders: The framing on a quilt that serves to visually hold in the design and give the eye a stopping point.

Broderie perse: A technique in which individual motifs are cut from one fabric and applied to another fabric foundation.

BSK: See "Basic sewing kit."

Bugle beads: Long, thin beads sometimes added to a quilt top for embellishment.

Burr: A nick or rough area on a needle that may snag fabric.

Butted corners: Term used when border pieces meet at a 90° angle or when binding pieces overlap in the corner at a 90° angle, rather than being mitered.

Buttonhole stitch: See "Blanket stitch."

C

Center-intersecting blocks: Block designs that have multiple pieces meeting in the center. Special piecing techniques are needed to prevent excess bulk or warping at the block's center.

Center points: The visual or actual center of a block where units come together.

Chain piecing: Sewing patchwork pieces in a continuous chain from edge to edge without backstitching. Short lengths of thread link the pieces.

Chain stitch: An embroidery stitch that appears to be a series of chain links.

Channel stitching: Parallel rows of straight-line quilting going in one direction across a quilt top.

Chenille needle: A long, oval-eye needle used for heavyweight thread, embroidery, and tying quilts.

Chevron stitch: A zigzag-type embroidery stitch used for decorative embellishment.

Color retention: A fabric's ability to retain its color when it is washed.

Color-wash quilt: See "Watercolor quilt."

Color wheel: Device used to see the relationships of primary, secondary, and tertiary colors and the tints and shades of each.

Complementary colors: Pairs of colors that sit opposite one another on the color wheel.

Continuous bias binding technique: A method of marking, sewing, and cutting a square of fabric so as to transform it into one long bias strip.

Continuous sashing: Strips of fabric that separate entire rows either vertically or horizontally.

Contrast: The differences between fabric values, which are described as light, medium, or dark. Contrast clarifies design and makes depth apparent.

Conversation print: See "Novelty print."

Cording foot: A specialty sewing machine foot that has a deep groove on the bottom to accommodate cording or piping.

Corner matching points: Marks made on templates and pattern pieces indicating where corners come together. Especially important when hand-piecing, as the seams are not sewn into.

Cornerstones: Squares of fabric pieced within sashing that align at the block corners.

Couching: A process of stitching thick threads, ribbons, beads, and other items to a quilt surface.

Covered cording: A trim or binding made by covering cording with fabric. Also called piping.

Crazy quilting: A type of quilting popularized in Victorian times. Crazy quilting is identified by odd-shaped pieces of fabric usually sewn onto a foundation and embellished with fancy embroidery, ribbons, and beading. Silk, velvet, cotton, and other fine fabrics are typically used in crazy quilting.

Crocking: The rubbing off of color from one fabric to another, caused by the friction of fabrics rubbing against one another during handling or washing.

Crosshatch: See "Grid quilting."

Cross-stitch: A decorative embroidery stitch that appears as a series of Xs.

Crosswise grain (cross grain): The threads running perpendicular to the selvage across the width of a woven fabric.

Curve, concave: A curve that bows inward.

Curve, convex: A curve that bows outward.

Curved rulers and templates: Made of acrylic plastic, these commercial products make it easier to rotary-cut intricate, curved pieces.

Cutting mat: Surface used for rotary cutting that protects the tabletop and keeps the fabric from shifting while cutting. Often mats are labeled as self-healing, meaning the blade does not leave slash marks or grooves in the surface even after repeated usage.

D

Darner (darning needle): A needle with a long, narrow eye. Used for basting, tying, or weaving.

Darning foot: An open-toe sewing machine foot that is used for free-motion quilting.

Design wall/surface: A vertical surface used to position and view fabric choices to see how they might appear in a quilt.

Diagonal set: A style of quilt top where the blocks are set "on-point" in diagonal rows.

Difficult to needle: The ease (or lack thereof) with which the needle glides through fabric.

Directional borders: Borders that have designs running in a particular sequence or order.

Directional clipping: Snipping seams on the bias to prevent raveling of fabric edges, such as in appliqué.

Directional pressing: Ironing seams in a designated direction to limit bulk in certain areas of a block. Commonly used in diamonds and other center-intersecting blocks.

Directional stitching: Sewing seams in a designated direction when piecing to prevent puckering. Commonly used in sewing diamonds and other center-intersecting blocks.

Dog-ears: Long points that extend beyond the seam allowance, block edge, or quilt top edge after the pieces are stitched together. Usually trimmed off to make aligning subsequent pieces easier.

Double-appliqué method: Finished-edge appliqué pieces created by facing them with a lightweight interfacing prior to stitching them to a foundation fabric.

Double-fold binding: Binding made from a fabric strip that is folded in half before being attached to the quilt. Also called French-fold binding.

Double- or triple-needle: Specialty sewing machine needles with two or three needles hooked together at the shank. Can be used for decorative stitching.

Drag: Caused by the weight of the quilt pulling while sewing. Drag can result in distortion of a finished quilt or uneven quilting stitches.

Drapability: The relative stiffness or softness of a fabric or quilted piece.

Drop: The part of a quilt that extends over the edge of the mattress.

E

Easing: The process of working in extra fabric where two pieces do not align precisely, especially when sewing curves.

Echo quilting: Stitching multiple lines that follow the outline of an appliqué or other design element, echoing its shape.

Embellishment: The process of adding decorative items or stitches to a quilt top. May include buttons, beads, heavyweight threads, or charms.

Embroidery: A type of embellishment or stitchery that can be created by hand or machine using a variety of threads.

English paper piecing: Technique of stabilizing fabric over a paper template. Frequently used for designs with set-in corners such as the hexagon shape. See also "Grandmother's Flower Garden."

Equilateral triangles: A triangle in which all three angles measure 60°. Six equilateral triangles combine to create a hexagon.

Ergonomics: The study of work space design to prevent injury.

Even-feed foot: See "Walking foot."

Extra-fine pins: Pins with a thinner shaft than standard pins, thus leaving smaller holes in fabric.

F

Fat eighth: A ⅛-yard fabric cut that is cut crosswise from a ¼-yard piece of fabric for a finished size of approximately 9×22".

Fat quarter: A ¼-yard fabric cut that is cut crosswise from a ½-yard piece of fabric for a finished size of approximately 18×22".

Featherstitch: A decorative embroidery stitch.

Feed dogs: The sawtooth-edge machine component that rests under the throat plate and aids in moving fabric beneath the presser foot.

Felted wool: Wool fabric which has been machine-washed and dried to create a napped, no-fray material.

Filler quilting: See "Background quilting."

Filler triangles: See "Setting triangles."

Finger-crease: See "Finger-press."

Finger-press: The process of pressing a small seam using a finger and pressure. Also called finger-crease.

Finishes: Created by mechanical or chemical processes used in fabric manufacturing that result in different surface characteristics, from a sheen to a nap. Finishes can be permanent or temporary and may have varying degrees of durability (ability to withstand washings).

Flannel: A 100%-cotton fabric that has a brushed, napped surface.

Flat flower pins: Pins with a unique flower-shape head. The long shaft makes these pins easy to grab and helps them stay in fabric.

Floating blocks: A look achieved by cutting side and corner setting pieces large enough that the block edges in the quilt center do not touch the border.

Flying Geese unit: An often-used unit in quilt making. It is identified by its rectangular shape created with a large 90° triangle in the center and two small 90° triangles on each side.

Foundation piecing: A method of sewing together fabric pieces on the reverse side of a paper pattern or foundation fabric. Sometimes preferred for joining very small or irregularly shaped fabric pieces.

Four-Patch: A block or unit comprised of four equal-size squares sewn in two horizontal rows, often with alternating color placement.

Framed block: A block with fabric strips around it that give it the appearance of being framed. This technique can be used to unify blocks or adjust block size.

Free-motion embroidery: Machine embroidery done with the feed dogs disengaged and using a darning presser foot so the quilt can be moved freely on the machine bed in any direction.

Free-motion quilting: A process of quilting done with the feed dogs disengaged and using a darning presser foot so the quilt can be moved freely on the machine bed in any direction.

Freezer paper: Paper commonly available at grocery stores that can be used to make appliqué patterns. The shiny coating on one side temporarily adheres to fabric when pressed with a warm iron.

French-fold binding: See "Double-fold binding."

French knot: A decorative embroidery stitch formed by wrapping thread around the needle.

Fusible web: A paper-backed adhesive that can be ironed to the back of fabric that is then cut into shapes. These fused shapes can then be adhered to a background fabric by pressing them with a warm iron. Frequently used in appliqué projects.

Fussy cutting: Isolating and cutting out a specific print or motif from a piece of fabric.

G

Gathering stitch: A long running stitch that can be pulled to draw up the fabric.

Glass-head pins: Pins with a glass head that won't melt when pressed.

Glazing: Treating thread and fabric with starches and special chemicals, as well as polishing, to create a high luster.

Grain (grain line, on grain, or grain perfect): Reference to the lengthwise or crosswise threads in a woven fabric.

Grandmother's Flower Garden: A traditional quilt design created entirely from joining hexagon shapes. See also "English paper piecing."

Greige goods: Fabric in a raw, unfinished state. Pronounced "gray-zh" goods.

Grid quilting: Quilting in vertical and horizontal lines across the quilt top. Also called cross-hatching.

Grid method: A system of dividing quilt blocks into smaller units to organize the design. Nine-patch and four-patch are two commonly used grids.

H

Half-square triangle: The 90° triangle formed when a square is cut in half diagonally once.

Hand: The feel of the fabric. Determined by the different greige goods and finishes used on fabric.

Hand appliqué: Using needle and thread to hand-sew fabric pieces onto a fabric foundation.

Hand ironing tool: A piece of hardwood that can be used to "press" open a seam.

Hand piecing: Using needle and thread to hand-sew seams while making a quilt top.

Hand-piecing templates: Pattern shapes used to trace and cut patches for hand-piecing projects. The pattern shapes do not include seam allowances.

Hand quilting: Series of running stitches made through all layers of a quilt with needle and thread.

Hanging sleeve: A piece of fabric sewn to the back of a quilt. The fabric holds a rod so a quilt can be hung for display.

Hawaiian appliqué: Intricate, symmetrical appliqué designs. The pattern-making process is similar to that used to create paper snowflakes.

Herringbone stitch: A decorative embroidery stitch.

Homespun: A fabric woven with colored threads rather than printed. The color is inherent in the fabric and not applied at a later time.

I

Inset seam: See "Set-in seam."

Intensity: The amount of pure color (saturated or brilliant) or muted color (grayed or subdued) present in a fabric.

In-the-ditch quilting: A process of stitching just next to the seams on the quilt surface, it is often used to define blocks or shapes. Also called stitch-in-the-ditch quilting.

Ironing: The process of moving the iron while it has contact with the fabric, which can stretch and distort fabrics and seams. Ironing is distinctly different from pressing.

Isosceles triangle: A triangle with two equal sides whose sum is longer than the base.

K

Kaleidoscope: A quilt block pattern in which fabric is pieced so that it resembles the variegated image seen through a kaleidoscope.

Knee-lift presser foot: A device attached to a sewing machine that allows the quilter to raise the machine presser foot with the knee, leaving the hands free to manipulate or hold the fabric.

Knife-edge self-binding: A binding alternative in which both the quilt top fabric and backing fabric are turned under to meet evenly at the edges of the quilt, leaving the quilt edges without an additional strip of binding fabric.

Knot on the needle: See "Quilter's knot."

L

Lap quilting: Hand quilting done while holding the quilt loosely in the lap without using a hoop.

Lattice: See "Sashing."

Lazy daisy stitch: A decorative embroidery stitch often combined to create a flowerlike design.

Lengthwise grain: The threads running parallel to the selvage in a woven fabric.

Light box: A translucent surface that is lit from below and is used for tracing patterns onto paper or fabric. Available in crafts or photo-supply stores.

Lingerie thread: See "Bobbin-fill thread."

Lockstitch: The stitch created by a sewing machine consisting of several very short stitches which serve the same purpose as a knot. Used to begin or end a row of stitching that will not be crossed by another seam.

Loft: The thickness of the batting.

Log Cabin: A block assembled in a numerical sequence with strips, or "logs," beginning at the center of the block and working in a clockwise direction around a square center.

Logs: Strips of fabric used to make a Log Cabin block.

Long-arm quilting machine: A quilting machine used by professional quilters in which the quilt is held taut on a frame that allows the quilter to work on a large portion of the quilt at a time. The machine head moves freely, allowing the operator to use free-motion to quilt in all directions.

M

Machine appliqué: Attaching fabric motifs onto a fabric foundation with a sewing machine.

Machine piecing: Machine-sewing patchwork pieces together with ¼" seam allowances while making a quilt top.

Machine quilting: Series of stitches made through all layers of a quilt sandwich with a sewing machine.

Machine tension: The balancing forces exerted on the needle and bobbin threads by the sewing machine that affect the quality of its stitch. Tension may be affected by the machine parts, how the machine and bobbin are threaded, thread type, needle type, and fabric choice.

Marking tools: A variety of pens, pencils, and chalks that can be used to mark fabric pieces or a quilt top.

Matching point: Where the seam line joining two pieces begins or ends. Also known as a joining point.

Meandering stitch: An allover quilting pattern characterized by a series of large, loosely curved lines that usually do not cross over one another. Commonly used to cover an entire quilt surface without regard for block or border seams or edges.

Metallic needle: A needle designed with a larger eye for use with metallic thread.

Metallic thread: A synthetic thread with a shiny, metallic appearance.

Milliners needle: A long needle with a small round eye. Used for basting, gathering, and needle-turn appliqué. Also called a straw needle.

Mirror image: The reverse of an image or how it might appear if held up to a mirror.

Mitered borders: Border strips that meet in the corner at a 45° angle.

Mock-hand appliqué: A method of using clear, monofilament thread in the needle, cotton thread in the bobbin, and a blind-hem stitch to make virtually invisible appliqué stitches by machine.

Monochromatic: Use of a single color, which may include tints and shades of that color.

Monofilament thread: A clear or smoke-colored thread made of polyester or nylon that is used for machine quilting. Finished stitches are virtually invisible.

N

Napping: A process wherein the fabric surface is brushed, creating soft texture. Process used to create flannel.

Needle threader: A device that helps in getting thread through the eye of the needle. Available for both hand and machine sewing.

Needle-punched: A process used in batting manufacture to entangle the fibers and stabilize the batting.

Needle-turn appliqué: An appliqué method in which the seams are turned under with the needle tip just ahead of the section being stitched.

Nine-Patch: A block or unit comprised of nine squares of fabric sewn together in three horizontal rows, often with alternating color placement. A common block configuration in quilting.

Notch: A small V shape clipped into a curved seam to reduce bulk and make seams lie flat when joined.

Novelty print: Fabric designed with a theme that may include holiday symbols, hobbies, or pet motifs. Also called a conversation print.

O

Off grain: When the lengthwise and crosswise grains of fabric don't intersect at a perfect right angle.

Oilcloth: A vinyl cloth with a napped, flannel backing. Used in quilting to hold fabric pieces as a portable design wall.

On point: Quilt blocks that are positioned on the diagonal are on point.

Outline quilting: Quilting done ¼" from a seam line or an edge of an appliqué shape.

Overprinted: Fabric that is first dyed and then printed.

P

Paper foundation: A thin piece of paper with a drawn, printed, or stitched pattern that becomes the base for a quilt block when fabric is sewn directly onto it.

Partial seams: A two-step process of seaming to avoid set-in seams.

Perle cotton thread: A soft, yarnlike cotton thread used for quilting, decorative stitching, or embellishment. Available in a variety of thicknesses.

Photo transfer: Technique for transferring photo images onto fabric for use in a quilt top.

Pieced border: Blocks or pieced units sewn together to make a single border unit that is then sewn to the quilt center.

Pillow tuck: The portion of a quilt that is tucked under the pillow(s).

Pin-baste: Process of basting together quilt layers using pins (most often safety pins).

Pinking blade or shears: Rotary-cutter blade or scissors with edges that cut a zigzag pattern in fabric.

Piping: See "Covered cording."

Pivot: The process of leaving the needle in the fabric and turning the fabric when machine-piecing or machine-quilting.

Ply: A single strand of fiber. Several are twisted together to create a thread.

Polychromatic combination: A multicolor mix.

Pounce: A chalk bag that can be patted over a stencil to transfer a pattern to fabric. Also called stamping powder.

Prairie points: Folded fabric triangles used as a quilt border or embellishment.

Preshrinking: Washing and drying of fabric by the quilter or manufacturer to remove finishes and shrink fabric before it is cut and sewn.

Presser foot: The removable machine accessory that holds fabric in place against the machine bed and accommodates the needle. A variety of presser feet styles are available for most machines.

Pressing: The process of picking up the iron off the fabric surface and putting it back down in another location, rather than sliding it across the fabric.

Primary colors: The three main colors from which all colors are built—red, blue, and yellow.

Puckered seams: Seams with uneven or pulled spots. Can be caused by pushing or pulling the fabric through the sewing machine, having unbalanced thread tension, or pulling the thread too taut when hand-sewing.

Q

Quarter-square triangle: The 90° triangle formed when a square is cut diagonally twice in an X.

Quilt center: The quilt top before borders are added.

Quilt sandwich: The three parts of a quilt layered together—the quilt top, batting, and backing.

Quilt top: The front of a quilt prior to layering and quilting. It can be pieced, appliquéd, or a single piece of fabric.

Quilter's knot: A knot used frequently in quilting in which thread is wrapped around the needle, then the needle is pulled through the wraps to create a knot. Also known as knot on the needle.

Quilting bar: A machine attachment used as a guide for channel or grid quilting.

Quilting distance: The space between quilting stitches. Batting manufacturers recommend different quilting distances for their products.

Quilting frame/hoop: Two pieces of wood or plastic that are placed on the top and bottom of a quilt to hold the fabric taut for quilting or surface embellishment.

Quilting stencils: Quilting patterns with open areas through which a design is transferred onto a quilt top. May be purchased or made from sturdy, reusable template plastic.

Quilting templates: Shapes that are traced around to mark a quilt top for quilting. May be purchased or made from sturdy, reusable template material.

R

Raw edge: An unfinished fabric edge. Sometimes used as a decorative element on quilt tops.

Rayon thread: A synthetic thread used for embroidery, embellishment, and sometimes quilting, but not piecing.

Reducing lens: A device that allows quilters to view fabric and projects as if they were several feet away. Distance may be valuable in determining design qualities.

Redwork: White or off-white fabric with images embroidered in red embroidery floss.

Relief: A raised surface, created in quilting by stuffing or filling an area, then quilting around it, as done for trapunto.

Repeat: Repetitions of a pattern or design in a fabric or repetition of a quilting design or motif.

Reproduction fabrics: Re-creations of fabrics from different time periods, such as the Civil War era or the 1930s.

Resiliency: The ability of a batting to resist creasing and regain its loft.

Reverse appliqué: An appliqué method in which the foundation fabric is on top of the appliqué fabric. The foundation is cut away to reveal the appliqué fabric underneath.

Right triangle: A triangle with one 90° angle.

Rock and roll motion: See "Rock the needle."

Rock the needle: The process of bringing the needle back to the surface of all the quilt layers by using a rocking motion. Also called a rock and roll motion.

Rotary cutter: Tool with a sharp, round blade attached to a handle that is used to cut fabric. The blade is available in different diameters.

Rotary-cutting mat: See "Cutting mat."

Row-by-row setting: A quilt layout in which a different type of block comprises each row.

Running stitch: A series of in and out stitches used in piecing, quilting, and embellishing.

S

Sampler quilt: A quilt in which each block is a different pattern.

Sandpaper: Typically used in woodworking and crafts. The fine-grit type can be used in quilting to hold fabric while marking to prevent distortion.

Sashiko: A type of Japanese embroidery traditionally using a thick white thread on layered indigo-color fabric to create geometric patterns.

Sashing: Strips of fabric used to separate or set off block designs.

Satin stitch: A compact zigzag stitch often used around appliqué pieces to enclose raw edges and attach the appliqués to a foundation fabric.

Scale: The size of a print in relationship to other fabrics.

Scalloped border: A border with multiple curves around the quilt's outer edges.

Screen-printing: The process of applying designs to a fabric surface in separate steps.

Scrim: A loosely woven fabric resembling a net. Used to contain fibers in some types of batting.

Seam allowance: Distance between the fabric raw edge and the seam line. Typically ¼" in machine piecing.

Seam line: The straight or curved line on which the stitches should be formed.

Seam ripper: A sharp, curved-tip tool used to lift and break thread when removing a seam.

Secondary colors: Colors created by combining the primary colors—orange, violet, and green.

Seed beads: Small, round beads used for embellishment.

Self-binding: Using backing fabric as binding, rather than attaching a separate binding strip.

Self-healing mat: See "Cutting mat."

Selvage: The lengthwise edge of woven fabric.

Serpentine stitch: A wavy-line stitch sometimes used in quilting.

Set: How blocks are arranged in a quilt top.

Set-in seam: The type of seam used when a continuous straight seam is not an option. Separate steps are necessary to sew a piece into an angled opening between other pieces that have already been joined.

Setting a seam: The first pressing of the seam as it comes from the sewing machine to lock threads together, smooth out puckers, and even out minor thread tension differences before pressing the seam open or to one side.

Setting squares: Solid, pieced, or appliquéd squares placed between the focal-point quilt blocks to set off a design.

Setting triangles: Triangles used to fill out a design when blocks are set on point. Also called filler triangles.

Shade: Black added to a color or hue creates a shade of that color.

Shaft: The body of the needle that extends below the shank.

Shank: The top part of the needle that is held by the machine.

Sharp: A thin hand or machine needle with an extremely sharp point that is used to piece woven fabrics.

Shrinkage: The amount of area a fabric or quilt loses after being washed, dried, or quilted.

Signature block: Quilt block with a blank area where a signature has been added with permanent ink pen or embroidery.

Silk pins: Thin-shaft pins with sharp points for easy insertion and tiny holes in delicate fabrics.

Single-block setting: Quilt created primarily from a single block shape, such as Tumbling Blocks or Grandmother's Flower Garden.

Single-fold binding: A single-thickness fabric strip used to enclose quilt edges. Most commonly used for quilts that will not be handled frequently.

Sizing: Product used to add body or stability to fabric, making it easier to handle.

Slipstitches: Small stitches used to stitch down binding.

Spacer border: Plain border sewn between a quilt center and an outer pieced border.

Split complement: A color grouping utilizing a primary, secondary, or tertiary color and the colors on either side of its complement.

Spool pin: The spindle that holds thread on the top of the sewing machine.

Spray starch or spray sizing: Liquid starch or sizing that can be sprayed over fabric to stabilize it before cutting.

Squaring a block: Measuring and, if necessary, trimming a block to ensure that it is the correct size.

Squaring fabric: Straightening one edge of the fabric prior to rotary cutting.

Squaring up a quilt: Straightening the edges of a quilt prior to sewing on the binding.

Stab stitch: A quilting stitch in which the needle and thread are brought to the back and up again in separate movements.

Stabilizer: A product used beneath an appliqué foundation to eliminate puckers and pulling on the fabric while machine-stitching. Stabilizers are often tear-away or water-soluble for easy removal after stitching is complete.

Stained-glass quilt: A quilt style with pieces outlined by black bias tape that simulates the leading in stained glass windows.

Stamping powder: See "Pounce."

Star stitch: A decorative embroidery stitch.

Stem stitch: An embroidery stitch frequently used to outline objects.

Stippling: An allover quilting pattern characterized by a series of randomly curved lines that do not cross. Stippling is used to fill in background areas, which allows motifs to be more prominent. Also called allover meandering or puzzle quilting.

Stitching sequence: A designated order in which appliqué pieces should be stitched to the foundation fabric. Normally notated on appliqué patterns or pieces by a number.

Stitch-in-the-ditch: See "In-the-ditch quilting."

Stitch length: The number of stitches per inch. On a sewing machine, stitch length is often in millimeters.

Stitch width: A term generally applied to machine satin or zigzag stitching where the stitch width can be adjusted.

Straightedge: A ruler or other rigid surface that can be placed on template material or fabric to position a cutting tool or draw a line.

Straight grain: See "Lengthwise grain."

Straight set: A quilt top setting with blocks aligned side by side in straight, even rows without sashing.

Straight-set borders: A border that has been added first to the top and bottom of the quilt, then to the side edges, or vice versa.

Straight-stitch throat plate: A sewing machine throat plate with a small round hole for the needle to pass through. This allows less area for the sewing machine to take in or "swallow" the fabric as it is being stitched.

Straw needle: See "Milliners needle."

String piecing: Sewing multiple strips of fabric to a foundation piece for use in a block.

Strip piecing: A process for accurately and quickly cutting multiple strips and joining them together prior to cutting them into units or subunits for blocks. Also known as the strip method.

Swallow the fabric: At the beginning of a seam, the fabric edge is sometimes pushed into the throat plate by the needle and it appears that the machine has "swallowed" the fabric.

Symmetry: When one-half of something is the mirror image of the opposite half.

Synthetic threads: Threads made from polyester, rayon, and nylon.

T

Tack stitch: A stitch used to secure appliqué pieces to a foundation.

Take-up lever: The sewing machine part that holds thread and pulls it up as the stitch is being made.

Tapestry needle: A needle with an oval eye that accommodates thick thread and creates a hole in the fabric big enough for thick or coarse fibers to pass through.

Temperature: A relative characteristic that denotes the warmth or coolness of a color.

Template: A pattern made from paper, cardboard, plastic, or other sturdy material used to cut pieces for patchwork or appliqué.

Template plastic: Easy to cut, translucent material available at quilt shops and crafts supply stores. Designs can be traced onto its surface with a marking tool to make templates, pattern pieces, or quilting stencils.

Tension: See "Machine tension."

Tension dial: A sewing machine part that allows for adjustment of the upper thread tension, important to achieving a balanced stitch.

Tension discs: Sewing machine parts that hold the thread and keep the tension appropriate for the stitch being sewn.

Tertiary colors: Colors that are combinations of primary colors (red, blue, yellow) and secondary colors (green, orange, violet)—red-orange, red-violet, blue-violet, blue-green, yellow-green, and yellow-orange.

Tessellating designs: When a single shape is repeated on a quilt top and covers the surface without holes or overlap.

Tetrad: A four-color combination of colors equidistant on the color wheel.

Thimble: A device to protect finger pads from needle pricks. Can be made of metal, leather, plastic, or rubber.

Thread-basting: Basting quilt layers together using a needle and thread and extra-long stitches that will be removed after the quilting is complete.

Thread count: The number of threads woven into a fabric. A higher number designates a more tightly woven fabric.

Thread finishes: Mechanical or chemical processes performed during thread manufacture to enhance the thread's ability to perform under certain sewing conditions.

Throat plate: The removable plate on the machine bed that covers the bobbin and has an opening for the feed dogs and needle. Throat plates can be changed depending on the type of project.

Tint: White added to a color or hue creates a tint of that color.

Tone-on-tone print: Fabric that appears solid from a distance but have areas of light and dark.

Topstitch: A machine straight stitch typically done on the right side of a project close to a seam.

Tracing paper: A thin, translucent paper used for copying patterns.

Trapunto: A method of adding raised texture to quilts by stuffing design areas. Trapunto is used frequently in stems, leaves, and other motifs.

Traveling (with the needle): Moving from one area to another without knotting the thread and starting again.

Triad: Three primary, secondary, or tertiary colors that are equidistant on the color wheel.

Triangle-square: The square unit created when two 90° triangles are sewn together on the diagonal.

True bias: Intersects the lengthwise grain and crosswise grain at a 45° angle.

Tufting: See "Tying."

Tying: Taking a stitch through all three layers of the quilt and knotting it on the quilt surface. Tying creates a loftier quilt. Also called tufting.

U

Unbalanced borders: Borders of different sizes resulting in an asymmetrical look.

Unit: A combination of at least two pieces of fabric sewn together that form part of a block.

Universal needle: A sewing machine needle type with a point and eye suited for multiple sewing and quilting applications.

Utility stitch: See "Big stitch."

V

V-clip: A notch taken out of a seam to reduce bulk.

Variegated thread: Thread in which the color changes throughout the strand.

Vertical set: A style of quilt top in which the blocks are set on point in vertical rows.

W

Walking foot: A sewing machine foot that has grippers on the bottom that act in tandem with the machine's feed dogs to evenly feed multiple layers of fabric and batting beneath the foot. Effective for machine quilting. Also called an even-feed foot.

Watercolor quilt: Quilt identified by the multiple squares of print fabrics positioned so the colors blend into the next and create a watercolor effect. Also called color-wash quilt.

Water-soluble: Threads, stabilizers, or marks that dissolve when wet.

Whipstitches: Small stitches used to join two finished edges, such as in English paper piecing.

Y

Yo-yos: Three-dimensional gathered fabric circles that may be sewn into quilt tops or used for decorative embellishments.

Z

Zigzag set: A style of quilt top in which the blocks are set on point in vertical rows that are slightly offset.

Zigzag stitch: A side-to-side stitch that can be used for machine appliqué. It can be shortened and very closely spaced to create a satin stitch.

Index

15

CREDITS

Special thanks to the following companies who contributed products and materials for use in the photography of this book.

AMERICAN & EFIRD INC.
Mount Holly, North Carolina
Mettler and Signature thread

BERNINA OF AMERICA, INC.
Aurora, Illinois
Sewing machines

CHERRYWOOD FABRICS INC.
Brainerd, Minnesota
Hand-dyed fabrics

CLOVER NEEDLECRAFT, INC.
Carson, California
Tools, notions, needles, scissors, silk thread, craft iron, Quick Bias

COATS & CLARK
Charlotte, North Carolina
Thread

ERGONOMIC ADVANTAGE
Englewood, Colorado
Tiltable, SureFoot System

EZ QUILTING BY WRIGHTS
West Warren, Massachusetts
Notions, rulers, stencils, marking tools

FAIRFIELD PROCESSING CORPORATION
Danbury, Connecticut
Batting

FISKARS CONSUMER PRODUCTS, INC.
Wausau, Wisconsin
Scissors, rotary cutters, rulers, mats

GINGHER SCISSORS
Greensboro, North Carolina
Scissors, shears, clips

GUTERMANN OF AMERICA
Charlotte, North Carolina
Thread, thread cabinet

HOBBS BONDED FIBERS
Waco, Texas
Batting

HUSQVARNA VIKING SEWING MACHINES
Westlake, Ohio
Sewing machines

J.T. TRADING CORPORATION
Newtown, Connecticut
Spray and Fix adhesive sprays, wool/polyester blend batting

JUNE TAILOR, INC.
Richfield, Wisconsin
Sewing and cutting supplies, fusible batting, photo-transfer supplies

MICHELL MARKETING
Atlanta, Georgia
Acrylic templates

MODA FABRICS
Dallas, Texas
Fabric

OLFA PRODUCTS GROUP
Terre Haute, Indiana
Rotary cutters, rulers, mats, weights, organizer

OTT-LITE TECHNOLOGY
Tampa, Florida
Lighting

PRYM-DRITZ CORPORATION
Spartanburg, South Carolina
Notions, W.H. Collins Inc. supplies and tools, guides, gauges, Omnigrid cutting supplies

THE QUILT BLOCK
Des Moines, Iowa
Machine accessories, notions, fabric

RICHLAND SILK COMPANY
Palmyra, Michigan
Silk batting

RJR FASHION FABRICS
Gardena, California
Fabric

ROWENTA IRONS
Medford, Massachusetts
Irons

SULKY OF AMERICA INC.
Punta Gorda, Florida
Decorative threads, marking tools, Solvy stabilizers, spray adhesives

SULLIVANS USA INC.
Downers Grove, Illinois
The Quilt Shop products, sprays, notions, tools

SUSAN MCKELVEY'S WALLFLOWER DESIGNS
Royal Oak, Maryland
Quilt label for Chapter 12 divider

TACONY CORPORATION
Fenton, Missouri
Baby Lock and Elna sewing machines

WIZARD ATTACHMENT COMPANY, INC.
Parker, Colorado
Specialty presser foot attachments

YLI CORPORATION
Rock Hill, South Carolina
Thread

Special thanks to the following individuals who also helped in the creation of this book.

CINDY BLACKBERG
MARY CECIL
DIANA MCLUN
MARTI MICHELL